Beyond the Obvious with SAS® Screen Control Language

by Don Stanley

The correct bibliographic citation for this manual is as follows: Don Stanley, *Beyond the Obvious with SAS® Screen Control Language*, Cary, NC: SAS Institute Inc., 1994. 347 pp.

Beyond the Obvious with SAS® Screen Control Language

Copyright © 1994 by SAS Institute Inc., Cary, NC, USA.

ISBN 1-55544-600-0

The SAS® System is an integrated system of software providing complete control over data access, management, analysis, and presentation. Base SAS software is the foundation of the SAS System. Products within the SAS System include SAS/ACCESS® SAS/AF® SAS/ASSIST® SAS/CALC® SAS/CONNECT® SAS/CPE® SAS/DMI® SAS/EIS® SAS/ENGLISH® SAS/ETS® SAS/FSP® SAS/GRAPH® SAS/IML® SAS/IMS-DL/I® SAS/INSIGHT® SAS/LAB® SAS/NVISION® SAS/OR® SAS/PH-Clinical® SAS/QC® SAS/REPLAY-CICS® SAS/SHARE® SAS/STAT® SAS/TOOLKIT® SAS/TUTOR® SAS/DB2™ SAS/GIS™ SAS/IMAGE™ SAS/PETRO™ SAS/SESSION™ SAS/SPECTRAVIEW™ and SAS/SQL-DS™ software. Other SAS Institute products are SYSTEM 2000® Data Management Software, with basic SYSTEM 2000, CREATE Multi-User QueX Screen Writer and CICS interface software; NeoVisuals® software; JMP® JMP IN® JMP Serve® and JMP *Design*® software; SAS/RTERM® software; and the SAS/C® Compiler and the SAS/CX® Compiler; and Emulus™ software. MultiVendor Architecture™ and MVA™ are trademarks of SAS Institute Inc. SAS Video Productions℠ and the SVP logo are service marks of SAS Institute Inc. Books by Users℠ and its logo are service marks of SAS Institute Inc. SAS Institute also offers SAS Consulting® Ambassador Select® and On-Site Ambassador℠ services. *Authorline® Observations®, SAS Communications® SAS Training® SAS Views®* the SASware Ballot® and JMPer Cable™ are published by SAS Institute Inc. All trademarks above are registered trademarks or trademarks of SAS Institute Inc. in the USA and other countries. ® indicates USA registration.

The Institute is a private company devoted to the support and further development of its software and related services.

OS/2® is a registered trademark or trademark of International Business Machines Corporation.

Other brand and product names are registered trademarks or trademarks of their respective companies.

SAS Institute does not assume responsibility for the accuracy of any material presented in this book.

Contents

Acknowledgments

Texts don't just magically appear from nowhere. Invariably, the fact that a text is published implies that many people have had input, often without even realizing it. That input, no matter how trivial it may appear, is a necessary part of writing a text such as this.

The following individuals have carried out tasks without which this text might still be a garbled collection of algorithms, ideas, and badly structured sentences scrawled at my desk (you are, of course, permitted to consider privately that this is still the case!):

Richard Gibson ... I have known Richard for many years. We both renovated Victorian houses at the same time and drew off each other's ideas and end-visions. Because he is a thorough proofreader and always enthusiastic to read and try new ideas with the SAS System, I knew Richard would appreciate some reading matter on long train trips home from work each day. His reading of the entire text, subsequent comments, and ideas for enhancement have steered me away from rambling and unclear statements in many places. Any rambling unclear statements left in the text are, of course, due entirely to my inadequacies.

Susann Ryan ... for reviewing the grammar and general use of the English language. That I still dont know when and where to place apostrophes is proved by at least one word in this sentence. Seriously, Susann's involvement has extended our marital relationship beyond the norm. I'll have to share the royalties now.

Databank SAS programmers ... Much of the Question and Answer section of the book came from questions from these people, as did the initial idea for the text.

Senior management of Development Division at Databank Systems Ltd ... for permission to use code from applications originally developed as part of the overall EDP strategy at Databank and for general support of the SAS product.

David Baggett, technical review staff, and documentation editors at SAS Institute Inc., including Marje Martin, Annette Harris, Greg Smith, Teresia Arthur, Ottis Cowper, Yao Chen, Helen Weeks, Jennifer Ginn, Hanna Schoenrock, Blanche Phillips ... for giving me the opportunity to work with them on this project. I'm sure there must have been some qualms about the sheer geographical distance that this text had to cover. The Books By Users program is unique in the software industry. That SAS Institute Inc. is prepared to give people a world away the go-ahead to do this is further proof of its commitment to high-quality software and supporting documentation.

The above people are those I had direct contact with over the development lifetime of this text. Many others at SAS Institute had input, as did SUGI and SUNZ (SAS Users New Zealand) conference attendees. To all those people who took the time to read, criticize, stare with glazed eyes, and provide encouragement, thank you.

Chapter 1: Introduction

Contents

Overview

If you have been using the SAS System since prior to 1984, there is a good chance that you started when the system comprised little more than base SAS. That product included a set of procedures that are now called SAS/STAT software.

In 1984 you may have marveled at a new product, SAS/FSP software, running as part of the interactive SAS System under TSO. That product hinted at the direction that SAS Institute was taking, but the hint is only apparent now with the release of Version 6. That direction was to develop a windows or display-oriented system to complement the existing batch approach. At about the same time as SAS/FSP came the macro language, providing extra functionality and the ability to generate code dynamically.

With Version 5 of SAS software came SAS/AF software, which allowed a methodology for controlling display screens in an interactive SAS application. This allowed SAS software to be

---

used as an online development system. While Version 5 SAS/AF development tools were rudimentary in comparison with Version 6, they provided a much needed ability in SAS software to develop interactive systems.

However, Version 5 SAS/AF was somewhat difficult to use and was limited in the richness of the macro based language and the methodology for creating applications. SAS software users developed many complex applications in Version 5 SAS/AF and contributed many ideas that were eventually incorporated in Version 6.

Version 6 of SAS software introduced Screen Control Language (SCL). This was a major enhancement to the Version 5 SAS/AF system (indeed it is effectively a new language). SCL is a very rich, powerful language designed for creating and manipulating display screens and databases. Full windowing ability is built in.

With Release 6.08 came an additional feature -- frame technology. This drives SAS software into object-oriented programming (OOP), where display screens are built from objects and SCL code defined behind objects. These objects become the building blocks of future applications.

Many of the features that are built into SCL allow extensive interfacing with the rest of SAS software. Such features as embedded SAS software code submission, SCL interface with procedures in the SAS/FSP product, ability to use standard structures such as formats, and SQL code submission all make for a language that is useful and relatively easy to learn.

This text is an attempt to add experiences with SCL to the SAS documentation set. It is not a SAS Institute manual, but rather a book by a user who has used SCL since 1988 when Release 6.03 was available under PC DOS. The text doesn't just describe functions; rather it attempts to show how SCL as a language can be applied to specific situations and just what difficulties you may encounter.

This text assumes that you have both SAS/AF and SAS/FSP available for use.

Applications Presented In This Text

The examples in this text are derived from applications I have developed for Databank Systems Limited in New Zealand. It is not necessary to discuss the mission of Databank Systems in detail, but some background of its use of SAS will provide an overview for the SCL applications discussed here.

Databank Systems provides a number of EDP facilities for New Zealand clients. SAS software is widely used in the internal systems area of Databank. That is the area of chargeback, operational reporting, operational job checking, capacity management, project management and charging (or costing), management reporting, and graphical analysis.

The SAS development team in the Development Division at Databank is charged with the development of many applications based on SAS and with the support of the SAS product. This group develops and supports resource chargeback systems, project costing and chargeback systems, and a number of other management systems in the payroll and systems development life cycle areas. Most use of SAS software revolves around the base product, SAS/AF and SAS/FSP systems based on SCL, and SAS/SHARE.

The SAS Usage Notes System (SUNS)

SUNS was written to enhance use of the SAS Notes. This application is a developer's system, which is to say that one of the reasons it exists is to have a functioning application on which new features or techniques can be tried before they are being used on production applications.

SAS Institute also provides an SCL-based method of accessing the usage notes. The Databank version was not written because of any apparent shortcoming in the Institute version; I just wanted a functional system on which coders could experiment with SCL and extend to suit their own needs as necessary. The application is constantly evolving, as different programmers add their code, or attempt to do things differently. For the SAS programming team in Databank's Internal Systems Department, the application can be looked upon as one means of learning and understanding SCL.

In this text, the usage notes system is referred to as SUNS (SAS Usage Notes System).

Features of SUNS include

- the ability to search by keys for specific products or keywords and have those keys validated before any searching occurs

- the ability to search by usage note number or other text in the MODULEN field (MODULEN is a key field in the SAS Notes, containing in one field the release, area of SAS the note refers to, and note number)

- the ability to link into a secondary set of site notes that allow site notes and call track details to be maintained

- extended tables for viewing matches from searches.

The Management Accounting Rate Table System (MARTS)

This application extensively uses SCL behind FSVIEW. FSVIEW is essentially a table-based system. Its interaction with SCL is much different from the interaction of SCL with either SAS/AF or SAS/FSP.

The application is a simple rate table system. It stores rates for various computer and people resources for chargeback purposes. It is a clearly defined relational database system that, despite its clear and apparently simple requirements, needed some interesting and sophisticated SCL.

This system is referred to as MARTS (Management Accounting Rate Table System) throughout this text. MARTS is not presented in full; rather, examples from MARTS are used to facilitate understanding of concepts throughout the book.

The Job Activity Recording System (JARS)

The third application presented here is Databank's means of compiling and charging for people resources used on projects. This system is the Job Activity Recording System and is referred to as JARS throughout.

JARS is a very large system that includes about 7,000 lines of SCL code. In addition to the SCL, JARS has some 3,000 lines of SAS code. The system can be envisaged as an online system with data capture, reporting, PC download, project cost management, and centralized project administration built in. Since I began writing this text, JARS has further expanded to allow a complete system for tracking and estimating the cost of phases in the development life cycle.

Supplementary to the online system is an overnight batch update, designed to allow JARS to interface with other systems and carry out tasks that require exclusive database accesses. JARS interacts with Databank's problem management and payroll systems via this mechanism.

Although users often do not realize it, JARS also runs a number of tasks in a batch environment by building and submitting report requests. This action prevents long reports from being run interactively. (Although it is a feature of SAS software that practically anything can be in interactive mode, experience has shown that it is sometimes a design advantage to get users off terminals as quickly as possible, especially when the user is not an experienced EDP person. Whether or not to discourage interactive processing is, of course, totally user base dependent.)

JARS was originally written using SAS/AF under MVS in Release 5.18 of SAS. Richard Gibson, now a technical consultant at SAS Institute in Wellington, New Zealand, wrote the original system while employed at Databank Systems in 1987. I wrote Version 2 of JARS using SCL in Release 6.06 in 1990. In 1992 I again substantially modified JARS to operate under SAS/SHARE using Release 6.07.

This product is constantly evolving as our company's needs evolve. At present I am adding a Systems Development Life Cycle tracking system onto JARS. This extends the JARS product into phase tracking and accurate phase estimates, phase and customer reviews, and other life cycle related activities. Some of the code and ideas from this system are also included in this text.

Using This Book

Audience For This Book

The text is aimed at people with a reasonable knowledge of SAS software, in particular the DATA and PROC steps, and an understanding of SCL.

No intention is made here to cover the whole topic of SCL. The book neither attempts nor pretends to replace existing SAS Institute documentation, but enhances SCL documentation with real life experiences and systems. Along with this text, you will probably want to read SCL documentation from SAS Institute.

It is assumed that

- you have attempted to use SCL
- you know how to use the SAS editor and PROC BUILD
- you are familiar with FSEDIT screen modification.

Experienced SCL users should find techniques in this text useful.

In practice, there are often many ways to accomplish a specific task in many languages. SCL is no exception. I do not pretend that the techniques used here are the only possible ways of coding, nor that any technique is the best in a given situation. Rather, the aim is to show what can be done. Where possible, techniques are compared and obviously unsuccessful techniques in some context are rejected.

One of the aims of the text is to illustrate that SCL can be used to create 'tight' systems. A 'tight' system is one that rigidly restricts users to using only the features available in the system. In contrast, a 'loose' system is one in which the user has all the facilities of the application available, but can also use features that are not specifically intended to be part of the system, like accessing operating system-specific windows.

Efficiency

Where possible, different ways of accomplishing some task are discussed and compared. That comparison includes considering resources used.

It is difficult to make definitive comments about efficiency with SCL. For example, obtaining statistics such as CPU time and I/O measurements is difficult for specific tasks in SCL, which leaves elapsed time as the most usable metric.

Unfortunately, the system clock is not a robust metric for comparing techniques for efficiency since elapsed time is subject to many other constraints outside of SAS software. Where elapsed times in V2.0 of the OS/2 operating system are presented, they are evaluated with only SAS software active under OS/2, but even these may not be very robust. Under OS/2, such timings can be affected by memory size, hard disk access speed, size of SWAPPER.DAT, and many other factors outside the control of SAS software. The same tasks illustrated here may show quite different outcomes on different hardware.

Elapsed time gives a feel for how well a technique performs against other techniques accomplishing the same end and is used in this text to evaluate methods under OS/2. In the absence of a means to gather SCL CPU and I/O under all systems, only the elapsed time metric is used and then only under OS/2.

All references in this book to OS/2 will be applicable to V2.0 and later versions.

Topics

The text goes into topics such as

- SCL coding standards and documentation
- topics specific to SAS/AF
- topics specific to SAS/FSP
- using SCL in an FSVIEW application
- undocumented features of some SCL commands
- use of macros
- window/screen design
- useful undocumented features
- using SCL in a noninteractive environment
- frame technology
- extended tables.

The subject of standards is covered here since far too many developers build systems that are either difficult or impossible to maintain because different people working on systems impart their own ideas without a common standard. Where a site forces adherence to standards, that problem is minimized. Standards and development life cycles should not imply inflexibility; rather they try to impart a development mechanism by which any developer can quickly understand systems and code in systems.

An additional chapter provides a collection of macros and screens that have been found useful in SCL systems I have worked on.

Note that the discussion of undocumented features is simply a reflection that vendors cannot document in official documentation absolutely everything their software can do. A prime example here is the COPY function in SCL. It has never been documented that the FROM and TO data sets can be the same.

I have chosen to discuss some feature of an SCL element if any of the following conditions apply:

- SAS Institute has published written documentation covering it
- it is described in the SAS Notes
- SAS Institute reviewers have verified (while this text was being written) that the feature will continue to be supported
- the feature is documented in online HELP screens supplied by SAS Institute.

The discussion includes side effects that may be detrimental in a given situation, as well as nifty features that have not been noted before. Completely undocumented SCL functions, commands, or statements are not discussed because they may not be supported in the future.

 There is no attempt in this text to cover in detail topics that are already adequately covered in SAS Institute documentation. I recommend that all readers of this text also read the text *SAS Screen Control Language: Usage, Version 6*.

Conventions

This book uses the following conventions:

 The bookworm icon is a pointer towards further reading on the subject under discussion.

 The unhappy face icon is a pointer towards some feature or programming approach that either doesn't work as expected or may lead to a lot of difficulty. Essentially, it is a wrong way icon.

 The arrow icon indicates an important point that I considered worth stressing.

Chapter 2 considers development standards. Where a standard is proposed, it is inside a shaded box, as is this text. Occasionally, such a box appears elsewhere in the book, indicating a proposed standard method of carrying out some task.

- Code is presented in monospace. Here is an example of code:

```
if x eq y then do ;
```

- Elements of SAS software are presented in uppercase.

- Variable names are presented in bold.

Chapter 2: Standards In SCL System Development

Contents

Overview

In the computer industry a large number of authors and texts devote much time and energy to discussing the need for standards in the industry. Despite all the written material available and the apparent wealth of experience with standards, the main criteria for some developers is getting the job done. They often overlook the need for adherence to standards.

One of the reasons is that standards tend to be site specific. Each site has its own idea for user documentation, written coding documentation, data set names, program module names, program internal documentation, use of programming aids such as macros, job names, screen layouts, and screen messages, and many more attributes of software. But some people find using written material impractical.

A further and frequently espoused reason for overlooking standards is that strict adherence can add considerably to the cost of developing software, particularly where standards demand project phase reviews and thorough internal documentation. I reject the cost issue as a valid reason for not following standards, as the consequences of lack of adherence are frequently more costly than the initial adherence to standards. Often this is a management issue -- if management rejects standards because adherence is expensive, the consequences are likely to be even more expensive.

The intention here is not to state absolute rules, rather to suggest ways of ensuring that SCL-based systems are easily constructed, maintained, and used. The ideas here are guidelines that can be modified to suit your site. The most important message is that once standards are decided upon, you should USE THEM.

The ideas in this chapter have been tried and work, but none will work successfully unless all members of development teams and management agree to implement them.

Many systems have more than one person working on them. In order to ensure that anybody can read the code, understand what each module does, and thus change or support the system, some standards in coding and documenting are necessary.

Standards extend beyond the programming task. User documentation should follow some standards. There is an excellent argument for all user documentation at a site following the same format. That ensures that once staff members understand the company's documentation standards, they can read any document with relative ease. Help screens are another candidate for standards. The argument for site documentation's following predefined rules applies to help screens also.

Standards also apply to the user interface, in other words the physical screens that make up an application from the user's viewpoint.

Case Study -- The Impact Of Lack Of Standards

An application had four developers coding. All were contractors and under the control of a project leader. The project was completed and functional, on time .

To get the project in on time, the project leader insisted on seeing results in the form of working code and screens. As the project evolved, the project leader totally overlooked the questions of standards, maintainability, and documentation. At completion, the contractors were immediately signed off.

The working code was given to a support team to maintain. Although proficient in the use of the software that the system was developed in, the support team required more time than did the original contractors to rewrite code in a manner that was consistent from screen to screen, to understand code, and to add documentation. They even had to rewrite display screens, as the look and feel of screens differed even to the point of how users selected menu items.

The point is that although the system came in on time, the overhead that the lack of standards generated actually more than doubled the cost. There will always be high priority, high impact systems that must be 'in by date x.' That is no excuse for not adhering to standards during development or not allowing time after production for completion of documentation.

Catalog Standards

SCL code is stored in entries in SAS catalogs. These catalogs are specific to SAS software. Catalogs themselves are stored in an operating system-dependent file.

Catalogs Versus Data Files

Keep catalogs in separate operating system files from SAS data sets.

There may be one or many catalogs in an application.

Data files have different optimum storage factors, such as block sizes and logical record lengths, than catalogs have. Code catalogs tend to be static; that is, a production application is unlikely to undergo frequent changes to code stored in catalogs, while data files tend to undergo more frequent change. The 'dynamic' data file has different back-up requirements than the catalog (for example it probably needs daily back-up, whereas the catalog doesn't). Often it is not a simple task to ensure that maintenance of either the code or the data doesn't have a negative impact on the other.

An example of such negative impact came in a system where the catalogs containing source code and databases were updated from a development system. Migration to production was done by moving the entire source code library -- accidentally including the development system databases. These were simply copied straight over the top of the production databases, causing the production system to be using nonproduction data.

In my applications, I have found that a workable rule is that program code, whether it be SAS/AF, SAS/FSP, PMENU, or some other catalog structure, should be stored in a separate application file from the application data files.

Code That Can Be Used In Many Applications

When code is being used with minor variations in many systems, it is a good idea to create a system library of frequently used SCL routines and make the code generic for reuse. Note that this standard suggests the use of parameters and method blocks.

From an application developer's viewpoint, there are two clearly separate types of code in SCL. These are application specific code and generic code that can be used in a multitude of applications.

Generic code in an SCL sense occupies a role in SCL similar to the role of the SASAUTOS library in the entire SAS system. That is, generic code consists of windows or SCL programs that can be used in several applications and should be stored in a system library accessible to all SCL programmers. This approach saves having multiple users developing similar code for different applications, just as the SASAUTOS library for macros does.

Some standards have to be applied to decide just what goes into a generic code library. It is pointless to put into such a library either code that is unlikely ever to be used in another application or code that is not generic enough to be useful.

A further advantage of generic code libraries is that needing to store source code in just one place saves disk space. This advantage can be particularly important in disk space-constrained sites or sites where each application is charged for its space. While this benefit should be obvious, the need for rapid development often causes such obvious benefits to be overlooked. I also find it an advantage not to store source code with my production applications, but to keep source code in a development (testing) system. This relieves space used but also removes any urge to alter the production source code!

Catalog Naming

Like all storage media, catalog names should be meaningful. A workable system is to have catalog names consist of 3 characters to describe the application, then 5 characters to describe what is in the catalog.

Nongeneric catalogs should reside in system libraries that reflect the application's name. This arrangement simplifies working out disk space in use by an application and in general assists system administration, tuning, and maintenance.

While the library names are often governed by site data set naming standards, it is rare that sites have developed such standards for SAS catalogs.

The convention of 8 characters for catalog names on many systems may appear to be restrictive but has rarely been a problem in my experience. A bigger bind occurs in the CMS operating system, where operating system constraints restrict catalog names to 7 characters.

My preference is to keep different types of catalog objects (such as FSEDIT, PROGRAM, and HELP) in different catalogs. For large systems, it can be helpful to know that all FSEDIT entries are in one place, while all AF entries are somewhere else.

For instance, in JARS, FSEDIT entries are in a catalog called JRSFSEDT, AF entries are in a catalog called JRSAFSCR, and PMENU entries are in a catalog called JRSPMENU. Under CMS, this convention would need to be altered, often a 2-character acronym can be used to describe the application.

If your system data sets will only hold code for single applications, the first 3 characters can be used for other purposes. However, keeping a unique prefix like this can be useful when copying catalogs and when viewing catalogs on screen as it provides a built-in masking feature.

For instance, if JARS, MARTS, and SUNS code all resided in the same SAS library, that library would contain catalog entries called JRSAFSCR, JRSFSEDT, JRSPMENU, MTSAFSCR, MTSFSEDT, MTSPMENU, SUNAFSCR, SUNFSEDT, SUNPMENU, as well as any other necessary catalogs.

Note that most sites under MVS include some system library that contains much of the site's source code for batch-based applications. There is no reason why such a library should not exist for SAS online systems as well, following the above naming conventions.

Program Code Standards

Source Entry Member Names

If there is one standard to be obeyed as a rule, it is to make member names and descriptions meaningful. It is always easier to have a meaningful name and associated description in a catalog, than to use something that has no relevance to the application.

For very large systems, it is useful to design a member naming convention for program entries; FSEDIT entries, and so on and stick to it. A useful one is to allow entry names to follow the menu choices they apply to.

An example of this naming convention is drawn from JARS. The main menu has eight options. Code for each of those options is in a set of AF programs called JRSxzyyy, where x is the menu number. If that option leads to a another menu, say with three options, you could generate program entries with names like JRSx1yyy, JRSx2yyy and JRSx3yyy. The yyy part of the name is at the programmer's discretion, but it may designate another menu option. When you view program entries under PROC BUILD and such a naming convention is in force, all entries for a specific option are together. You may be surprised at how much easier it is to work with all entries together than to work with them spread about.

Obviously such a convention may require some modification to work with different applications. An immediate problem occurs when the number of menu items increases so that altering one character does not allow distinction between items. The point is to develop workable standards in names, stick with them, and not randomly assign names to entries.

A major advantage of such a naming convention is that it enables you to see at a glance which pieces of code apply to individual menu options. When debugging, documenting, or simply talking about options, you will find this convention has been found to be very helpful.

☹ *Meaningful names that try to describe a screen's function can look very random when being viewed in a BUILD list unless they follow a naming convention that causes them to be logically grouped.*

Variable Names

Meaningfulness can be hard to achieve within the eight character limits for SCL window fields. How does one assign a readable, instantly identifiable name to a field that describes a person's productivity for a month? Maybe a field called **product** already exists and describes products that have been worked on. On the other hand, **prodtiv** and other such corruptions are difficult to interpret.

The answers are not obvious and may come down to personal preference. To allow maximum flexibility with names, you should use comments to describe the program's variables.

That sounds like overkill. An often heard programmer's response is 'I know what the variables mean...' My response to that is generally unrelenting. The fact that you wrote a program doesn't mean that you and only you will ever look at it or that even you will remember in a few months just what everything means.

Describing the variables is a useful documentation technique. SAS Institute supplies this as an integral part of fields in a SAS data set using the variable label. SCL programs and FSEDIT screens should not be ignored just because the data dictionary ability is not currently built in.

The following example is the start of an entry's source code from JARS. It illustrates the idea of labeling variable names in a variable descriptor area at the top of source code:

```
/*********************************************************
Variable Descriptor Block:

MESS              : array of screen messages
*MESSAGE          : currently active screen message
*JARSDEPT         : list of departments user can access
*DP               : department selected by this user
RC00              : return code from FIELD function

* means a variable displayed on screen
*********************************************************/
```

Description Of Program Entry

For each program or SCL entry, a short description of what it does can be useful.

Generally that is not absolutely necessary with FSEDIT screens, as they are devoted to controlling a particular database update.

It is not necessary to write a novel to describe what the role of a program entry is. Usually, as the code is developed, specific notes must be made to describe just what certain sections are doing. These notes are code specific and need not be included at the top.

An example of such a note from MARTS is the following:

```
/************************************************************

Allows user to update machine type database using FSVIEW and
creates format tables to check validity of machine types
when entered in other screens

************************************************************/
```

That is straight to the point, describes the function of the entry, and doesn't clutter up the code. Details of particular pieces of code are described later when the code is written.

Change History

A description of each change to the program is useful. This helps later when you try to understand program logic (particularly as program changes may cause variations in design documents), and it may prevent previous bad code from being coded back in later. It also serves to state exactly who has altered the system code and when.

For want of a better or more standard name, I will refer to this descriptive area of an entry as a change block. At a minimum, a change block should state who made a change, when, why, and exactly what the change entailed. A further tip is to give each change an identifier and add this to each line changed in the program.

Change blocks generally are kept at the start of source code members. Throughout the computer industry, this is a well used and accepted place to put change blocks. While it would be nice to have an integrated window in SCL to store change blocks as part of the program, that is not available and there is no need to attempt to change the industry standard.

As an example, in JARS we have the following change block in one of the program entries' source code:

```
/***********************************************************
-----------------------------------------------------------
Date Changed: 15jul91     By: DGS_____     ID: CHG0001

Reason: When users selected option 7, if they had
        used option 6 earlier the macro variable EDTYPE
        was not reset, and they were placed in the
        administrator's project list in edit rather than
        browse mode.

Details Of Change

Explicitly reset &EDTYPE before entering option 7
-----------------------------------------------------------
***********************************************************/
```

An entry is made each time a program is modified. This procedure allows a trail of changes to be maintained easily. In the program code, each changed line includes the identifier in the comment, as shown below:

```
call symputc('edtype','BROWSE') ; /* CHG0001 */
```

Whether the code that is being replaced should be removed is really up to coders. I prefer to leave the old code in the source stream but comment it out. That makes it simple to see what caused an old error. If you do delete the prior code, the change block description can become somewhat meaningless.

Using a change block may raise the question of when to purge old entries. If many change blocks are filling the program entry, finding the program code becomes difficult, especially when you are also using variable descriptor blocks and code description blocks.

To get around this problem, you can maintain a separate database for change blocks. However, this strategy creates the overhead of maintaining a separate database and of remembering to update it. Also, it defeats part of the purpose of keeping change blocks, that is, to have changes described accurately and succinctly at the source code.

Change blocks at the beginning of a program module are a standard method of recording changes in the EDP industry. There is no reason why SCL programs should not follow the tried, tested, and workable standard. It seems to add more problems than it solves to use a separate file, or as has been suggested, to place change blocks at the end of the source code.

The problem of old change blocks no longer being required is simple to get around. Using your discretion as to when a change becomes part of the system, ultimately you may be able to delete them (assuming that external documentation is updated to reflect this change). Always ensure that documentation about all changes is kept, as it is quite plausible that someone could put the same code back in later.

Storing Error Messages

Most systems have error, warning, or note messages that can be displayed under various circumstances. The physical placement of these messages on screen is described under 'Screen Display Standards' later in this chapter. Here I address just where and how the messages should be stored in a program.

The rest of this section describes several options.

Embedding Messages In Code

The simplest method of storing error messages is to imbed messages within the code at the point where they will be displayed.

With this method, messages are scattered throughout the program. Two immediate disadvantages occur:

- Coding this way makes error numbering difficult.
- If messages are used throughout a program, they may be duplicated.

The advantage of coding error messages this way is that the message always appears right where you want it. This is helpful when viewing code; you see the error messages right where they are used.

I use this method in situations where I do not need an error number. However, if an SCL entry has repeated messages, I prefer not to code messages this way.

Storing Messages In An Array

An alternative is to store the messages in an array at the AF or FSP entry beginning.

Storing messages this way concentrates all the error, warning, or information messages for an entry together in one place and makes error numbering simple. To display a message, assign the relevant message number to the message field or legend field being used.

This method has the disadvantage that if the same error message is required in multiple entries, that message must be duplicated in each screen. However, in the context of an SCL system such duplication is likely to be minor.

An example of using arrays for message storage follows:

```
array mess {*} $ 70 (
'ERROR 001:  - No Department Selected -- Use Option 1'
'ERROR 002:  - Access To Administrators Options Invalid'
'ERROR 003:  - Access Denied While Department Selected'
'ERROR:  - Administration Options In Use By'
'NOTE: Data Downloader Complete'
'ERROR 004:  - Please Enter A Valid Value'
'NOTE: JARS Administration Options Complete'
'Department Not Yet Selected'
'Welcome To JARS '
'No Verification Report As No Units Selected'
'Unit Level Verification Report Completed'
'Unit Level Verification Report Started'
                    ) ;
```

Note that for ease of maintenance, the maximum array size is not coded. This ensures that when items are added to the array, changing the maximum size is not overlooked.

To assign a message to a display field, simply use an assignment statement:

```
_msg_ = mess{10} ;
```

Note that array references can use either round brackets or curly brackets. Curly brackets are recommended, as they make it obvious that an array rather than a function is being referenced.

Storing Messages In An Application-Wide List

> *You could store messages in an SCL list, thus avoiding the inherent problem of messages being duplicated between entries. As SCL lists can be defined over a whole application rather than entry by entry, this method removes the requirement to store arrays in each entry.*

The list approach has the overhead of setting the list up once at the application start. Given that many other tasks tend to occur at startup, this is not likely to be a major burden unless a large number of messages exist. On memory constrained systems with large lists being used, this approach may cause some slowdown.

The list approach has the distinct advantage of allowing the messages to be stored in a SAS data set, which makes updating very easy.

Messages are easily assigned to a message field from a list. Use the GETITEMC function to assign the tenth item of the list to the standard SAS message field, as follows:

```
_msg_ = getitemc(listid,10) ;
```

Using Compile-Time Macro Variables

> *This method, along with hard coding the messages at the point they are to be issued, minimizes run-time resources, as the message is hardwired into the code at compile time. By contrast, the array and list methods require run-time resources to fetch the message text.*

I find this method of storing messages really useful. If you use a string of macro assignments in each program, the method becomes similar to an array-based approach. The main difference is that the array uses run-time resources, so it may appear to be a little slower to the end user.

To use this macro variable approach, just code all the error messages at the entry beginning, assigning each message to a macro variable. As with a named list, you can use a name (in this case the macro variable name) to refer to error messages.

The equivalent to the previous array example is the following:

```
%let nodept='ERROR 001:  - No Department Selected -- Use Option 1';
%let noaccess='ERROR 002:  - Access To Administrators Options Invalid';
%let denyaccs='ERROR 003:  - Access Denied While Department Selected';

%let optinuse='ERROR:  - Administration Options In Use By';
%let download='NOTE: Data Downloader Complete';
%let invalid='ERROR 004:  - Please Enter A Valid Value';
%let admncomp='NOTE: JARS Administration Options Complete';
%let nodept='Department Not Yet Selected';
%let welcome='Welcome To JARS ';
%let noverify='No Verification Report As No Units Selected';
%let verfcomp='Unit Level Verification Report Completed';
%let verfstrt='Unit Level Verification Report Started';
```

To fetch a particular message (done at compile time), use code like the following:

```
_msg_ = &noverify ;
```

The clear disadvantage here is that often you can write code in such a way that message text is not known until run time. You cannot use this method in that case because the macro variable variables are substituted at compile time.

> *I recommend using the macro approach where possible for readability. That and the hard-coded approach are functionally equivalent, but the macro approach has the advantage of clustering the messages in one place.*

Tests I have done indicate the list method requires most storage (due to the need to maintain code to create and populate the list) and time to extract a message and insert a variable value. The need to store array elements makes the array approach expensive in terms of storage, but it is fast. The macro and hard-coded approaches are very fast and conservative on storage.

Readability

> *You should avoid placing several statements on a physical line.*

There is little if any justification for having more than one statement to a line. It simply makes code difficult to read and understand. Furthermore, since the SCL debugger is line oriented, it can be difficult to work out exactly which statement is being executed if there is more than one to a line.

> *Statements that begin on one line and end several lines later (If Then Do, Do, SUBMIT, WHEN, SELECT, and so on) should follow simple indenting rules.*

Indent the second and following lines 2 or 3 characters under the first. Either line the end of blocks up with the start of the first line or indent the final line as well.

Examples taken from JARS follow:

(1) Example of indenting in an IF statement:

```
/* check validity of selected printer id by attempting to
   allocate as a SYSOUT and returning non zero if we cannot
   allocate, in which case tell user to try again */
%valprt(prt)
if retcode ne 0 then do ; /* not a prter */
   message=mess{2} ;       /* bad printer message */
   prt = _blank_ ;         /* empty the printer field */
   rc00=field('colour yellow highlight',
              'message') ;/* highlight the message */
   cursor prt ;            /* position cursor */
   return ;                /* control back to user */
end ;
```

(2) Example of indenting code within an already indented WHEN condition:

```
when('8') do ;
/* access the JARS administrator options. First check the
   user is allowed to access these*/
   if not index(jarsdept,'***') then do ; /* no access */
      message = mess{2} ;       /* issue message */
```

```
      %highligh                        /* highlight message */
      return ;                         /* back to user */
   end ;

/* ensure that the user is not currently accessing a
   department as the admin options may update tables for
   departments and a conflict could arise*/
   if symgetc('dp') ne _blank_ then do ; /* dept alloced */
     message = mess{3} ;       /* disallow access message */
     %highligh                        /* highlight message */
     return ;                         /* back to user */
   end ;

/* start up the admin options*/
   call display('catlg.jarscde.jarsp500.program') ;

/* and return control to the user*/
   message=mess{7} ;
   %highligh
   return ;
 end ;                                /* of the WHEN clause */
```

Note that in the first example above, the FIELD function extends over more than one line. It is usually easier to read such code by adopting further indenting. The example code illustrates this by indenting the second line under the parameter list from the first.

The above examples illustrate documentation and indenting standards. (Note that you may have other preferred methods. The point, again, is to be consistent.)

Code Documentation

Document code by giving a description of blocks of code stating exactly what the code does. The amount of documentation in program code should not be excessive. The point is to indicate quickly and succinctly just what a piece of code does.

Consider the following example from JARS:

```
/* check if data set has any observations, if so just invoke
   FSEDIT, otherwise invoke FSEDIT with the ADD option
   enabled so user doesn't see the 'PRESS END or ADD'
   screen */

dsid01= open(dsname,'i') ;
nobs  = attrn(dsid01,'any') ;
rc    = close(dsid01) ;

if nobs ne 1 then /* no observations on database */
   call fsedit(dsname,'ddname.screens.option.screen',,'add') ;
else            /* observations available */
   call fsedit(dsname,'ddname.screens.option.screen') ;
```

The short comment succinctly sums up just what the block of code does.

If a SAS software function is being used in a nonstandard or undocumented (by SAS Institute) method, either include some pointer to site documentation or document it in code. For maximum usefulness, such documentation should be kept in a place where all developers in an organization have access. This goal may require extending the SASHELP system to allow site information to be used.

Variable Names

> *Window variable names should be meaningful within the current 8-character restriction. Special purpose variables such as return codes, data set identifiers, and so on should be given names that reflect that special usage and can be greater than 8 characters if not window variables.*

A standard I follow is that return codes are named RCxx where xx range from 01 through 99.

Extend as necessary if you require more return codes in a program. However, it should be noted that it is rare for a return code to be required throughout a program; usually a return code is tested and handled immediately. There is no reason why a return code field like this cannot be reused.

The above comments also apply to data set identifiers (for example, from OPEN function calls, although these have a much greater likelihood of being required throughout a program).

Adopting such a naming convention means that it is immediately clear that a certain subset of the possible variables (return code, data set identifier, and so on) is being used. This aids readability and means a consistent coding style.

Following is a useful naming convention for various items such as return codes:

Return codes	RCxx
Data set Identifiers	DSIDxx
File Identifiers	FIDxx

Array names should follow the same rules as non-array variables; that is, they should be meaningful. An array that contains values of project identifiers should be called PROJIDS, not, as I have often seen, ARRAY1 or PRJARRAY.

Resist the urge to call parameters (for example, to DISPLAY, FSEDIT, FSVIEW) PARM01, PARM02, and so on. These names are meaningless.

> **As with any programming language, keep code simple and code tasks in the simplest, rather than most complex, manner.**

It is often necessary to come up with complex solutions to evidently simple problems. It is never necessary to code complex solutions to any problem when a simple solution will suffice.

Naturally, it is not always obvious that a simple solution may exist. If it is not possible to code a simple solution, ensure that code documentation is clear and concise. The next programmer who works on the task may have a better solution.

While unnecessarily clever code is frowned upon, experienced SAS programmers know that often there are many ways to accomplish a task. You may want to experiment with alternatives, as resource consumption can often be minimized by looking beyond the obvious solution. It is not unusual to have to make a decision as to whether readability and ease of maintenance should take priority over resource reduction.

Screen Display Standards

Certain attributes of display screens recur time and time again and should be standardized at least in an application and preferably across the site. In this section, discussion includes

- message standards (error, warning, and information)
- function key layouts
- screen names/titles
- position of legends
- size of windows
- placement of help screens.

Message Standards

A decision regarding messages needs to be made and stuck to at the start of an application. You must decide whether to use

- the default SAS message line and variable (_MSG_)
- your own message line
- legends for all messages
- the WNAME function to display messages in the top left hand corner
- some combination of the above.

Using The SAS Message Line

The obvious way to display messages is to use the SAS message line.

This appears immediately under the command line. It has the immediate disadvantage that messages placed in here by SAS software cannot always be overwritten as they may be initialized after SCL has completed. Hence user-written messages cannot always overwrite the SAS ones. The SAS message line is not available when a SAS/AF entry has the BANNER attribute switched off. It is available when you are using the PMENU facility.

The advantage of using this line is that you do not use any extra part of the screen over that which SAS already uses. Hence you are maximizing screen usage.

Displaying Messages Using A Screen Field

Create a screen variable to place messages into.

Application messages can coexist with SAS internal messages, and a message line is available when the BANNER general attribute is set to NONE in a SAS/AF program entry. A reasonable standard is to reserve the first line after the SAS message line for such an application message line. However, this standard is very dependent on your site standards. If other applications display messages at the screen bottom, place your message field there.

An example display screen under AF appears in Figure 2.1:

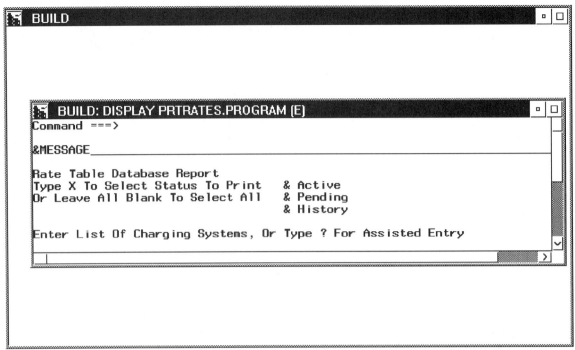

Figure 2.1: Using A Field To Display Messages

In Figure 2.1 we are using the variable name **message**. SAS/AF assigns these attributes as follows (only attributes changed from the default are listed):

Attribute	Value
Pad	BLANK
Type	CHAR
Protect	YES
Just	CENTER

Note that the PAD option is used to set the message field to blank, thus hiding the field from display when no message is present. This is quite different from the NODISPLAY option, which allows a field to exist on the screen but never to be shown to the user. Though PAD=' ' is *always* displayed, the characters are often blanks.

To display the message in SAS/AF, it may be desirable to add some color or attribute to the field. Use the FIELD function to do this.

In FSEDIT, the message field is added to the screen using the MOD;2 option. It is a 'computed' field; in other words, it does not exist on the database being displayed by FSEDIT, but rather is computed in the SCL program. The message can be assigned a display color in the FCOLOR screen and attributes in the FATTR screen. In my applications, it is also necessary to use the CAPS screen to remove capitalization, the PROTECT screen to protect the field, the JUSTIFY screen to CENTER the field, and the PAD screen to set a pad character of ' ' (or blank).

Using Legends For Displaying Messages

You could use legends, which have the definite advantages that an eyecatching window pops up and also that you can use several lines for messages without interrupting your own screen display.

The legend overlays your screen with a new window, rather than taking up space in the current window.

Full control over attributes such as highlighting and color is built in. Defining a legend is simple and quick, and the developer has full control over how long it is displayed on the screen.

Legends provide a neat and visually attractive interface that fits in well with the window oriented language that SCL features. For example, the screen in Figure 2.2 demonstrates how SUNS error messages are reported.

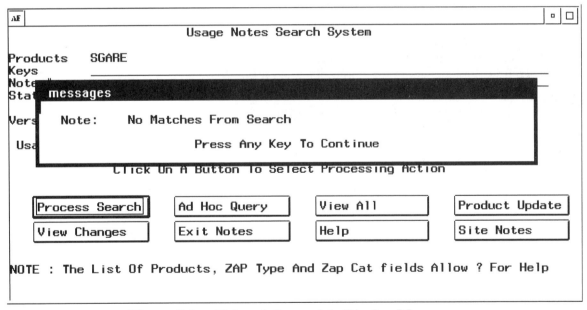

Figure 2.2:   Using A Legend to Display Messages

The CALL WAIT routine (available from Release 6.08) can be used to suspend SCL execution for a period, as in the following program:

```
call putlegend(2,'NOTE: No Matches From Search');
call legend() ;
call wait(20) ;
call endlegend() ;
```

This holds the legend on screen for a period of 20 seconds, then hands control back to the user.

Using CALL WAIT means that the developer, rather than the user, has control over how long the message stays on screen. This condition is not always appropriate or desirable. The user can control this timeout period using the following code:

```
call putlegend(2,'NOTE: No Matches From Search');
call putlegend(4,'  Press Any Key To Continue') ;
call legend('Messages') ;
call execcmdi('next messages','noexec') ;
call endlegend() ;
```

This strategy works because the EXECCMDI routine makes the legend active. Pressing the ENTER key (or a number of other keys) in that screen reactivates the entry that displayed the legend. Note that once the legend is activated, then EXECCMDI gives it control. Placing these the other way around is futile as the window named MESSAGES doesn't exist at the time the EXECCMDI is called.

It has been noted under OS/2 (in Release 6.08) that an annoying flicker can occur as the legend window is made active, as though the legend rapidly disappears and reappears. This occurs once and seems unavoidable. Under MVS, the user is placed in the legend, and the legend window is active; but the border appears like that of an inactive window.

If you decide to use legends, settle on a consistent position for placing them on screens throughout a whole application. Do not make the mistake of moving legends to different positions on different screens. This looks unprofessional and is difficult for users to adjust to.

If using legends, customize the following macro and place it in SASAUTOS. Calling this macro with the appropriate parameters will ensure that the legend is always placed in a consistent manner.

```
%macro legit(line,message) ;
  call wregion(10,10,5,60,'') ;
  call putlegend(&line,&message,'','highlight');
%mend legit ;
```

To customize, decide on your appropriate placement for the legend window and alter the WREGION to reflect this. You may want to add more parameters and PUTLEGEND calls to accommodate more messages or to include an EXECCMDI as above to give the user control over how long the legend remains on screen.

Call the macro in the following manner:

```
%legit(2,'Processing Request, Please Wait')
call legend(,,,'highlight') ;
.....
call endlegend() ;
```

Note that legends are the only means discusssed here of issuing messages that can be used in SCL entries. They do not rely on the presence of a display screen.

Using The Window NAME Area For Messages

The Window NAME area provides a predefined area of the program screen that is entirely under program control and thus is not affected by SAS messages, does not take up screen space, and does not require extensive coding to set up.

WNAME puts text onscreen starting in the top left hand corner of the window border area. Text can be updated at any time and is displayed when the screen is next rewritten.

JARS uses WNAME to set up the physical placement onscreen of all its messages. Databank adopted a standard that any message would be concatenated to a screen name. This provided the distinct advantage that if users report a problem of any description, the screen name is embedded within the message. Coding is very simple, and WNAME removes the possible problem of extra variable space being used. The screen that is presented to the user is shown in Figure 2.3.

```
┌─────────────────────────────────────────────────────────────────────────┐
│ ▞ JARSP000 ERROR: JR000003 - Access Denied While Department Selected  ▫ □ │
├─────────────────────────────────────────────────────────────────────────┤
│              Welcome To JARS               Department 746 Selected         │
│                                                                           │
│                                                                           │
│            Please Select An Option And Press ENTER    8                    │
│                                                                           │
│                1   Select Working Department                               │
│                                                                           │
│                2   Add/Edit This Weeks Activity Sheets                     │
│                3   Data Verification Report                                │
│                4   Data Verification Report For Individual Units           │
│                5   Reporting Options                                       │
│                6   Department Support Options                              │
│                                                                           │
│                7   Project Leaders Activity Sheet Review Option            │
│                8   Administrators Support Options                          │
│                9   Use Data Downloader To PC                               │
│                X   Exit JARS (Or Press PF3)                                │
│                                                                           │
│ PF1= Help      PF2= View Rpt  PF3= End       PF4= Unselect  PF5= -Unused-  │
│ PF6= -Unused-  PF7= -Unused-  PF8= -Unused-  PF9= SDSF      PF10= -Unused- │
└─────────────────────────────────────────────────────────────────────────┘
```

Figure 2.3:   Using A WNAME Area To Display Messages

An example of usage of WNAME in this context follows. Here I am assigning an error message in a JARS screen. The code to do this can be any one of the following, depending on whether embedded messages, lists, or arrays are used to store the error messages:

```
call wname('JARSP000 Error: JR000003-Access Denied While Department
Selected') ;
```

or,

```
call wname('JARSP000 ' || getitem(listid,12)) ;
```

or,

```
call wname('JARSP000 ' || mess{12}) ;
```

Note that the message is displayed when the screen in Figure 2.3 is refreshed, not when the WNAME function is called. To get the message updated without using a RETURN, use the REFRESH statement.

Combining Message Styles

It is possible that none of the above will completely cover an application's messaging requirements. The advice is simple. Choose a workable combination and stick with it on all screens.

Using legends in conjunction with other messaging may be inappropriate because the legend is so eyecatching that users tend to miss the other message. Popping up successive legends can be irritating, so you are really left with using either WNAME and a special message field or multiple message fields. However, note that legend windows can be set big enough to place multiple messages in one legend.

In my applications, I use either LEGENDS or WNAME to display messages. I prefer WNAME because it is such an easy routine to use and our site's MVS standards for messages are not aligned to legends. However, I feel that legends look better and are more eyecatching. They require a little extra work to set up.

Function Key Layouts

This is a rule, not a tip or suggestion, but an absolute rule. Function key values must be consistent from screen to screen. Furthermore, they should follow the same standards that other applications in the site already use.

It is generally standard in IBM shops that PF1 means HELP, PF3 means END, PF7 is BACKWARD, and PF8 means FORWARD. This convention is generally used by SAS software, but as such it merely follows from a standard evolved over operating systems over many years. Other operating systems may adopt similar or even very different standards; the point is, again, to be consistent.

Other keys may be application dependent, but the rule still exists. If a key is to be a standard command such as RIGHT or LEFT, use the usually accepted keys in your site for that command, in the IBM case PF10 and PF11.

Application design frequently dictates that function key meanings be displayed on screen. Over the years, a de facto standard of using the bottom lines of a screen for this purpose has developed as shown in Figure 2.4. In general, this is a usable and consistent standard.

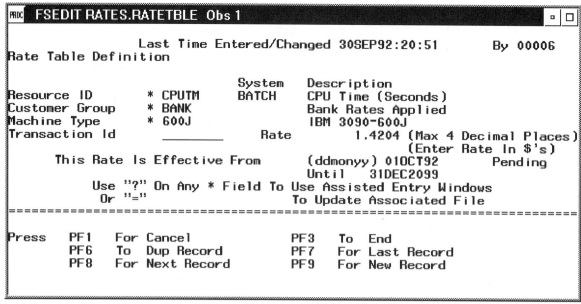

```
PROC  FSEDIT RATES.RATETBLE Obs 1                                    □ │□

                    Last Time Entered/Changed 30SEP92:20:51      By 00006
Rate Table Definition

                              System     Description
Resource ID        * CPUTM    BATCH      CPU Time (Seconds)
Customer Group     * BANK                Bank Rates Applied
Machine Type       * 600J               IBM 3090-600J
Transaction Id       _____   Rate         1.4204 (Max 4 Decimal Places)
                                                   (Enter Rate In $'s)
         This Rate Is Effective From      (ddmonyy) 01OCT92        Pending
                                          Until    31DEC2099
              Use "?" On Any * Field To Use Assisted Entry Windows
              Or  "="                     To Update Associated File
=============================================================================

Press    PF1   For Cancel          PF3   To   End
         PF6   To  Dup Record       PF7   For  Last Record
         PF8   For Next Record      PF9   For  New Record
```

Figure 2.4:   Displaying Function Key Settings On Screen

The KEYS entries that SAS Institute supplies as an integral part of the SAS System have the disadvantage that no text other than the key value can be displayed. It is not always the case that the key's value reflects its meaning, especially to a naive user. For displaying keys, the recommendation is that lines be displayed at the screen base with a short, succinct description of each key. There is another, more practical reason for not using the KEYS window as a prompt for users, namely that you may not want the command line and may require all function keys for purposes other than displaying a KEYS window.

Note that even if the window does not occupy the whole physical screen, consistency suggests that the bottom lines be reserved for key definitions.

There is no reason why a description of key definitions could not be placed in HELP screens.

FSVIEW presents a different situation due to its different screen handling and will be discussed separately in the later FSVIEW chapter.

Further discussion on operating system-specific aspects of function keys is found in the later section on portability.

> *Extended tables are a special case due to the inability to use the scrollable area for static key definitions. One option I find works well is to display a legend with the key settings in the bottom few lines of the screen and fit the extended table to the remaining space. This can also be applied to native SAS windows such as PREVIEW.*

Screen Names And Descriptions

For error reporting, it is useful to display the screen name (that is, the SAS/AF program entry name or the FSEDIT screen name) in the WNAME area. This helps problem solving as problems are reported by screen name.

SAS software supplies a means of placing a screen description via the WNAME function. This description is placed in the top left hand corner of the display and is a useful means of identification, particularly when users want to report problems with a screen. As previously discussed, it can also be a useful place to display error messages.

For straight-out screen naming, WNAME is most useful under FSEDIT. SAS/AF program entries have the ability to specify an entry name from the GATTR window associated with the entry. However, you may wish to have different messages in the top right-hand corner dependent on events occurring within the system. Since WNAME updates the description when the screen is next seen, it can be used to change the message at will.

There is no reason why the WNAME function shouldn't be used in FSEDIT to display a short comment about the screen. A very useful example of the way WNAME can enhance a screen can be found in the modified FSEDIT screen that SAS Institute supplies with the SAS Notes.

WNAME is called on each observation and places text indicating the type of note in the top left corner. Figure 2.5 shows a screen with a compatibility note:

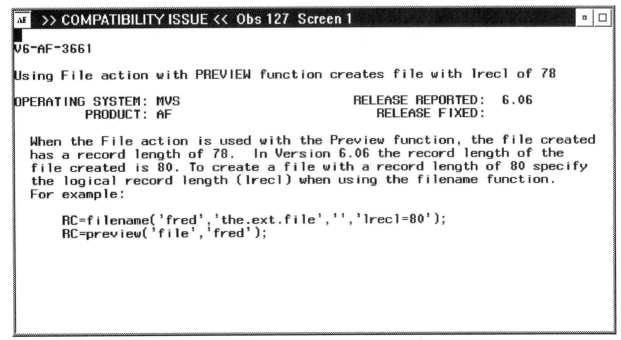

Figure 2.5: Describing A Screen Using WNAME

Note that while this section has revolved around using WNAME purely as a screen descriptive mechanism, WNAME was discussed earlier as a means of providing systems messages.

Help Screens

> *Online help screens require certain standards to be met. They should be context sensitive. For instance, a HELP key pressed on the command line should pop up help in the application window, while a HELP key pressed in a window field should offer specific help on that field.*

It is a simple task to make HELP screens context sensitive in both SAS/AF and SAS/FSP. In SAS/AF, use the help entry on each field's ATTR screen and ensure a function key is set up to initiate the help. In FSEDIT, use the ALLCMDS option of the CONTROL statement and also the CURFLD function.

The following example demonstrates this task in FSEDIT. The intention is to allow users to press PF1 and receive HELP on the field they are in, or if not currently in a field, to receive help for the screen. In the INIT section code, enter the following:

```
control allcmds <other options> ;
```

Then, in the main section, use the following code:

```
if word(1,'u') eq 'HELP' then do ;
 select (curfld()) ;
   when ('field1') call display('field1.help') ;
   when ('field2') call display('field2.help') ;
   otherwise call display('screen.help') ;
 end ;
 return ;
end ;
```

Unless the NO EXIT SAS/AF attribute is used, using the CURFLD approach is totally unnecessary in SAS/AF entries, as HELP is an attribute available for each field.

> *It is reasonable to accept that end users, rather than developers, should have some control over just what is placed in a HELP screen. As developers, we need to be aware that what we consider trivial may be a user's nightmare. HELP screens can be a high maintenance overhead, but they can provide concise easy-to-access documentation.*

CBT screens, while not covered in this text, are an excellent means of providing help. The ability to provide HELP screens that allow users to effectively select further help on specific topics is supplied by CBT, whereas the standard SAS/AF HELP window is purely textual. In JARS, it is possible to select HELP in the main menu and from that HELP, using CBT, access the help for any of the menu options. Thus the main menu, as well as being the entry point into the system, also becomes the entry point into the HELP system. In time, JARS developers will allow HELP options in specific windows to directly access the help for those windows.

Although HELP screens are text, you can make them look very professional and visually appealing. This is accomplished by means of screen attributes and colors.

To utilize color and attributes in a HELP screen, you need the display manager COLOR command. This command causes any text typed after the command is entered to appear on screen in the new color. Thus you have the bulk of the HELP screen appear in, say, CYAN, and can then issue the command COLOR TEXT YELLOW and highlight a particular part of the screen to have it stand out.

Attributes that can be entered are Reverse, Blink, Underline, and Highlight. These are set up by adding the capitalized letter to the COLOR command. Thus COLOR TEXT YELLOW R would cause all text entered in the HELP screen to be yellow reverse video after the COLOR command is entered.

Alternatively, use the SAS software escape sequences, discussed under the HOST INFORMATION topic of the SAS System help facility in an interactive SAS session.

The major catch with using these sequences is moving between operating environments. This is discussed in the later section on portability. It may be necessary to modify your HELP screen attributes after porting to utilize these features in a meaningful manner. For instance, under OS/2 a help screen may use a different color to make text stand out; under MVS it may use highlighting and ignore the color.

In a nongraphical operating environment (MVS, for example) you may be restricted as to how much you can use color. However, attributes such as highlighting may be available.

Note that it is also possible to use the EDPARMS entry in SAS/AF to set up defaults for each screen. This is useful to ensure that all screens are the same color when you are coding multiple screens in other than the default color and not using escape sequences or the COLOR TEXT command.

If you want to make help screens look really appealing, consider the use of extended tables scrolling in a region on a FRAME entry. A further region would exist on screen containing help information for the currently selected entry. As the user scrolls the table, the text in the help region changes to reflect the current extended table selection. This strategy is just an extension of FRAME entries; I haven't seen them suggested in a help context, but they are so flexible that this should be a simple and useful exercise.

Chapter 3: Some Useful Concepts

Contents

Subsetting And Deleting Observations

Where Clauses

With Version 6, SAS software introduced a number of fundamental changes to the SAS database structure. Among these changes is the ability to subset data sets using a WHERE clause.

The FSEDIT and FSVIEW procedures allow users to issue WHERE clauses in two ways:

- The WHERE clause can be applied when calling the procedure; thus the procedure will only operate on those observations that satisfied the WHERE clause. The user cannot overwrite this, but can issue another WHERE clause (not necessarily a WHERE ALSO) that further subsets the current observations. An example is

```
proc fsedit data = <libref>.<data set name> ;
  where <where clause > ;
run ;
```

- The user can issue a WHERE clause from the command line. All observations are available to the procedure when a WHERE UNDO or WHERE CLEAR is used, but until one of those commands is executed, the user only accesses the subset. However, the user can issue a WHERE ALSO command to restrict the current subset further.

Additionally, you may desire to force a WHERE clause using the SCL EXECCMD routine, thus forcing the user to access only a particular subset. This action is equivalent to the one described in the second bulleted point above, except that the application, not the user, is charged with issuing the command. However, the user can undo or overwrite this WHERE clause, as it is issued from the command line.

To avoid this overwriting of the WHERE clause, you can either

- use a WHERE data set option in the CALL FSEDIT routine

- if necessary, use SUBMIT to submit a PROC FSEDIT or PROC FSVIEW and issue a WHERE clause in that SUBMIT.

When a WHERE clause is in effect, the user can still carry out normal actions such as FORWARD, BACKWARD, and so on. The difference is that the WHERE clause forces these commands to access the next observation satisfying the clause, not necessarily the next consecutive observation in the database. In this situation, the access is described as accessing the next logical observation, as opposed to a usual FORWARD or BACKWARD on an unsubsetted database that accesses the next physical observation (if no observations are deleted). Note that some texts may use the words 'relative' instead of 'logical' and 'absolute' instead of 'physical'.

Using a WHERE causes FSEDIT to behave in a slightly different manner than usual. For instance, you cannot jump directly to an observation. Because logical observations are being used, FSEDIT does not know where any particular observation number is to be found. Even if it did, it still would not know whether accessing a particular observation meant to access the physical observation number (and thus issue an error if the observation did not satisfy the WHERE) or to access the nth logical observation when you jumped to observation n.

Deleting Observations

Observation deletion from FSEDIT is not a new feature in Version 6. However, its ramifications for SCL are useful to explore.

When an observation is deleted using an in-place editor such as FSEDIT or FSVIEW (or using the SCL DELOBS function), it is not physically removed from the data set. That 'deleted' observation stays there until the entire data set is written back out again. Physically the observation still exists; logically, it does not. All that the DELETE accomplishes is to set a flag in the observation to tell SAS not to process it in future reads.

 Although a deleted observation still physically exists, it is not currently (Release 6.08) possible to 'undelete' it. The delete is final.

Effectively, when any part of SAS software reads an observation, it does so using internal routines that check for deleted observations and issues a return code to the caller that the observation is not available if it is deleted. SAS software routines then request that the next observation be read.

Writing the entire data set back out (thus physically removing the deleted observations) can be accomplished in many ways, for example using the SORT routine. When an observation is deleted in place, the flag set on the observation tells SAS to remove that observation when the data set is next written.

As a further illustration, consider the following. I have a data set with 5 observations and delete observation 3. When the data set is next read sequentially, the observations are processed in the order 1,2,4,5. Because observation 3 is deleted, it is skipped over. Until that data set is rewritten, it has 5 physical observations, but SAS software will only allow access to the 4 observations that logically exist. Using FETCHOBS(<dsid>,3) would return physical observation 4, not observation 3.

Enhancing SCL With Methods And Macros

Run-Time Macros

➡️ *A macro called in an SCL program (except in a submit block) is loaded, compiled, and executed when the SCL is compiled, not when a user executes the code that physically contains the macro call.*

This process differs from the DATA/PROC step of SAS software (assuming the step does not use saved compiled code), where the code is compiled and run each time a user submits a program and thus the user may change macros and macro variables in each run. Therefore, in SCL programs, macro variables referenced by name in a program as in

```
if "&mvarname" then ...
```

will have the value of the macro variable at compile time hard coded into the program. To avoid this, it is necessary to make extensive use of the SYMGETx and SYMPUTx functions. These will allow returning of the run-time values of macro variables.

☹️ *Suppose you want to display today's date on screen. You may try to use the* **&sysdate** *macro variable to do this. If the following program line is used, then the program screen will always show the date the program was compiled, irrespective of when the program entry is executed:*

```
datefld = "&sysdate"d ;
```

That line of code is physically equivalent to using

```
datefld = date the program is compiled ;
```

You need to pick up the macro variable value at run time, which you can do using the SYMGET routine, as in the following example:

```
datefld = input(symget('sysdate'),date7.) ;
```

This line of code, because it is executed at run time, always picks up the date of execution, not compile.

The concept of run-time macros, in other words, SCL code that is different each time the SCL program runs, does not exist unless your application also permits and causes SCL programs to be recompiled. However, for submitted code (using the SCL SUBMIT statement), macros can be different each time code is submitted. They compile and run when the SAS code is submitted, not when the SCL code containing the SUBMIT call is compiled.

Macros effectively become a developer's tool in SCL. Through the use of macros, certain repetitive tasks can be reduced to simple macro calls. Frequently, these macro calls contain SCL code that is compiled into the SCL program.

*Using macros requires a great deal of care. You must be aware that if a macro is changed, all SCL programs that used the macro need to be recompiled. If they are not, then any programs not recompiled will still be running the old code. **They will not fail to run, but they may fail to do what is now intended.** Conversely, when changing macros, ensure that changes will not compromise any existing programs.*

When changing existing macros in an SCL application, you need to be aware of the following:

● Any changes to parameters are likely to cause code currently using the macro to have to be altered

● You must ensure you do not alter the macro in such a way that existing calls to the macro fail to work at all. If a recompile is overlooked, it may be several days, weeks, or months before the problem is picked up.

● You can recompile an entire application by using the BUILD procedure as follows:

```
proc build c=<catalog name> batch ; compile ; run ;
```

Compile-Time Macros

Given that the concept of macros resolved at the time the program is run does not exist under SCL, you need to consider carefully just what can be done with macros. You need to consider whether macros or SCL programs with parameters (or method blocks) should be used.

There is definitely a place for macros in SCL. As with base SAS software, macros can reduce long, tedious programming tasks to simple chunks. They have the distinct advantage of generating instream SCL code, while method blocks require a call to an additional entry to access them.

Macros can be used in the following situations:

- The code in the macro is stable.

  The implication is that once the code has been written it is unlikely to be changed. This requirement addresses the fact that if a macro is changed, every SCL program or FSEDIT program that calls that macro must be recompiled. While the SAS/AF program entries can be easily compiled under PROC BUILD, it is a more difficult task to quickly recompile every FSEDIT SCL program.

- The code will be used in more than one program, or if only in one program it will be used multiple times.

  The requirement is not strict; generally, macros are written to build a library of code that can be used multiple times. However, experience has shown that placing code that will only be called once into a macro can often substantially improve readability of code.

- The code carries out a specific task.

  Do not attempt to clutter macros up with code that carries out multiple tasks. A good rule of thumb is that if the macro is much over a screen long, there may be too much code in it.

- The code cannot easily be placed in a method block.

  I recommend that reusable code should reside in a method block. However, this is not always possible. But the distinct advantage of it is that only the method needs changing and compiling; programs that call the method will not need to be recompiled.

  You cannot use a method block if the intention is to generate and compile code. The usefulness of method blocks is restricted to code that operates in the same manner on different variables at run time, while macros can generate different code in different situations at SCL compile time.

If a macro will only be used in one program, store the macro definition in the program also. This ensures that changing the macro will see the program recompiled. It also allows more than one macro of the same name to be used in the application. It is not unusual in SCL to require a macro many times in a specific program, but not elsewhere.

An example of macro usage in SCL from JARS concerns the FSEDIT screens. In order to avoid having the SCL executed on DELETED observations, every FSEDIT program in JARS starts MAIN with the following code:

```
MAIN:
  cmd = upcase(word(1));
  %obsdel

  ... rest of main code

RETURN;
```

The macro OBSDEL resolves to

```
if obsinfo('DELETED') or cmd = 'DELETE' then return ;
```

Call this macro to check if the observation has been deleted and consequently ensure MAIN does not run in that situation. It cannot be called as a method without having to carry out a lot more code to accomplish the RETURN. The reason is that a RETURN from a method returns back to the calling screen, which must then decide whether to return to the user; on the other hand, the instream RETURN generated at compile time by the macro returns control immediately to the user.

You might attempt to code the above macro as a method as follows:

```
chkdel:
method  del $ 1;
  if obsinfo('deleted') or cmd = 'DELETE' then del= 'Y' ;
endmethod;
return ;
```

Your call would have to be as follows:

```
del = 'N' ;
call method('chkdel',del) ;
if del = 'Y' then return ;
```

*Think again about the use of the method above. The method does not work at all. The reason is that the OBSINFO function has no meaning to the SCL program because it only applies to FSEDIT. The method, while it was called from FSEDIT, does not have the ability to execute the FSEDIT SCL specific routines (OBSINFO, for example). In fact, the variable **cmd** would be uninitialized in the method.*

Using Methods

The fundamental difference between macros and methods is that a method is a program rather than code compiled instream. As such, methods can accept run-time parameters.

Run-time parameters are important. Macros generate code and compile it instream at compile time. Methods take variable values at run time and apply a fixed precompiled set of instructions to those values.

➡ *Because methods are free-standing programs, they have the advantage that any changes are local to the method. Thus a single recompile completely prepares the method for use.*

In contrast, when you use macros, a change in a macro requires every program that calls the macro to be recompiled. Of course, if you change a method in such a way that you affect the parameters, either by adding, deleting, or altering their meaning, all programs using the method may need to be altered and recompiled.

In practice, it is often the case that an application uses both macros and methods. JARS, for instance, has a 30-program compile time macro library of useful SCL code and also has a large library of method blocks.

It is useful to keep SAS code for submission in methods rather than instream to SCL programs. This can concentrate all SAS code in one place, which allows relatively easy maintenance and also allows code to be reused easily. SAS code can make the structure of an SCL program difficult to read if there is a lot of it; placing it in a run-time METHOD library helps readability.

The SCL List Structure

What Is A List in The SCL Context?

A list is an in-memory array of data that can be accessed at any stage of an SCL application after definition. Lists can be application defined or defined by SAS software. They can be defined in either SAS/AF or SAS/FSP software.

Lists and arrays are quite different in their definition and use.

- Arrays are strictly defined in the context of an SCL program (although they can be passed as parameters between programs). Lists are available to any entry in an application from the time they are defined.

- Lists need not contain just one data type. They can mix numeric and character data. Arrays have a fixed data type.

- Lists can be saved to SAS catalog entries easily using SCL commands and can be reused in any application. Achieving the same with arrays requires coding the entire SAVE/RECALL code.

- Lists may contain other lists; arrays cannot contain other arrays, although the effect can be emulated by using multidimensional arrays.

- Many items defined in SAS software are automatically placed in lists. The SCL built-in selection list windows are further enhanced by the SCL list structure.

An SCL list can be either local or global. A local list exists from the time it is defined until the end of the application (or deliberate deletion within the application). At the application end, the list is removed from memory by SAS software.

Global lists, on the other hand, exist from the time of definition until either the SAS/AF session ends or the user explicitly deletes the list. It is possible to use a list to pass information from one application to another if both applications start in the same SAS session.

It is very easy to populate a list from an external file. It is much more difficult to populate an array. A single command, FILLIST, will fill a list with records from an external file. To fill an array from the same file requires writing many lines of SCL code as well as checking for end of file.

Since a list can be easily saved to disk, it is possible to use the disk-save feature as an exchange of information between different sessions. One user may cause a list to be filled or altered, and another user's session could immediately read that list. An example of this use is presented in the following case study.

Case Study -- Passing Lists Between Application Sessions

This case study arises as a result of SAS/SHARE software being implemented in a system (JARS) originally coded without SAS/SHARE (in Release 6.06). The situation is as follows.

The application had a number of formats that a system administrator could update. Updating is accomplished by editing a SAS data set. The application sets up that data set for entry into the CNTLIN option of PROC FORMAT and carries out the format creation.

Prior to the installation of SAS/SHARE, formats could only be updated when all users were off the system. With the integration of SAS/SHARE into the system, the administrator can now update a format while users are logged on.

Difficulty arises when a user has already loaded a format. Updating by the administrator is successful, but the user is no longer using the most up-to-date version of the format. To reload the format, the user must log off and restart the application as SAS software does not allow a format to be unloaded and reloaded under application control.

The following discussion revolves around one specific format. This is $OPNPRJ, which simply mapped open projects onto the letter Y and had an 'other' category of N. The principles discussed here can apply to any formats. Open projects are defined as any observation in our LIBRARY.PROJLIST (the master project register) which has the **status** field not equal to C or W. At time of writing, JARS contained some 1,500 open projects in a project register containing 5,500 projects.

Suppose a project was closed, but then someone put time into it later. JARS will not allow that project to be used, as our business rules do not permit time being put into an expired project. If the time is valid, the administrator must reactivate the project, placing it back in the valid projects table by changing the **status** field. On exit from LIBRARY.PROJLIST, JARS immediately rebuilds the formats that are affected by the change.

The administrator can make the change immediately, but any user already on JARS needs to completely exit the application to use the changed table, even though under SAS/SHARE the format catalog is updated.

A possible solution to this problem is not to use formats, but instead to use a table lookup routine such as LOCATEx or a WHERE clause. WHERE clauses can be prohibitively expensive (we have the situation that for a particular piece of data entry, up to 16 checks are required and up to 80 pieces of data entry can occur in a session) on large nonindexed data sets, and after a short test they were not considered further. The LOCATEC function would have worked here, but tests showed it also to be appreciably slow compared with formats. Both were slow here because they involve a lot of I/O in this situation. They are **not** uniformly slow, but they did not work well in **this** situation.

To get around the problem, the following strategy was adopted. Instead of a format-based table lookup, checks for valid projects would be done in the following manner:

- At startup, a list would be created of all valid projects.

- Format table lookup would be replaced by a search of the list.

- If the database that the list is based on changes, the list is reloaded, allowing immediate use without needing to deaccess the application.

The reload is done by calling a program module triggered by the user pressing a function key. That module checks for the administrator's data set being updated and reloads the list if it has been updated.

The initial load is achieved by the following code in the INIT section of the same entry that the user will issue the reload from (in this case the main menu):

```
loaprjlist = makelist() ;dtime = 0 ;
mlevel = 0 ;
link tablechk ;
```

The following code is executed in the LINKed section:

```
tablechk:
  submit continue sql;
    select modate into :modate from dictionary.tables
    where libname eq 'LIBRARY' and memname eq 'PROJLIST' ;
  endsubmit ;

  modate = input(symgetc('modate'),datetime16.) ;

  if modate gt loadtime then do ;
    loadtime = modate ;
    dsid = open('library.projlist','i') ;
    rc = where(dsid,'status not in ("C" "W")') ;
    rc= lvarlevel(dsid,'project',mlevel,prjlist);
    call close(dsid) ;
  end ;
return ;
```

The SQL dictionary feature is used to extract the latest date and time that the LIBRARY.PROJLIST file was updated. That time is loaded into a macro variable called **&modate**. The SQL does not print any output, as its only function is to populate the **&modate** macro variable.

Once the SUBMIT is finished, SCL creates a variable containing the macro variable **modate** value. This is compared with the value of **loadtime**, which is the date and time that the table was last loaded. Note the defaulting of **loadtime** to 0 in INIT to force the initial load.

Loading is a simple application of the LVARLEVEL function. A WHERE clause is in existence to prevent any closed or withdrawn projects from being loaded.

To actually reload the table, the user defines a function key, PF5, to execute a command RELOAD. The user determines when to use this, usually on advice of a system administrator. When the user presses PF5, the following code is executed in MAIN:

```
if word(1) eq 'RELOAD' then do ;
  call nextcmd() ;
  link tablechk ;
  return ;
end ;
```

Some discussion is warranted as to how to use the list to replace the use of a format. The above example from JARS is used in FSEDIT to compare an entered project id with a list of valid project ids. Consider the following code:

```
if put(project,$opnprj.) eq 'Y' then ....
else ... error condition ...
```

This use of a user-defined format is standard SAS usage. You have a field called **project** and apply the $OPNPRJ format. The output from this is either 'Y' or 'N'. If a formatted value returns

'Y' it is valid; otherwise it returns 'N', which corresponds to the other category. If a PROC FORMAT existed, it could look as follows:

```
proc format ;
value $opnprj 'PROJ001' -- 'PROJ099' = 'Y'
              other                   = 'N' ;
run ;
```

To use a list structure instead of a format, just fill the list (perhaps using the LVARLEVEL function as above) with all the valid project identifiers. Then wherever the format would have been used, use the SEARCHC function as follows:

```
if searchc(listid,project) ne 0 then .... ;
else ... error condition ... ;
```

In practice, the list search seems as quick as using a format, as both are in-memory operations. Initial loading of the list seems to be somewhat quicker than loading the format. Even though formats use a binary search and list searches are sequential, from the user's viewpoint there is no perceivable difference in the above example. Intuition suggests that as the size of the list increases, the format would perform faster due to its binary search. However, that threshold will be both application and system dependent.

> *There is an added benefit to using lists over formats. In a memory-constrained system, you can delete the list after use and reuse the memory it occupied. Developers have no control over formats; they are deleted from memory when SAS wants to remove them, which can sometimes lead to memory bottlenecks when large formats are in use.*

Using Built -In Lists From Selection Windows

Beginning with Release 6.07, SAS software places selected information in a local list when items are chosen from built-in selection lists. This enhances the flexibility of windows such as DATALISTC.

In earlier releases, you could return only the nominated variable as follows:

```
varname = datalistc(dsid,'var1 var2 var3','','',1) ;
```

The code would fill the SCL variable **varname** with the value of **var1** from the last observation that the user selected.

The list feature now causes an SCL list to be created with the values of all three variables available for all selected items. This feature prevents you from having to code a data set search and fetch of an observation which, even though the observation has already been loaded into the DATALISTC window, would be necessary without the use of the list structure.

The advantages of returning data in a list should be readily apparent. It is not necessary to read the database using SCL to pick up the values of the **var2** and **var3** variables when the list window has finished. This cuts down considerably on I/O if the additional values are required to be fetched.

List output is available with most selection list windows. For instance, the FILELIST window will now allow a selection to be made and the fileref returned as previously, but all filerefs selected will also have the corresponding FILENAME available in the list. Also available is the number of items selected, which means that it is no longer necessary to use coded counting algorithms to find out just how many words are in the list of words returned from the function call.

For example, suppose you want to allow a user to return up to 5 items from a DATALISTC window. Additionally, you want to know how many items were returned. The following code accomplishes your objective:

```
main:

    if _status_ in ('E' 'H' 'C') then return  ;



    listid = makelist() ;

    rc = curlist(listid) ;



    dsid = open('usage.usage') ;

    r= where(dsid,'modulen contains "TABULATE"') ;

/* at end of this DATALISTC, the FLIST variable has the value corresponding
to the
    first selected record from the list window. The SCL LIST  in CURLIST has
ALL
    the values selected */

    flist = datalistc(dsid,'modulen title keys',

                    'Press Enter To Select Up To 5 Items',
                    'N',5) ;



    call close(dsid) ;



    if flist eq _blank_ then return ;

    list = _blank_ ;
```

```
/* at end of this loop, the variable list is a string of all selected
values */

   ncount = getitemc(listid,count) ;
   do i=1 to ncount ;
     list = list || getitemc(listid,modulen) ;
   end ;
return ;
```

Note that the **flist** variable is used only to store the last value returned from DATALISTC.

At the conclusion of this MAIN section, the list referred to as LISTID will contain each selected observation from the USAGE.USAGE file. For each observation, the list will contain the three variables **modulen, title,** and **keys.** Furthermore, the variable **list** will contain a string of the selected values of **modulen.**

Using Lists For Storing Global System Messages

Here I discuss the use of a list as a storage area for system messages. This was discussed earlier in Chapter 2, 'Standards in SCL System Development.' The intention here is to have a single source of all system error messages, rather than having them scattered throughout code.

Two methods are presented here. The first uses a SAS data set to store the messages in while the application is not running. The second uses an array in an SCL entry. It is necessary to store the messages somewhere before loading the list, and these two methods give fairly flexible storage means.

Method 1

The SUNS application maintains a data set named LIBRARY.MESSAGES. In this library are all the application messages plus an identifying number. The contents of this data set are loaded into a list of system startup.

When you want to display an error message, the message is fetched from the list. You need to know only the identifying number.

Defining the list is simple. At application start up, the following code reads the messages data set into a local list:

```
init:
  mlevel = 0 ;
  dsid = open('library.messages','i') ;
  messlist = makelist(nobs(dsid),'L') ;
  call symputn('listid',messlist) ;
  rc= lvarlevel(dsid,'message',mlevel,messlist);
  rc= revlist(messlist) ;
  call close(dsid) ;
return ;
```

The macro variable **&listid** is used to hold the list number. This is used in windows that require a displayed message. To display an item from the list, all that is required is the list identifier value in **&listid**, the GETITEMC function, and code to display the message.

The REVLIST function is necessary because the LVARLEVEL function loads the list in back-to-front manner. The first list item is entered into the list, and successive items are loaded at the top of the list. If it is necessary to maintain a one-to-one mapping between a database and a list, reverse the list. In this application you want to maintain that mapping because the error numbers referenced in the SCL programs are the observation numbers of the messages in the SAS data set.

An example of extracting a list item is

```
listid = symgetn('listid') ;
call putlegend(2,getitemc(listid,12)) ;
```

The list structure is very fast as the entire list is in memory. For this error handling application, it also removes the need to store long text strings in screens and ensures that messages only need be defined once.

Method 2

The second method stores the messages in an array in an SCL entry, then loads them into the SCL list as part of the application startup routine.

The array approach has some advantages over the data set approach. First, all the messages are in a single SCL catalog entry. This makes it simple to update messages, and all can be seen at once without having to access a SAS data set. Second, populating the error message list is simpler because you can avoid all I/O. Third, using this approach, it becomes very easy to implement a named list and hence to refer to error messages by name in the code.

Disadvantages include that the SCL needs compiling each time it is added to, a minor overhead given that you must edit the list and thus do not need to go to any lengths to accomplish this.

The following example SCL entry contains all error messages for the usage notes example, stored in an array in a program entry. Included in the message is an 8-character name used for naming each item in the list. The name is at the start of each entry, followed by the message. This SCL entry is the one that starts our application; it loads the application error list and then triggers the initial screen that the users interact with.

```
array messages (*) $ (75) (
'ENDSEARCNote:    Search Complete, Matches Follow '
'SEARCHINNote:    Searching ............ '
'NOMATCH Note:    No Matches From Search '
'WAIT1   Note:    Extracting Altered Records -- Please Wait '
'NOACCESSNote:    Update Access Not Presently Available '
'BADINPUTERROR:   A Product, Keyword Or Modulen Text Must Be Present '
'UPDATINGNote:    Product Update In Progress -- Please Wait '
'UPDATE  Note:    File Update Completed '
'USEBUTONERROR:   Use A Button To Activate Request '
```

```
'BADDATE Note:    No Processing As Date Left Blank '
'IOERROR1ERROR:   USAGE Note Data set Not Found In Database '
'NOTEXT  Note:    No Text Is Associated With This Entry '
'CLOSED  Note:    Record Is Already Closed '
'CLOSEERRERROR:   Closed Records Must Have All Close Fields Entered '
'ESCALATENote:    Record Has Been Escalated '
'ESCALAT1ERROR:   Fill In All Escalation Fields '
'NODESC  ERROR:   You Must Enter A Problem Description '
'FATALERRERROR:   A FATAL ERROR HAS OCCURRED -- SYSTEM ENDING '
'RECORDIDERROR:   The Selected Record Id Does Not Exist '
'NOPROB  ERROR:   You Must Enter A Problem Number For The Command To Use '
'PROBERR ERROR:   The Second Parameter Must Be A Problem Number '
'DATAERR ERROR:   Invalid PRODUCT, ZAP TYPE or ZAP Status Value '
          ) ;

init:
  messlist = makelist(dim(messages),'L') ;

  do i=1 to dim(messages) ;
    messlist = insertc(messlist,substr(messages(i),9),1,
                  substr(messages(i),1,8)) ;
  end ;
  call symputn('messlist',messlist) ;
  call display('library.usagenew.userparm.program') ;
return ;
```

Notice how the first 8 characters are reserved to be the name that will be used in the named list to reference the error message, with the message itself being the ninth through the last characters. When it is necessary to make use of the list to extract an error message, use the GETNITEMC function.

Portability -- Coding For Multiple Platforms

All the applications discussed in this text were initially coded under Release 6.06 or 6.07 using MVS. They were later ported to Release 6.08 under Version 2.0 of OS/2.

Porting was simple. Under MVS the catalogs were copied to a transport file; the data files were copied to a different transport file, then downloaded to a PC. Release 6.08 easily read the Release 6.07 files.

 SAS Technical Report P-195, Transporting SAS Files between Host Systems, describes all the necessary mechanisms for accomplishing file transfers between systems.

Under Release 6.08 MARTS required a two-line change to accommodate the different filename terminology and then ran almost exactly as under MVS. Porting was so simple and quick that it quickly became apparent that SAS Institute's efforts at ensuring compatibility across platforms worked well for this application.

Programs do not need recompiling in order to function on a different platform unless platform-dependent code is present in the code stream.

SCL generates intermediate code, which is converted to system-specific object code at run time, ensuring no requirement for recompiling when moving between platforms and releases. Experience showed, though, that some differences could occur between releases at run time, particularly in the windowing areas. The intermediate code may be different and cause subtle changes when recompiling.

One difficulty immediately emerged with porting from mainframe to graphical environments. The application was developed under MVS using nongraphics terminals. Although SAS software made menus and push buttons consistent with the OS/2 standards, the data entry screens left a lot to be desired.

The difficulty was due mainly to the lack of color on the MVS terminals. These were able to handle few extended attributes, and only highlighting was used. This meant that in the graphically superior OS/2 environment, the application screens looked jaded and unprofessional.

Another problem was that Release 6.07 under MVS has a display manager command CLOCK. This does not appear to be available under OS/2.

Other than these difficulties, the application worked as intended. Some MVS-specific code did exist to facilitate printing under MVS writers, and it needed to be rewritten. Otherwise, the system worked as intended prior to recompiling.

Porting SUNS was equally as simple, and the response time in searching and retrieving usage notes was impressive. From the user point of view, SUNS performed far better under Version 2 of OS/2 than it did under MVS, even using the same MVS usage notes database.

The only immediate problem noted with SUNS (other than the problems already mentioned with MARTS) was that the FSEDIT screens seemed to have 'lost' any function key screen definitions that existed under MVS. This is not a bug and is discussed in usage note V6-CIMPORT-2267.

The first attempts to compile code were dismal failures. Fortunately the problem here was simple and due to character translation in the download process from the MVS system. All concatenation characters had been changed to]] in the download process, and these characters are not understood as concatenation characters by SAS.

Changing to !! fixed this problem. (Don't forget that if the change was to a previously compiled macro, you must recompile the macro. This may require that the currently compiled macro be deleted from WORK.SASMACRO catalog and MRECALL be switched on).

Compilation was now successful and the application behaved similarly to the MVS application.

Screen Interfaces

It is an unfortunate fact of life that MVS is not a graphically oriented operating system. Few sites afford the luxury of having all users able to use color graphics terminals, and as a consequence SAS full screen applications at our site rarely consider color and extended field attributes.

Reverse video and highlighting under MVS are frequently the only ways to draw attention to a field. Under OS/2, reversed video fields defaulted to a dark blue box with black text after porting. This text was barely readable. Your results will depend on your SAS defaults.

Standard fields under AF and FSEDIT, that is, those with no extended attributes, appear under MVS the same color as protected (non user-changeable) fields. Under OS/2 they had color and defaulted to yellow. This was difficult to read as all the text and fields were the same color (although the text occasionally managed to incorporate multiple colors, I assume this was due to SAS software supporting ESC sequences which mainframe programmers managed to accidentally trigger occasionally).

 It is evident that if porting from mainframe to a graphical environment, you should expect to spend time resetting the colors and extended field attributes.

Of interest in many sites is developing on the PC and porting to the mainframe. This avoids the often heavy mainframe development costs.

Unfortunately, it has not been possible to explore portability in this direction. Release 6.08 was available under OS/2, but had not yet been made available under MVS as this book was being developed.

Function keys turned out to be a major cause of difficulty. The first problem, already mentioned, was that key definitions disappear when porting. According to usage note V6-CIMPORT-2267, this situation works as intended, so I assume it will continue. This means from the developer's viewpoint it will be necessary to edit a ported application to reset the key definitions.

☹ *A further source of difficulty emerged under OS/2 with function keys. Quite simply put, they are not all available.*

Due to the requirements of the operating system, SAS cannot always utilize every function key. It is also the case that some operating systems may allow more 'function keys', for example, the CNTL keys under OS/2. When you access a KEYS window under OS/2, a message appears stating 'MANY KEYS ARE RESERVED BY OPERATING SYSTEM'. Version 2 of OS/2 does reserve use of some keys. To preserve the integrity of the operating system keys, SAS software will not allow access to these keys, nor does it show them in the KEYS window. (This situation may also occur on other platforms.)

Of immediate interest is the F10 key. The inability of SAS software to use F10 makes coding in a situation where all keys are required rather difficult. In the site notes entry and edit part of SUNS, 12 function key definitions are required and available under MVS. When one key is missing, consistent screen layout and key usage are difficult.

In SUNS, F10 is required in an FSEDIT program to flag a problem observation as CLOSED. To attempt to make it available, the SCL SETFKEY routine was used in the INIT section. This strategy caused a problem in that the SETFKEY command worked but assigned the command to the F11 key, which holds the position of the F10 key in the KEYS window. Thus the F11 key's definition was lost.

☹ *The LASTKEY() function cannot be used to detect the last key pressed if it is an operating system reserved key.*

Documentation makes it clear that the LASTKEY function returns a value based on position in the KEYS window. Thus the following statement returns the value 10 only when F11 is pressed:

```
if lastkey() eq 10 then do ....
```

It was necessary to compromise somewhat here. The absence of F10 can be overcome by allowing an explicit command from the command line. But SUNS does not utilize a command line in the site notes section. However, for each observation in the site notes file, there is a field called **status**.

The original intention was that pressing F10 would internally set **status** to 'C' and trigger close processing. Design changed slightly so that if the user explicitly changes this field to 'C', an observation is closed and close operations are carried out.

It should be realized that although SAS does give excellent portability between platforms, some aspects of one platform may be inappropriate on another platform. Operating systems such as OS/2 are themselves based on push-button operations, and few applications use function keys as the **main** means of executing commands. The reverse is true for MVS; it is a function key-oriented system and applications should generally reflect that.

The above comment is intended as a warning for programmers, not as any criticism of the implementation of SAS on various platforms. SAS software is maintaining its own integrity by following the development guidelines set by operating system vendors; unfortunately, if we as developers are not aware of those restrictions, that unawareness can at the least hinder our development effort.

System-Dependent Code

No matter how hard a vendor tries to provide platform-independent software, complete platform independence is very difficult to accomplish. SAS software attempts to provide many functions that will accomplish tasks that would otherwise require some form of system dependent code (for example, LIBNAME and FILENAME to replace the vastly differing means of allocating files for a SAS session).

The preceding sections discuss how the look and feel of an application might differ between operating systems. This section discusses how you might code tasks that SAS software does not provide code for or that have different syntax on different platforms. First, consider just what is meant here by system-dependent code.

There are two types of system-dependent code:

1. SAS syntax that differs between platforms (the LIBNAME command, for example)

Fortunately, this is a rarity in SAS software and even more of a rarity in SCL. In general, syntax of commands is consistent.

One area of concern is the LIBNAME and FILENAME commands. These commands have to provide options that are system dependent. Ideally, porting a system should see any options that don't work on the target system ignored. That is not the case with SCL.

Consider the following code from MVS:

```
if libname('global','jars.global.database','','disp=shr') then ....
```

Under OS/2, after you adjust the filename, this code does not accomplish the allocation because it treats the 'disp=shr' as a possible valid option on the OS/2 platform. However, it is not valid and thus a run-time error occurs.

➡ *To successfully write SAS code that differs across operating systems you will find the* **&sysscp** *macro variable very useful.*

&sysscp contains a description of the operating system. Using this allows both development and production environments, possibly on different operating systems, to be coded without need to change code when the system is ported. Under MVS, **&sysscp** returns the characters OS. For OS/2, it returns the characters OS2. The value for other platforms will be in the SAS operating system companion.

&sysscp can be used as follows:

```
opsys = symgetc('sysscp') ;
select(opsys) ;
    when ('OS') rc=libname('global','jars.global.database','','disp=shr');
    when ('OS2') rc=libname('global','e:\jars\global\');
    otherwise ;
end ;
```

All this code is executed at run time, allowing both the MVS and the OS/2 code to coexist in the application. At run time, the correct operating system-dependent code is executed. Note that the SYMGETC function is used to extract the value of **&sysscp**; this returns the value at execution time. Using the following program would cause the value of **&sysscp** to be hardwired into the program at the time it is compiled:

```
opsys = "&sysscp" ;
select(opsys) ;
    when ('OS') rc=libname('global','jars.global.database','','disp=shr');
    when ('OS2') rc=libname('global','e:\jars\global\');
    otherwise ;
end ;
```

Thus at run time **&sysscp** is treated as a constant and will NOT operate correctly in any environment except that in which it was compiled. The **&sysscp** macro variable is a most useful and powerful tool. It should be used in the above form in any situation where you desire to move system-dependent compiled (intermediate) code to a different platform.

An alternative to using **&sysscp** is to keep a library of system-dependent METHODS or DISPLAY entries on each platform that the application is targeted for. In your application, just code the entry as that operating system requires it. When you port your application, all that needs to be done is to ensure that a LIBNAME to the system-dependent library is set up, and then the code should run. However, whatever you do, don't put system-dependent code in macros; you will have to recompile your whole application on the target system to ensure it is running correct code.

You need to be wary of writing code that uses the SYSTEM function or macros such as %SYSEXEC. These will generally fail if code is ported. This problem is covered in the discussion that follows.

2. Operating system routines that can be called from within SAS

There are some features that it may be desirable to use that are not available within SAS software, but are only available at the operating system level. Consider the following examples:

- You want to initiate a job to run in a different SAS session.

  Under MVS it is necessary to run a batch job, under OS/2 to start a second SAS session and execute the job in that session in the background (similar analogies exist for other operating systems).

  In the MVS situation, you accomplish this task by writing the JCL and SAS code to an external file and then using the TSO SUBMIT command. Alternatively, SAS software allows a DATA step to write directly to the JES internal reader for execution in a batch address space. This action requires the INFILE option.

  Under OS/2, you can run multiple SAS sessions. You want to run a program in the background entirely without user intervention (indeed ideally without the user even being aware of the task's existence).

- Often you cannot make any assumptions about the user's ability to set up and maintain SAS printer forms. This happens frequently when the users have no computer experience and are to be shielded from all but the application.

  Under MVS you may want to execute a command such as TSO PRINTOFF or TSO PRINTDS. Under OS/2 you want to just spool output to a printer attached to the computer.

- Under MVS, you can give an application added flexibility by allowing the application to invoke SPF (assuming it was invoked from a native TSO session). The comparable option under OS/2 is to execute CMD.EXE to open an OS/2 command-line window.

Executing external commands is simple in that all platforms allow the X command, which either executes operating system commands or places the user in a window in that operating system. For instance, under TSO typing X in any SAS window command line places you in native TSO.

➡ *Be aware that on most platforms many programs external to SAS do not require you to exit SAS or use the X command to run.*

For instance, the CALL SYSTEM command simply executes an external program if it is available. For example, if you are running SDSF (Spool Display Search Facility) under MVS from an SCL window, just issue the following line in your SCL:

```
call system('sdsf') ;
```

Provided SDSF is in a library in your operating system's automatic program search list, it will be run.

You should be wary of using CALL SYSTEM without making use of the **&sysscp** macro variable. The program will still be run if it exists, but there is no guarantee that a program under one operating system will have the same function as an identically named program on another system.

The Command Line

A design decision in an application may be to allow or disallow access to the window command line. This may include a decision to use the pmenu facility or to completely disable any form of command line.

The following discussion uses the terms 'pmenu' and 'wpopup' as if they were interchangeable. Pop-up windows are another way of looking at the pmenu facility's pull down menus, but they are triggered by cursor position and appear at the cursor point. Pull-down menus by contrast are always in a static position starting in the upper left-hand corner of the screen area (excluding the border area). Under OS/2, the Preferences dialog box, selected from the Options menu, allows you to permanently select COMMAND LINE, MENU BAR (PMENU), or POPUP.

It should be realized that a pull-down menu is only a different way of viewing a command line. Experience under MVS has shown that for that operating system, the pmenu facility can be difficult to work with. Despite that, all the applications discussed in this text use the pmenu facility at some stage because it allows a greater level of control within an application than does a command line.

Because a pull-down menu is just another way of viewing a command line, popping up a menu option and entering END (via a function key) while the menu option is active is equivalent to typing END on the command line. The entry will attempt to carry out TERM processing.

I find the pmenu facility is most useful on mouse-based systems. Tabbing and pressing the enter key works fine, but it is both an unwieldy and error-prone operation. Under MVS if no mouse is available, pull-down menus may have to be justified in other terms than ease of use. Having said that, I use pmenus under MVS to replace command lines in native windows such as PREVIEW. I have to say that they are universally unpopular with our user community, but they provide a higher level of control over an application than can be achieved with a command line.

It is easy to remove a command line in SAS/AF. That functionality is built into each SAS/AF program screen. Just access the GENERAL ATTRIBUTES (GATTR) screen and select NONE for the BANNER value.

It is more difficult to remove a command line in FSEDIT or native SAS windows (PREVIEW and CATALOG, for example).

Why would you want to remove a command line? There are several possible reasons:

- It has no use in the application; in other words, all commands are function key driven or push-button driven, or the application has no commands.

- The application has commands, but you want to make the application really tight (for example, you don't want users to be able to carry out any commands other than those relevant to the application).

- You want more room on the screen. The command line uses space that may be better employed in the screen layout.

Several options will enable you to replace a command line:

- If the SAS/AF application has no commands at all, just switch the command line off in each entry's GATTR window. (See item 1 in the list that follows this section.)

- If the SAS/AF application has commands, but they require no extra dialog with the user, assign the commands to function keys or push buttons and switch off the command line in the entry's GATTR window. (See item 2 in the list that follows this section.)

- If the SAS/FSP application requires no command line, the only way the command line can be 'removed' is to replace it with a dummy pmenu that does nothing. This does not give any extra space on the screen but does remove the command line. (See item 3 in the list that follows this section.)

- If the SAS/AF application has commands, and they require dialog with the user, you can do one of the following:

  - use PROC PMENU to set up dialog boxes.
  - call another display screen with no command line to carry out the dialog and pass values as parameters.
  (See item 4 in the list that follows this section.)

- SAS/FSP applications can have commands assigned to pmenus or function keys.

- SAS/AF entries can use the NO EXIT option in the GATTR window to disable commands that would open another window. All other commands are still available. If your only criterion is to prevent access to other windows (KEYS, X, and so on) this option allows a command line to remain for other commands while ignoring the window opening commands.

To investigate how each of the above might be used, I will consider situations that use each approach.

1. Switching off the command line completely in SAS/AF is simple. Enter the GATTR window when using BUILD to edit the entry. Change the BANNER selection field to NONE.

   Note that switching off the command line in SAS/AF also switches off the _MSG_ line.

2. To switch off the command line and allow commands to be assigned to function keys requires more work. First, use PROC BUILD to create a KEYS entry for the screen and assign the commands you want to use to function keys.

   Second, use the GATTR window of the SAS/AF entry to switch off the command line as in 1. above and also to define the KEYS entry. Alternatively, your application may need to define the keys using the SETFKEY function.

   The final step is to code the SCL to check for the command being entered (pressing a function key with a command attached to it looks to the SCL program like the command came from the command line).

   Suppose it is necessary to allow your users to access the SDSF program under MVS. Set up a function key at the main menu and assign the text 'SDSF' to that key.

In the SCL it may be necessary to code CONTROL ALLCMDS in the INIT section. This is not necessary if the only commands to be trapped are those being set up for the application. CONTROL ALLCMDS is only necessary if you want to trap and handle SAS software commands rather than allowing SAS to carry out the processing associated with the command. This strategy allows you to assign commands such as KEYS to a function key and causes your program to override the default SAS processing.

Whether CONTROL ALLCMDS is switched on or not, the MAIN section looks as follows:

```
if word(1) eq 'SDSF' then do ;
  call nextcmd() ;
  call system('sdsf') ;
  return ;
end ;
```

The idea is to check for the command being passed to the program. If it is found, purge the command line buffer (to ensure that SAS does not attempt to process it as a SAS command), set up the code to carry out the processing associated with the command (in this example only one line), and then return control back to the user.

3. You can use the pmenu facility to completely switch off any ability to interact with SAS software except using the application's built-in features.

Do this using a dummy action bar, in other words a menu that literally contains nothing. It is necessary to

- code the pmenu using PROC PMENU
- invoke the pmenu facility in FSEDIT.

First set up the action bar. This is not an SCL task; it is done completely outside SCL control using PROC PMENU.

When setting up a pull-down menu in the program editor, remember that the compiled code and the source code are two separate entities. Do not overlook the saving of the source code to either an external file or a SAS catalog entry.

There is only one way to remove the command line in FSEDIT. The application must issue a PMENU ON command to replace the command line with the action bar. To avoid using the default SAS software action bar, you must also use the SETPMENU command or the PMENU function. This defines the menu to be displayed.

Issuing the SETPMENU command has to be done via CALL EXECCMD or EXECCMDI. The only alternative is to have the user switch on the pmenu facility, which completely defeats the purpose of denying users access to the command line. You can use CALL EXECCMD in the screen that calls the FSEDIT, as in the following:

```
call execcmd('setpmenu library.pmenu.fsedit.pmenu;pmenu on');
call fsedit ....
```

Or you can use it in the FSEINIT section of the FSEDIT entry:

```
fseinit:
  call execcmd('setpmenu library.pmenu.fsedit.pmenu;pmenu on');
return ;
```

Alternatively, you can use CALL EXECCMDI in the FSEDIT FSEINIT section. You cannot use CALL EXECCMDI in the calling program, as that would cause an action bar to be set in that entry and leave the FSEDIT entry at the SAS default action bar.

If you are using the PMENU function, it must be used in the FSEINIT section, as it applies only to the currently displayed window.

Now the action bar can be set up in FSEDIT. You need to create the menu. The following PROC PMENU program provides the functionality required above:

```
proc pmenu c=library.usagenew ;
  menu null;
    item ' ';
run ;
quit ;
```

Note that even though a dummy action bar is used, under OS/2 clicking the right mouse button will show a small unusable empty PMENU window if WPOPUP is used.

Full SAS Institute documentation of PROC PMENU is provided in the *SAS Procedures Guide, Version 6, Third Edition*.

4. PROC PMENU gives simple, yet powerful ability to interact with the user when a command is entered.

The procedure is used to define a menu that the user will pop up on screen and carry out an interactive dialog with. This example is from MARTS and has the following requirements:

- no FSEDIT command line
- ability to jump to a specific observation number
- issue a WHERE clause
- clear a WHERE clause

- issue an STR command to specify a search field
- carry out a search using the S command.

You can code the entire action bar using PROC PMENU as follows:

```
proc pmenu c=rates.pmenu ;
  menu dbox ;
  item 'Options' menu=choice ;
  menu choice ;
  item 'Search' dialog=getstr ;
  item 'Where ' dialog=whrstr ;
  item 'Select ' dialog=chgstr ;
  item 'Repeat Search ' selection=repsel ;
  item 'Jump Observation ' dialog=firsel ;
  item 'Exit  ' selection=goback ;
  selection goback ' ';
  dialog getstr 's @1' ;
    text #1 @1 'Enter The String To Search For';
    text #4 @4 len=15 ;
  dialog whrstr 'where @1' ;
    text #1 @1 'Enter The String To Subset For';
    text #2 @1 'Enter A Blank String To Clear Any Existing WHERE';
    text #4 @4 len=75 ;
  dialog chgstr 'str @1' ;
    text #1 @1 'Enter The Field To Search On';
    text #4 @4 len=15 ;
  selection repsel 'rfind' ;
  dialog firsel ' @1';
    text #1 @1 'Enter Observation To Jump To';
    text #4 @4 len=6 ;
  run ;
  quit ;
```

All the required functions of the screen, plus the ability to repeat a search, are coded in that PROC PMENU. In FSEDIT under MVS, the user will see the word OPTIONS in the top left hand corner without a command line. Under OS/2, clicking the right mouse button will display the menu if WPOPUP rather than MENU BAR is the default.

When an option is selected, the user sees the list of functions that can be carried out displayed as a menu list. Under MVS this is displayed under the word OPTIONS, while under OS/2 with WPOPUP as the default menu option it is displayed at the point where the mouse had moved the cursor before clicking. Wherever the list appears, it looks like the example from an OS/2 screen in Figure 3.1.

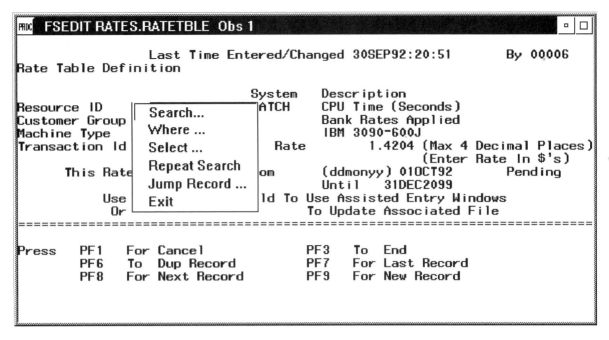

Figure 3.1:   WPOPUP Menu Under OS/2

Selecting an option leads to a further dialog box; selecting the WHERE option in the action bar in Figure 3.1 results in the dialog box shown in Figure 3.2:

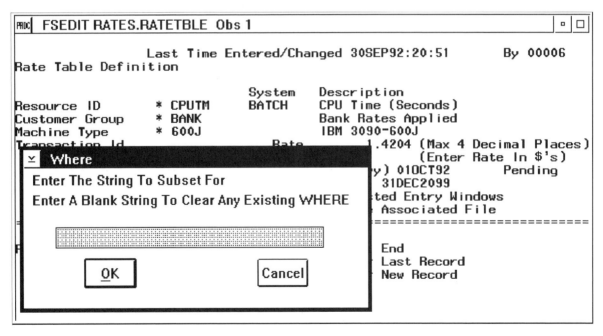

Figure 3.2:   Dialog Box In A Menu

It is necessary to consider how to standardize code structure when commands and menus are used. JARS allows many screens to have the user select a numeric option or press a function key to trigger a command. I generally use a program flow in MAIN similar to the following:

- Check if END key pressed and exit if so. (END is often used to exit with no further processing while ENTER is a trigger to continue processing.)

- Check if a command and process if so. (Don't get overly complicated by allowing the user to select both a menu option and a function key driven command.) Return to the user as soon as the command is complete.

- If the user selected an option, process that option.

The code layout in MAIN follows the above list:

- See if the user wants to end and exit the screen if so. (It is not recommended that commands such as END or the PF3 key be used to trigger processing except for exit processing, as it is frequently standard outside of SAS software that END does not imply any processing except an exit.)

- If not an END, check if a valid command and process the command, returning control to the user at the end. (You may wish to include the ability to process multiple commands separated by commas.)

- If a window menu option, process that option.

Handling Application Errors

In this section I discuss strategies for dealing with unexpected situations in an application. These are run-time rather than compile-time errors.

The topic is independent of the programming language being used. The handling of an exceptional condition in one language should be similar in its user interface and outcome to the handling of it in any other language. However, the means of achieving that outcome will be language dependent.

Function Return Codes

Consider the following function call:

```
rc = append(dsid00) ;
```

This attempts to write an observation from an SCL data vector to the end of a SAS database. Generally this is a straightforward task, with the simple syntax above accomplishing the highly complex task of moving data from the SCL-based application to the external data storage location.

Although the task appears simple, you should always check that the operation actually worked. Here are some situations that should be considered:

1. the SAS data set or the storage medium has been corrupted

2. the SAS data set has been deleted (unlikely, as the earlier file OPEN function would have failed and your return code checking would have dealt with that)

3. your coding was in error and the file has inadvertently been closed or was never opened

4. the file was opened, but your code inadvertently used the wrong open mode

5. the SAS database has run out of space.

I have managed to code myself into situations where all these have occurred. It is unlikely that situations 3 and 4 will get past rigorous system and user testing; however, situations 1 and 2 are generally difficult to avoid. Situation 5 is so common that it should always be checked for.

An example of situations 1 and 2 was that a disk pack VTOC under MVS once got corrupted while an SCL application was running (this is analogous to the file allocation tables being trashed somehow under PC DOS or OS/2). This is totally outside the SCL programmer's scope, but the possibility of these errors must be considered. After all, our end-user base should not be considered to have any particular knowledge, so the more the application can deal with error situations the better.

Many other situations could occur to destroy an application's integrity. These range from simple events, such as no observations satisfying a WHERE clause, to potentially catastrophic events like the ones described above. Whatever the event, you need to devise and code strategies for dealing with these events.

Where a return code is available, it is simple to test that return code and take appropriate action. The SYSRC macro (discussed in the next section), the SYSMSG() and SYSRC() functions, and the SCL return code are all useful here. An example follows:

```
rc = append(dsid00) ;
if rc then do ;
  _msg_ = sysmsg() ;
  return ;
end ;
```

The disadvantage here is the need to carry an extra variable and to do a comparison as well as the function operation.

It is not necessary to generate a variable containing the return code in all situations. For instance, you could call the APPEND function this way:

```
if append(dsid00) then do ;
....
end ;
```

Thus the function becomes the comparison operator, which saves having to test a variable later and, of course, saves having to carry an additional variable. In memory-constrained systems, that may be important.

The disadvantage here is that it is a little more difficult to use the SYSRC macro. Normally the macro is called this way:

```
rc = append(dsid00) ;
if rc eq %sysrc(_SWEOF) then do ;
...
end ;
```

This rather trivial example writes to the end of a file, then tests for end of file. The equivalent without the variable is

```
if append(dsid00) eq %sysrc(_SWEOF) then do ;
...
end ;
```

SYSMSG() use does not change at all. This function always generates a message based on the internal workings of SCL, not on parameters that developers pass to it. Thus the following code will work perfectly satisfactorily:

```
if append(dsid00) eq %sysrc(_SWEOF) then do ;
  _msg_= sysmsg() ;
  return ;
end ;
```

Note the immediate problem here, though. It is not possible to report the actual return code, only the message associated with it. That is not a problem in the above example because the SYSMSG() is only invoked for one return code anyway, but the following code cannot return the code:

```
if append(dsid00) then do ;
  _msg_ = sysmsg() ;
  return ;
end ;
```

However, SCL provides the SYSRC function. This can be used to provide the most recent return code. Hence the above code can be altered to

```
if append(dsid00) then do ;
  _msg_ = sysrc() || '-' || sysmsg() ;
  return ;
end ;
```

Using The SYSMSG() Function

The SYSMSG function returns a blank if the last operation that could generate a return code succeeded. Otherwise, it contains a message relating to the last operation.

The message returned here provides much more information than just the return code. This function is useful behind the scenes, rather than as a direct user interface. To avoid having naive end users facing complex messages that are (to them) meaningless, JARS reports fatal error conditions with a simple message that the application is about to stop and that the user should contact JARS developers.

The real error message generated by SYSMSG() is written to the SASLOG, along with a dump of just what values of fields are at the time. Thus SYSMSG() is often used as a developer's field support tool.

It is possible to introduce strict standard usage of SYSMSG. If the first word is 'WARNING' inform users that a problem has occurred and ask them to contact system support, but let the application continue. If the first word is 'ERROR', force an end to the application and ask users to contact support. This avoids the need to check return codes. The validity of this system depends on SAS Institute's continuing to use those terms at the start of system messages.

Here it is assumed that SAS Institute's decision about what type of condition constitutes a WARNING and what is an ERROR is appropriate for the task at hand. You may want to consider this further if relying on SYSMSG().

It is generally simpler to use the return code and generate a message if necessary from SYSMSG(); however, I have shown that it is not strictly necessary to carry an extra field for storing return codes.

SAS Software Return Codes

SAS software does not always finish a successful function call with a zero return code.

Consider the following situation. Your SCL program issues a LIBNAME as follows:

```
rc = libname('usage',dsetname,'disp=shr') ;
```

You now want to ensure that the allocation was successful and prevent further processing if the function call did not succeed.

SCL documentation from SAS Institute makes clear that the LIBNAME function returns a zero return code if the function was successful. However, it also makes clear that a non-zero return code will be produced if the function issues a WARNING.

What is not defined is just what a WARNING means. For example, if the LIBNAME allocates a libref to an already allocated file, the return code is -70004. The allocation is perfectly valid; the LIBNAME has been allocated, yet it does not result in a zero return code.

The difficulty here is just what return codes to report and which to ignore. Using a check such as

```
if rc then do ;  /* error occurred */
```

and subsequent error processing is not always successful; as shown, some return codes that are non-zero may be perfectly valid.

It may be necessary to carefully check the %SYSRC macro in the supplied SASAUTOS library to check all possible return codes and decide which should be treated as if they were zero. Unfortunately, this may add considerably to overheads as that macro is not static (in other words, there is no reason why SAS Institute should not add to it). Coding a check for several return codes may also add to the time taken for background processing to complete and for control to be passed back to the user.

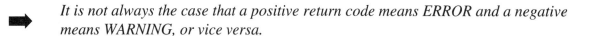

It is not always the case that a positive return code means ERROR and a negative means WARNING, or vice versa.

For instance, the return code -70008 means a library does not exist; attempting to allocate a LIBNAME in such a situation is an error. That particular return code also points out what may be a potential problem in some applications: it appears to have two meanings. -70008 is also a warning message in SYSRC but still means a library does not exist. By contrast, in the situation described above, the negative code for an already allocated data set is a warning.

Hence an application can consider a nonexistent library an ERROR or a WARNING. Usage of %SYSRC in the application code should make it clear which context the error message applies to. However, how you treat return codes is entirely up to you in the context of the application. You can elect to treat a WARNING as an ERROR in your application and vice versa.

The discussion is not limited to LIBNAME return codes. The same comments apply to WHERE processing. %SYSRC reveals some non-zero return codes for perfectly valid situations; for example, successfully augmenting a WHERE clause with an ALSO returns a code of -580015. There are sure to be more.

You cannot get around this problem using just the return code. However, SAS software is fairly specific about naming of fields in the %SYSRC macro. The error names for SCL start _SE or _SW. The E is for ERROR, while the W is for WARNING. To use this information, you need to include some more code in your return code checks. Instead of relying on the return code, look instead at %SYSRC.

It is only of interest whether the LIBNAME call succeeded or not. For example, it is usually not necessary to draw any distinction between a zero return code and a -70004 (the return code returned when a library is reallocated under a different libref). This reallocation is done as follows for the above LIBNAME example:

```
if rc not in (0,%sysrc(_SWDUPLB)) then do ;
```

Using SYSRC accomplishes the aim of allowing a LIBNAME to be treated as successful when the file is already allocated to another library. However, it does introduce the difficulty that you must check the %SYSRC macro whenever it is updated, as our application may strike other valid non-zero codes otherwise.

SCL Code Versus Submitted Code

When coding SCL you can often accomplish a task using code submitted to SAS. This section discusses just how you might determine when to use SCL and when to submit code.

> *An application developed under SCL need not be fully coded in SCL. A feature of SCL is that it allows embedded execution of SAS code, and that should be treated as an extension of SCL and used as a functional extra in SCL as necessary.*

- Consider whether the task can be accomplished **at all** in SCL. For example, would you code an entire SCL program to accomplish a PROC SUMMARY? Hopefully not!

- Can the task be accomplished **easily** in SCL? An example here is the task of appending a SAS data set to the end of another existing data set. In SCL the task is rather complex, requiring explicit file opens, observation fetchings, observation appends, and file closes. In addition, the extra time spent debugging and ultimately maintaining the code should all indicate that a submitted PROC APPEND is more sensible.

- Consider the question of what goes on in the background when you submit code. Code submission demands that SAS software carry out some tasks not associated with SCL. These include loading any software that SAS rather than SCL requires. Depending on the memory usage by SCL, extra I/O may be required to set up the environment for SAS to run submitted code and additional required memory that an SCL approach would not need.

  In many situations, what goes on in the background is likely to be of little consequence, and submitted code will not place a high (or noticeable) burden on the system. However, it has been noted that under Version 2.0 of OS/2 extensive use of SWAPPER.DAT occurred when submitting code after using a number of purely SCL screens. However, it is very difficult to quantify when this is likely to happen, as it is very dependent on data and SCL program size.

Experience has shown that some programmers want to do little more with SCL than place a menu-driven front end around a lot of submitted SAS code. This is a perfectly valid use of SCL if you have working programs that you just want to automate for ease of use. The fact that SCL, with its rich instruction set, can do much more **does not** imply that every SCL program has to use all (or even very much of) that richness.

One of the most strategic systems I have seen has a large number of management reports behind a menu screen. Each report is a separate option on the menu, and the SCL for each option only consists of an INIT section that submits the report. That system freed up a programmer's time by allowing the users to run the reports. Not only was the entire SCL system written in less than a day, but also the programmer's task of manually running the jobs (a task taking nearly a full day each month), was eliminated.The users simply selected and ran the reports online with no overhead on the programmer.

It is my opinion that when a task can be done in SCL and coding that task is within the programmer's ability, then SCL should be used. However, I do not consider that code should always be done in SCL just because SCL exists. After all, computers are used to get quick, accurate solutions to business problems. If a combination of SCL and submitted code can do that quicker than pure SCL, then use it.

Using ARRAYS In SCL

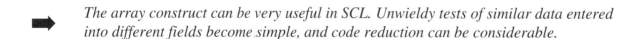 *The array construct can be very useful in SCL. Unwieldy tests of similar data entered into different fields become simple, and code reduction can be considerable.*

Consider the situation where an entry (AF or FSEDIT) requires a number of fields to be entered that all have the same meaning. Perhaps you are having a list of project codes entered or a list of vehicle registrations. Either way, although many fields can be entered, the processing on those fields is likely to be identical.

Without using an array to store the entered data, from the code viewpoint you effectively treat each piece of data as a separate entity. That means that code has to be duplicated, as in the following example. Here I have requested the user to enter up to 10 project codes into SCL window variables **project0 - project9**.

Behind the screen, I could have the following code to check that the project code is valid if it is entered:

```
if project0 ne _blank_ then do ;
    if put(project0,$valprj.) eq 'INV' then do ;
      erroron project0 ;
      call wname('Invalid Project Code Entered') ;
    end ;
end ;
if project1 ne _blank_ then do ;
    if put(project1,$valprj.) eq 'INV' then do ;
      erroron project1 ;
      call wname('Invalid Project Code Entered') ;
    end ;
end ;
if project2 ne _blank_ then do ;
    if put(project2,$valprj.) eq 'INV' then do ;
      erroron project2 ;
      call wname('Invalid Project Code Entered') ;
    end ;
end ;
if project3 ne _blank_ then do ;
    if put(project3,$valprj.) eq 'INV' then do ;
      erroron project3 ;
      call wname('Invalid Project Code Entered') ;
    end ;
end ;
```

Let's leave things there. The message should be clear that a large amount of practically identical code is being created. Now let's look at the same situation using an array:

```
array projects (10) $ 8 project0 - project9 ;
array projflds (10) $ 8 (
                  'project0' 'project1' 'project2' 'project3'
                  'project4' 'project5' 'project6' 'project7'
                  'project8' 'project9') ;

main:
erroroff _all_ ;
do i=1 to dim(projects) ;
  if projects(i) ne _blank_ then do ;
    if put(projects(i),$valprj.) eq 'INV' then do ;
        rc = field('erroron',projflds(i)) ;
        call wname('Invalid Project Code Entered') ;
    end ;
  end ;
end ;
return ;
```

That has reduced the amount of code carried, made the code much more maintainable and easier to read. There are some obvious changes in how the task is coded; these arise out of the different ways that array elements interface with some SCL elements, such as error handling.

Note that the array allows us to loop through each element one at a time. Each iteration of the DO loop processes just one screen field, the one identified by being in position **i** in the array PROJECTS.

 *Using arrays, you **cannot** write code like*

```
rc = field('erroron',projects(i)) ;
```

because even though an array element can be used as the second argument to FIELD, that second element must be a variable name. The above incorrect use of **projects(i)** *in the field function is invalid because the value of the array element will be seen by the FIELD function, and that value is what the user entered into the field rather than the field name.*

To get around this problem, create a secondary array that contains as its elements the names of the fields whose values make up the first array. The two arrays must be set up in such a way that the correct mapping between value and name is maintained as above.

Note that base SAS software includes a routine, VNAME, that is designed to return array element names when given the element value. This is mentioned because it is an example that not the entire base SAS software function set is available in SCL. VNAME would remove the need to create the second array, but it is not available in SCL.

Debugging SCL Programs

Debugging is the task of taking the entries that you have created and ensuring that

- the programs are syntactically correct (in other words, they conform to the rules of SAS software)

- the programs do as required

- the programs are stable (in other words, in the presence of unexpected inputs by users, the programs do not cease to work)

- the screens that you create are correct.

This section explores briefly some principles of ensuring that the above are correct for your application.

Syntax Errors

There are two possible situations to consider:

- The SCL compiler detects errors.

- Syntax errors have occurred that the compiler cannot find.

An example of the first item is the incorrect spelling of a keyword. For instance, consider the following code:

```
if project in ('F03432') thne do ;
```

The incorrect spelling of THEN as THNE is a syntax error, and because the error renders the statement uninterpretable, the SCL compiler will flag an error at the compile stage.

In practice, SAS software finds strict syntax errors at compile time (a strict syntax error is one that causes the compiler to be unable to interpret the code), and you have to correct them then. Rigorous program testing should be employed to find your other errors.

You may think that if the compiler does not find an error, then the error is in logic, not syntax. However, in languages like SCL, not all code is compiled. The primary situation here is submitted code. To illustrate the second potential problem, the following has a syntax error that will not be picked up by the SCL compiler; furthermore, it will not even be picked up by SAS software:

```
submit continue ;
  data temp
   set library.test ;
   ....
endsubmit ;
```

The error is a missing semicolon at the end of the DATA statement. The impact is rather drastic and the lesson simple. Even when you break some of the rules of SAS software, SAS may still find an interpretable, compilable, and executable program. But the results can be unpredictable.

Errors may in fact be missed despite the most rigorous testing. Take the example above with the missing semicolon. It is likely that the first indication of an error will come when a following step attempts to use either TEMP or LIBRARY.TEST and finds data missing. But what if missing data is actually possible and your program is coded to work around missing data? The system may get right through testing and into production -- and destroy some vital data.

Testing an SCL program may appear somewhat different from checking DATA/PROC step-oriented programs. In the DATA/PROC step situation, there are very definite step boundaries and you can easily check intermediate output. However, it should be realized that within a DATA step you still have to ensure code works. The major difference between how to debug DATA steps and how to debug SCL is in the different structure; SCL has defined sections and can run and pass data between other SCL programs. The DATA step has some comparative features such as %INCLUDE and LINKED code, so the basis of testing is similar.

It is not enough to ensure that your program does as expected when it gets the input that it expects. Users of your systems have a right to expect that when they accidentally enter unexpected data the system will continue to run with minimum (preferably no) disruption.

The above comments are all well-documented and well-known concepts. The rest of this section covers some ideas for finding out why an SCL program does not do as expected.

Non-Syntax Errors

The first rule when a program fails is to find out just what values variables have at the stage where the program failed.

 It is important to understand that where the program fails may not be where the error occurred.

For instance, if a file OPEN fails, the first error is noted when the program tries to use the opened file. The data set identifier will have been given a missing value, but it's only when you use it that you see a problem. Even if you make a syntax error and spell the file name wrong, the error will be picked up at run time, not compile time.

You can track program flow and trace variable values in two ways, by using carefully placed PUT statements or by using the SCL debugger.

PUT statements can be used liberally in code for testing purposes. Statements such as the following display all program variable values both before and after the call to 'TEST.PROGRAM':

```
put 'BEFORE ENTERING TEST.PROGRAM ' _all_ ;
call display('test.program',project,rc,planitem) ;
put 'AFTER ENTERING TEST.PROGRAM ' _all_ ;
```

When you need to trace program flow, a series of PUT statements in strategic places will help show where the program is going.

PUT statements have some difficulties. For instance, you may use a number of PUTS and isolate a problem to a specific section of code. You now need to go back and enter more PUTS in that section of code to narrow the problem down further. This means recompiling, and you must remember to remove all the PUTS before going to production. Also, when using PUT, you may have to let a program completely finish before you can examine the output.

The use of PUT statements (or their equivalents in other languages) is a simple and fairly trustworthy form of debugging that also has the distinct advantage of leaving the user in control. A more powerful tool, and consequently one with a higher conceptual learning overhead, is the SCL debugger. This is at a much lower level than the coded PUT statement; with the debugger you can start and stop programs anywhere as you desire while the program is executing. Furthermore, you can both examine and change values of variables while the program executes.

The main uses that I have put the debugger to are examining program flow and verifying values of variables. The debugger has proven invaluable as an aid in showing where a program has gone (when it doesn't go where I think it should). The ability to examine variable values without having to stop, enter PUT statements, and recompile is very useful.

This book won't go further into the debugger, except to say that as a programmer you have no option but to attempt to provide functional software, and the debugger is a tool for assisting with that. It does not have to be used, and indeed there are many cases when the use of simple PUT statements will suffice. However, every SCL programmer should at least know the basics of the debugger.

Some errors are introduced by incorrect data, but the actual error is not at the SAS level.For example, consider the situation in which a user has to enter a system library name but accidentally enters a nonexistent library name. The user then attempts unsuccessfully to open that library. The error is at the operating system level, and all SAS does is pass the filename to existing routines and accept a return code back from those routines. In that situation, use the SYSMSG() function, which will tell you the actual operating system error message.

 A useful debugging hint is to pre-empt the debugging process by checking return codes from all function calls and ensuring that file opens succeed.

SCL has a wealth of useful functions such as FEXIST and EXIST that can check whether tasks such as library or data set opens will work by first verifying that files do exist. The extra overhead in checking all function calls is small in computer-resource and user-response time; it may, however, be large in extra programmer effort. That is *not* a valid excuse for assuming that all function calls will succeed.

Chapter 4: Code Submission And The PREVIEW Window

Contents

An Overview Of Code Submission

➡️ *Submission of SAS code is SCL's interface with SAS software. The combination of SCL, SAS software and SQL makes for one of the richest, most powerful languages in existence today.*

Submitted code utilizes a preview buffer. This buffer is an area in memory where code is placed before actually being executed by SAS software.

You are not limited to placing SAS code in the preview buffer. There is no reason why JCL or other text could not be placed in the buffer. The user can access the preview buffer, and the text in there does not have to be passed to SAS software. Furthermore, the preview buffer can be used to allow users to enter their own programs, which can be passed to SAS software.

Submitting code is simple. Just use the SCL SUBMIT command, and all that follows up to the ENDSUBMIT command is passed to the preview buffer for subsequent SAS software or other processing.

The interface between SCL and SAS software allows SCL field values to be passed to the SAS program and also allows macro variables to be passed via the SYMGET and SYMPUT family of routines. Thus, your submitted program can draw upon variables created using the SCL user interface.

Code submission occurs as follows:

- At SCL compile time, the code between the SUBMIT and the ENDSUBMIT (including comments) is treated by SCL as a string of noncompilable text to be passed to SAS for execution later. This code includes possible macro variables (for example, &xxx) that are NOT resolved at SCL compile time.

- At SCL run time, when the SUBMIT statement is executed, the noncompilable text is scanned by SCL for any SCL variable references. These are denoted in the SAS code by using & prefixes as with macro variables. Any such variables are replaced by the value of the corresponding SCL variable. Therefore, submitted code must not use MACRO variables with the same name as an SCL window variable. If that cannot be avoided, there are two options:

  - submitted code must use SYMGETx functions to get the value of the macro variable.

  - use **&&mvarname** instead of **&mvarname**. Standard macro symbolic resolution causes the && to resolve to & on the first pass of the macro processor. This substitution occurs after SCL has handed control to SAS. The second pass does not attempt to place the AF variable in the field, as AF variable replacement has already occurred. The && is resolved when the code is submitted, while the AF replacement occurs before submitting.

- At run time, the SUBMIT statement places the text in a preview buffer. Mechanisms are built into SCL for programmers to modify the code in this buffer before submitting. This uses the SCL PREVIEW routine.

- Depending on the type of SUBMIT that the SCL uses, the code is either immediately submitted to SAS or not submitted at all. If it is immediately submitted, the action taken at the end of the SUBMIT statement depends on the options. You can use the SUBMIT statement with no options, or you can use any of the following options, discussed in the sections below: CONTINUE, CONTINUE SQL, IMMEDIATE, PRIMARY, COMMAND CONTINUE, TERMINATE.

When a field in an AF entry has a format associated, the formatted value is passed through if the variable is used in submitted code. Be very careful with time and datetime variables. A field named **time**, *containing a SAS time value and formatted with TIME8., appears in the submitted code as a character string in the format HH:MM:SS. Using this as a time variable ("HH:MM:SS"t) in the following code will not result in a successful match with a data set variable derived from a time function because the formatted value does not have the same precision as the data set variable named* **time** *that it is being compared to.*

```
submit continue ;
...
   where "&time"t eq time ;
...
endsubmit ;
```

You need to change the WHERE clause as follows for a successful match:

```
submit continue ;
....
   where put(time,time8.) eq "&time" ;
....
endsubmit ;
```

SUBMIT With No Options

The code is placed in the preview buffer, but it is not submitted for execution by SAS software. This allows some code to be readied, and other code to be added. Applications can thus stack up code and permit users to select coded options that continue to stack more code. Thus your SCL program structure could resemble the following:

```
submit ;
....
endsubmit ;
```

(more SCL code)

```
submit ;
....
endsubmit ;
```

(more SCL code)

```
submit ;
....
endsubmit ;
```

Each of the SUBMIT/ENDSUBMIT segments is called a submit block.

At the end of this segment of code, the preview buffer would contain all the code contained in the submit blocks. The SCL code between the submit blocks could include code to carry out the SUBMIT statements conditionally.

SAS code submitted in this manner can still be executed by SAS software if you issue the statements

```
submit <submit option>;
endsubmit ;
```

This has the effect of submitting whatever is in the preview buffer to SAS software for execution and emptying the preview buffer. Alternatively, ending a task stream causes code in the buffer to be submitted. Any of the valid submit options (CONTINUE SQL , IMMEDIATE, PRIMARY, TERMINATE, or COMMAND) can be used.

Once code is placed in the preview buffer, it can then be manipulated. Items manipulated in this manner do not have to be valid SAS code. For example, in your screen you can prompt users to enter fields that are required to build up JCL to be submitted to MVS.

JARS does this for some long running reports, requesting a job account code and floor for delivery from the user via SAS/AF program entries. Other screen fields may determine which parts of a program are to be run. The whole program, including JCL, is built and stored in the preview buffer. When it is complete, JARS issues a PREVIEW('file'...) command to store the JCL and program in an external library, then uses the TSO SUBMIT command to execute the program as a background task.

SUBMIT CONTINUE

Using the CONTINUE option on the SUBMIT statement allows the SAS code to appear as if it is part of the SCL code stream. The code is submitted, SCL is suspended until the submitted code is complete, and then the SCL that follows the submitted code continues. The SAS process and the SCL process can communicate variable values as follows:

- SCL to SAS (before the SUBMIT is triggered)

    via SCL variables or macro variables set in the SCL and resolved in the submitted code. An example is

    ```
    jobname = symgetc('sysjobid') || '01' ;
    submit continue ;
     data _null_ ;
      put "//&jobname" ;
      run ;
    endsubmit ;
    ```

    The example assigns a value to the SCL variable **jobname**, and that value is resolved before either the macro processor or SAS software sees the submitted code. Suppose instead of the AF variable, **jobname** is a macro variable instead. The equivalent of the above would be

    ```
    call symputc('jobname',symgetc('sysjobid') || '01') ;
    submit continue ;
      data _null_ ;
    ```

```
      put "//&jobname" ;
    run ;
  endsubmit ;
```

This time, because the variable is a macro variable rather than an SCL variable, the code that gets submitted to SAS would include the **&jobname**, and the macro processor would substitute the required value. Note that this assumes no existence of an SCL variable named **jobname**.

Finally, suppose both an SCL variable and a macro variable exist, and the intention is to use the macro variable value. Use the following code:

```
jobname = symgetc('sysjobid') ;
call symputc('jobname',jobname || '01') ;
submit continue ;
  data _null_ ;
    put "//&&jobname" ;
  run ;
endsubmit ;
```

SCL will make no attempt to resolve the double ampersand; rather it will be passed to the macro processor to sort out. Thus the macro variable **jobname** value will be correctly used.

- SAS to SCL (for SCL to use values created in the executed submitted code)

The submitted code creates macro variables that the following SCL code can use through the SYMGETx functions. For instance, suppose you read an external file and want to return how many records were read. The DATA step might look like this:

```
data _null_ ;
  infile external ;
  input .... ;
  count + 1 ;
run ;
```

The easiest way to get this count into an SCL variable is to store it in a macro variable. A slight change is needed to the above:

```
data _null_ ;
  infile external end = eof ;
  input .... ;
  count + 1 ;
  if eof then call symput('count',count) ;
run ;
```

Then in SCL all that is needed is to use the SYMGET function to extract the **count** value.

Output from this form of the SUBMIT appears in the SASLOG and SASLIST files. To keep a tight hold on an application, it may be necessary to reroute these files using PROC PRINTTO. An example of this situation is discussed in the section "The PREVIEW Window" later in this chapter. However, you can use the CONTINUE option of the DM command if you start your application with the DM command, and this will cause the OUTPUT and LOG windows to return control back to the application when the user ends out of them.

 A SUBMIT with the CONTINUE option may disable any active legends. The display manager STATUS OFF command will override this behavior under Release 6.07 on MVS and maintain legends during a SUBMIT, but under OS/2 and Windows it does not appear to.

SUBMIT CONTINUE SQL

This acts the same as SUBMIT CONTINUE, except the code is passed directly to SQL rather than SAS software. It is not necessary to code either a PROC SQL statement nor an ending QUIT.

This form of the SUBMIT statement does not appear to disable any active legends under any release (from 6.06 on) or platform that I have seen.

Although this command places CPU and I/O information in the SASLOG, as well as error messages, the program listing does not appear. So it may be difficult to see just what may have gone wrong when a program fails. Using SUBMIT CONTINUE and running PROC SQL does put the program listing in the log, so it may be preferable.

SUBMIT IMMEDIATE

This form of the statement does execute the submitted code immediately, but it does not execute any SCL following the ENDSUBMIT. Control passes back to the user when the SUBMIT has completed. The window is not exited, and the MAIN section will be executed next time the user enters a value (or presses ENTER without altering a field if CONTROL ALWAYS is on).

SUBMIT IMMEDIATE is intended for use in those situations where the code effectively ends the current execution of a section, but you wish the user to then explicitly exit or carry out another task (For example, choose another option to submit another program). You can certainly have code after the SUBMIT; to access that code you will need to branch around the SUBMIT.

This is a good option when you want to submit one of a number of programs and return control to the user when the program is completed. Branch to the program you want to run, and no other program following is executed. An example follows:

```
init:
  control always ;
return ;

main:
  if _status_ eq 'E' then return ;

  if pname eq 'USAGE1' then
                    submit immediate ;
```

```
                    proc print data=usage.usage ;
                       where modulen contains 'SQL' ;
                       var modulen prod keys ;
                    run ;
                  endsubmit ;
  put 'USAGE1 Completed' ;
  if pname eq 'USAGE2' then
                  submit immediate ;
                    proc print data=usage.usage ;
                       where modulen contains 'SCL' ;
                       var modulen prod keys ;
                    run ;
                  endsubmit ;
  put 'USAGE2 Completed' ;
  if pname eq 'USAGE3' then
                  submit immediate ;
                    proc print data=usage.usage ;
                       where modulen contains 'OPERATE' ;
                       var modulen prod keys ;
                    run ;
                  endsubmit ;
  put 'USAGE3 Completed' ;
return ;
```

In the above program, a display screen also exists that allows the name of the program (USAGE1, USAGE2, or USAGE3) to be run to be entered into field **pname**. If USAGE1 is entered, the code in the first SUBMIT block is executed and control immediately returns to the user. The message USAGE1 COMPLETED does not appear because the SUBMIT IMMEDIATE already caused control to be passed back to the user.

Selecting one of the other SUBMIT blocks has a similar impact.

SUBMIT PRIMARY

This is similar to SUBMIT IMMEDIATE in that no code is carried out after the SUBMIT. This statement has the added feature that it ends the current entry and fasttracks back to the entry that was called to start the current task stream.

☹ *Experience has taught that careless use of SUBMIT PRIMARY can cause an infinite loop and a rather tight one! If you place a SUBMIT PRIMARY in the INIT block of an entry that starts a task stream, then termination of the SUBMIT PRIMARY causes return to the entry that started the current task stream (in other words, itself), which retriggers the INIT section just exited, and so on (ad infinitum). Beware.*

The action here is similar in concept to the CALL GOTO routine (although it will not exit the current task stream) and carries all the same warnings that function does. You are responsible for ensuring that all open files are closed to maintain system integrity.

Considerable analysis should be carried out before you use SUBMIT PRIMARY. It is very possible that you may code this carefully and ensure that no databases are left open, but a later programmer may alter code and attempt to close a file after the SUBMIT PRIMARY. If using this form of the SUBMIT statement, ensure all screens that make up the task stream before the SUBMIT PRIMARY are carefully documented to minimize the possibility of this happening.

SUBMIT COMMAND CONTINUE

This form of the SUBMIT statement is specifically intended to allow the user to issue display manager commands rather than SAS program statements.

Note that this statement is documented in usage note V6-SCL-4075 and is available in Release 6.07.

This statement differs from the EXECCMD function in that

- the command is carried out immediately as part of the SCL program stream
- EXECCMD flushes the command buffer at the end of a task stream (this form of SUBMIT does not)
- the SUBMIT has no (known to me) restrictions on the length of the arguments (EXECCMD is limited to 200 characters).

SUBMIT TERMINATE

Use this option when code is submitted to cause the application task stream to end.

Note that when PROC V5TOV6 is used to convert SAS/AF entries, the default for converting Version 5-pushed SAS code into Version 6 SCL is to place the code in a submit block that uses the TERMINATE option. This is likely to cause a major difference in the running of the application compared with Version 5, namely that the application may end after a single code submission.

The PREVIEW Window

At first glance, it is far from obvious just why the PREVIEW window exists. Surely the application developer has placed SAS code in the SCL in order to shield programming from the user -- so why let them have access to such a window?

There are many answers, ranging from "it might be useful sometime, somewhere, just don't ask me where yet," to the PREVIEW window's being another tool in the experienced SAS programmer's toolbox since it allows manipulation of the text or code that users have submitted. It is also SCL's interface with the preview buffer, and that is a most useful tool.

Consider the following possibility. You have coded a system that allows a lot of reports to be run online. However, your users want more. In particular, they want to be able to code ad hoc reports themselves under application control.

I will assume that the users know SQL. Of course, that's not always an accurate assumption, but for any application that allows access to the PREVIEW window, familiarity with SQL should at least be a prerequisite. If your users don't have this ability, you should be wary about giving them any access to write their own programs.

In your program, you can give users access to the PREVIEW window and they can enter their own SQL queries. There is no need to have any code already in the preview buffer. In fact, to avoid confusion it is useful to empty the buffer first.

This is accomplished as follows:

```
main:
  rc = preview('clear') ;
  if preview('edit') eq -1 then rc=preview('clear') ;
  else
    submit continue sql;
    endsubmit ;
return ;
```

This simple code allows users to code their own queries directly into the PREVIEW window. If they exit the window using CANCEL (return code is -1), the preview buffer is emptied and no code is submitted. Otherwise, the code is submitted.

It could be the case, depending on the user base, that allowing users access to the preview buffer is self destructive. For users with little SAS background, questions such as "*Why do I have no output?*", "*How do I get back my program?*" in a later session (note, NOT "*How do I save my program?*"), "*How do I print the output?*" and so on can raise both the work load and blood pressure of developers by a rather large amount. Be wary about whom you let at the preview buffer for the purpose of creating code.

A question that arises with the above example is why use the preview buffer -- what about just giving users access to the program editor? The answer for my applications has been that the preview function allows the application to maintain control easily. The program editor effectively requires the SCL to be halted (or prohibits use of SCL at all), which requires all sorts of assumptions about user knowledge and what the user won't do to opened files. It also raises the question of how to encourage users to restart the application.

Using the PREVIEW window allows the application to control file handling and timing when the code is submitted. Thus, the user need know little more than librefs and data set structure.

The above discussion focused on the entering of code into the PREVIEW window. This window could allow entry of text -- allow the user to enter text and then under application control save it in a catalog or external file. This is used in Databank's JARS application, where project leaders maintain a diary of events. The diary is created and maintained by reading it into the preview buffer, allowing editing and addition to the text, then saving it again. The entire SAS System text editor is available for use with this.

You need to use the COPY or INCLUDE argument as the first parameter to CALL PREVIEW to load the PREVIEW window, and then use SAVE or FILE to save the user's work. The difference is that the COPY/SAVE pair will read/write the data from and to a SAS catalog entry, while the INCLUDE/FILE pair uses an external file. It is totally up to the application designers whether you use external or SAS files, but you should bear in mind that external files can be edited outside the control of SAS software, while SAS catalog entries are easier to keep under application control.

Case Study 1   Using The PREVIEW Window For Code Entry

This case study shows how a user can interact with the SAS System by means of the PREVIEW window. The example is from the usage notes system, SUNS.

The first issue that needs to be addressed is how to allow users to interact with the output and log. If they make a mistake, how do you tell them? How do you allow access to windows that they may have no idea how to communicate with (the LOG and LISTING windows, for example)?

Careful use of PROC PRINTTO can help here. To maintain total application control, simply route the LOG and PRINT files away from the LOG and LISTING windows. Then, completely under application control, permit viewing of those windows. Following is the complete program that allows SQL program entry via the PREVIEW window and also maintains application control. Figure 4.1 shows the display screen that sets up the access, seen from the programmer's viewpoint.

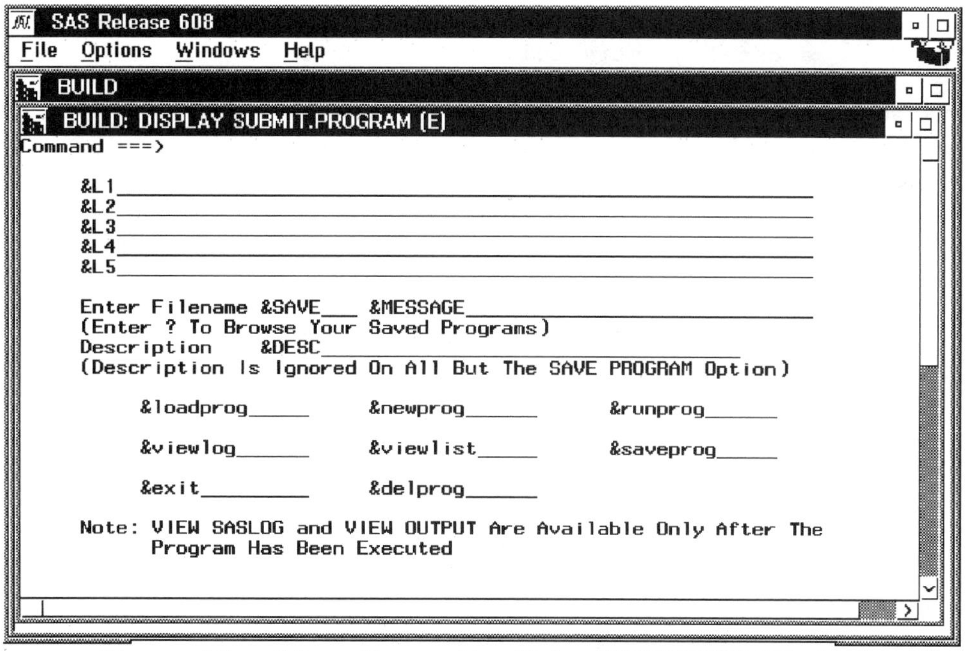

```
┌──────────────────────────────────────────────────────────────┐
│ ░▒ SAS Release 608                                      ░ │□│ │
├──────────────────────────────────────────────────────────────┤
│  File   Options   Windows   Help                           🖐 │
│ ┌────────────────────────────────────────────────────────────┐│
│ │▓ BUILD                                              ░ │ □ │ ││
│ │┌───────────────────────────────────────────────────────────┐│
│ ││▓ BUILD: DISPLAY SUBMIT.PROGRAM (E)                 ░ │ □ │││
│ │├───────────────────────────────────────────────────────────┤
│ ││Command ===>                                              ^  │
│ ││                                                         ░  │
│ ││     &L1_____    ░  │
│ ││     &L2_____    ░  │
│ ││     &L3_____    ░  │
│ ││     &L4_____    ░  │
│ ││     &L5_____    ░  │
│ ││                                                         ░  │
│ ││     Enter Filename &SAVE___  &MESSAGE_____    ░  │
│ ││     (Enter ? To Browse Your Saved Programs)             ░  │
│ ││     Description    &DESC_____    ░  │
│ ││     (Description Is Ignored On All But The SAVE PROGRAM Option) │
│ ││                                                         ░  │
│ ││        &loadprog_____    &newprog_____   &runprog_____ │
│ ││                                                         ░  │
│ ││        &viewlog_____    &viewlist_____   &saveprog_____  │
│ ││                                                         ░  │
│ ││        &exit_____    &delprog_____                 ░  │
│ ││                                                         ░  │
│ ││     Note: VIEW SASLOG and VIEW OUTPUT Are Available Only After The │
│ ││           Program Has Been Executed                     ░  │
│ ││                                                         v  │
│ │└───────────────────────────────────────────────────────────┘│
│ │└──────────────────────────────────────────────────────> ┘ ││
│ └────────────────────────────────────────────────────────────┘│
└──────────────────────────────────────────────────────────────┘
```

Figure 4.1:   Menu Screen For Using PREVIEW Window

Notes about the code are at the end of the listing.

❶`entry logname $ 44 prtname $ 44 ;`

```
/****************** PROGRAM DESCRIPTION ********************
This screen permits a user to interact with the PREVIEW window
and write simple queries to be executed by the SAS SQL system.
Total control over the user is maintained by the application.

***********END****** PROGRAM DESCRIPTION ********************/

/****************** VARIABLE DESCRIPTOR BLOCK *****************

 logname    -- passed from calling program, it is the file that
               the SASLOG is rerouted to for the user program
   prtname   -- passed from calling program, it is the file that
               the SASLIST is rerouted to for the user program
   des1      -- array containing the screen fields that are seen
               by the user on first entering the screen. These
               make up a set of dynamic instructions that tell
               the user what to do at this stage
   des2      -- array containing the screen fields that are seen
               by the user after running the coded program. These
               make up a set of dynamic instructions that tell
               the user what to do at this stage
   l1 - l5   -- the screen fields that make up the list of
               instructions stored in des1 and des2
   rc        -- used for storing return codes
```

```
       save     -- 8 character screen entry for saving a program
       filesave -- full SAS name for saving a program, this field is
                   a catalog entry built around SAVE


*****END*********** VARIABLE DESCRIPTOR BLOCK *****************/

❷array des1 $ 80 (
          'Now That Your Program Is Entered, It Needs To Be Saved And'
          'Submitted For Processing By The SAS Software. Please Enter'
          'The File Name To Save The Program To. If You Do Not Enter'
          'A File Name, The Program Is Not Saved, But May Still Be'
          'Submitted To SAS Software For Execution:') ;

array des2 $ 80 (
          'The Program You Entered Has Been Processed By SAS Software.'
          'You Should View Both The SASLOG (To Check For Any Errors)'
          'And The Output File Which Contains The Report You Coded'
          ' '
          '          Select An Option From The Buttons Below') ;

❸init:
  control always label allcmds;
  l1 = 'Select A Button To Initiate An Action' ;
  l2 = _blank_ ; l3 = _blank_ ; l4 = _blank_ ; l5 = _blank_ ;
  call execcmd('setpmenu library.usagenew.null2.pmenu;pmenu on');
  rc = field('color yellow highlight','save desc') ;
  ❺ rc = field('color pink highlight','message') ;
return ;


term:
  ❹call execcmd('pmenu off') ;


return ;


/*-----------------------------------------------------------------*/
reroute:
/* start by rerouting LOG and PRINT so the application can keep
   control; if this isn't done user is placed in OUTPUT window and
   needs SAS knowledge to view the LOG; we don't presume any
   knowledge of DMS here, only the ability to code a simple or
   otherwise SQL command

   Note the PROC SQL at the end; this forces whatever the user
   enters to be submitted to SQL. This is done in preference to
   a SUBMIT CONTINUE SQL later as that does not write the code
   out to the SASLOG */



  submit continue ;
   proc printto print="&prt"  new; run ;
   proc printto log  ="&log"  new; run ;
   proc sql ;
  endsubmit ;
return ;
```

```
/*------------------------------------------------------------------*/
normal:

/* end any submitted SQL and execute it, reroute the logs back
   where they belong */

  submit continue ;
    ;quit ;
    proc printto print=print ; run ;
    proc printto log  =log   ; run ;
  endsubmit ;
return ;

/*------------------------------------------------------------------*/
subtext:

/* redisplay the default message when a program is loaded */

  l1 = des1(1) ; l2 = des1(2) ; l3 = des1(3) ; l4 = des1(4) ; l5 = des1(5) ;
return ;

/*------------------------------------------------------------------*/
save:
  if save eq: '?' then do ;                /* user wants help */
/* first step is to verify that they have some saved files */
    submit continue sql ;
      create table temp as
        select * from dictionary.catalogs
          where libname eq 'SASUSER' and
                memname eq 'SQLQUERY' ;
    endsubmit ;

    if symgetn('sqlobs') eq 0 then do ;
      %legit('Note: No Saved Querys Exist',Y)
      return ;
    end ;

    call wregion(21,10,4,65,' ') ;
    call putlegend(2,'Use B To Browse An Entry') ;
    call legend() ;

    call wregion(1,10,20,65,' ') ;
    call execcmd("keydef f3 'END'") ;
    rc = catalog('sasuser.sqlquery' , 'source' , 'b');
    call endlegend() ;
    call nextword() ;
    return ;
  end ;
  else do ;                                /* name entered, check */
    erroroff save ;                        /* for validity        */
  ❻ if sasname(save) ne 1 then do ;     /* Not Valid            */
      %legit('ERROR: Invalid Name Entered For File',Y)
      erroron save ;
      return ;
    end ;
  end ;                                    /* all ok              */
return ;
```

```
/*-----------------------------------------------------------------*/
loadprog:
  if error(save) then return ;

  if save eq _blank_ then do ;
     %legit('ERROR: You Must Enter A Program Name',Y)
     return ;
  end ;

  filesave = 'sasuser.sqlquery.' || save || '.SOURCE' ;

  if cexist(filesave) eq 0 then do ;
     %legit('ERROR: The Program Does Not Exist',Y)
     return ;
  end ;

  call wregion(6,1,16,80) ;

/* call the PREVIEW window, place the user in there in EDIT mode,
   if they cancel CLEAR the PREVIEW window, return to main menu */

  rc = preview('clear') ;                /* empty preview buffer */
  link reroute ;                         /* log/prt to app files */
  call execcmd('copy ' || filesave) ;    /* push load to buffer  */
  if preview('edit') eq -1 then do ;     /* enter preview, check */
    rc = preview('clear') ;              /* for CANCEL and clear */
    link normal ;                        /* buffer/log/prt       */
    return ;
  end ;                                  /* all ok, new text disp*/
  link subtext ;
  cursor save ;
return ;

/*-----------------------------------------------------------------*/
newprog:
  if error(save) then return ;

  call wregion(6,1,16,80) ;

/* call the PREVIEW window, place the user in there in EDIT mode,
   if they cancel CLEAR the PREVIEW window, return to main menu */

  rc = preview('clear') ;
  link reroute ;
  if preview('edit') eq -1 then do ;
    rc = preview('clear') ;
    link normal ;
    return ;
  end ;
  link subtext ;
  cursor save ;
return ;
```

```
/*------------------------------------------------------------*/
runprog:
  if error(save) then return ;

/* check if already run and disallow action if it has been (this is
   because the preview buffer is now empty) */

  if l1 eq des2(1) then do ;
    %legit('ERROR: Program Already Executed -- Cannot ReRun',Y)
    return ;
  end ;


/* otherwise run the program. To do this just issue a dummy SUBMIT
   which executes the code in the preview buffer */

  %legit('Processing .. Please Wait')
  submit continue ;
  endsubmit ;

/* now set up the new message so the user has instructions on what
   to do next */

  l1=des2(1) ; l2=des2(2) ; l3=des2(3) ; l4=des2(4) ; l5=des2(5);

/* reroute the log and print back so the user can now view the
   program information */

  link normal ;
  cursor save ;
return ;

/*------------------------------------------------------------*/
viewlog:
  if error(save) then return ;

/* set up the LOG filename in the format that FSLIST wants and use
   FSLIST to display it */

  if l1 ne des2(1) then return ;
  logname = '"' || logname || '"' ;
  call fslist(logname) ;
  cursor save ;
return ;

/*------------------------------------------------------------*/
viewlist:
  if error(save) then return ;

/* set up the PRT filename in the format that FSLIST wants and use
   FSLIST to display it */

  if l1 ne des2(1) then return ;
  prtname = '"' || prtname || '"' ;
  call fslist(prtname) ;
  cursor save ;
return ;
```

```
/*---------------------------------------------------------------*/
saveprog:
  if error(save) then return ;

  if save eq _blank_ then do ;
    %legit('ERROR: Cannot SAVE Without A SAVE File Name',Y)
    return ;
  end ;

  if l1 eq des2(1) then do ;
    %legit('ERROR: Cannot SAVE After Program Was Run',Y)
    return ;
  end ;

/* if the program has not been run and the user selected to save
   then write to a SOURCE catalog entry. */

  filesave = 'sasuser.sqlquery.' || save || '.SOURCE' ;
  call preview('save',filesave,desc) ;


  message = 'Saved As ' || filesave ;
  cursor save ;
return ;

/*---------------------------------------------------------------*/
exit:
/* end of program; empty the PREVIEW window (we do not assume the
   program was run), point the log and list file back to their
   defaults, and exit */

  rc = preview('clear') ;
  link normal ;
  call execcmd('end') ;
return ;

/*---------------------------------------------------------------*/
delprog:
/* delete catalog entry. */

  if error(save) then return ;

  if save eq _blank_ then do ;
    %legit('ERROR: Cannot DELETE Without A SAVED File Name',Y)
    return ;
  end ;


  filesave = 'sasuser.sqlquery.' || save || '.SOURCE' ;

  if cexist(filesave) eq 0 then do ;
    %legit('ERROR: The Program Does Not Exist',Y)
    return ;
  end ;

  rc = delete(filesave,'catalog') ;

return ;
```

The following notes accompany the above program.

1. There are two parameters, the names of files to write the SASLOG to and the LISTING file to. These are operating system dependent and are set up in the initial program that starts up the application.

2. The arrays DES1 and DES2 are descriptive fields that are seen on screen by the user as various events occur in the application.

   At the start of the screen, these fields are blank. After selecting the &NEWPROG or &LOADPROG option, users see text that helps them select what to do next. When users have entered a program in the PREVIEW window and pressed END to exit back to the main window, they now see the screen in Figure 4.2.

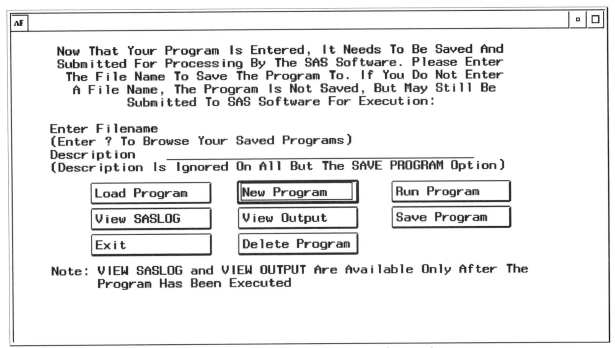

Figure 4.2: On-Screen Help Information

After users have submitted code to SAS for execution (using the RUN PROGRAM button), the text changes (see Figure 4.3) to assist them to view the log and list files.

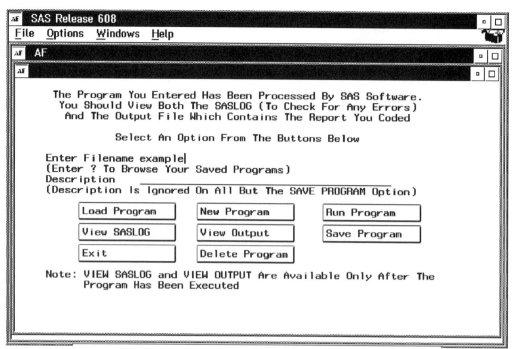

Figure 4.3: On Screen Help Information

The objective of the text changes that are occurring on screen here is to keep users informed without making them go to extra lengths such as using HELP screens. Remember, our users' objective is to code and submit an SQL program and view the output, so why inflict extra tasks upon them?

3. The INIT section sets up an initial text entry in one of the descriptive fields. It uses CONTROL LABEL to allow labeled sections of code to execute when the user enters fields or uses the push button options.

4. EXECCMD removes the command line. The command line is not needed because in this application it is not necessary to allow users to issue any commands. The EXECCMD argument is executed when INIT is finished (because EXECCMD arguments execute when a window is next displayed -- they do not execute at the stage that the execute occurs in the code stream), which is when the screen is displayed. The WREGION command does not remove the PREVIEW window command line, although it does set up the window placement on screen.

5. The FIELD command assigns colors and attributes to various fields. This only needs to be done once in the screen; those colors and attributes remain for the rest of the usage of the screen.

6. The field **save** is checked using the SASNAME function in the SAVE label to verify that the user entered a name that SAS software can work with.

At the start of each labeled section, the variable **save** (which contains the name of a member to be saved/loaded) is checked to see if the **save** label has placed it in error. If so, the other labeled sections do not execute. This prevents the situation where a user types an invalid value for **save** and uses a button to initiate an action on that value. Without the check for **save** being in error, the labeled section for the button would still execute and attempt to process an invalid value.

The **save** field can have a ? entered, in which case the CATALOG window is used to display all the user's saved entries. The user can browse them to decide which entry is to be loaded.

Note that although SUNS uses a list to store the system messages, the messages are expanded in full in the above program to aid reading here.

The use of the push-button fields requires some explanation here. The fields do not belong to a choice group. Thus each field is a stand alone button. When the button is clicked on, it is considered to be MODIFIED. Hence a labeled section with the name of that button is executed.

The attributes for each of the push-button fields are shown in Figure 4.4. Only one field is shown because all are identical except the initial message.

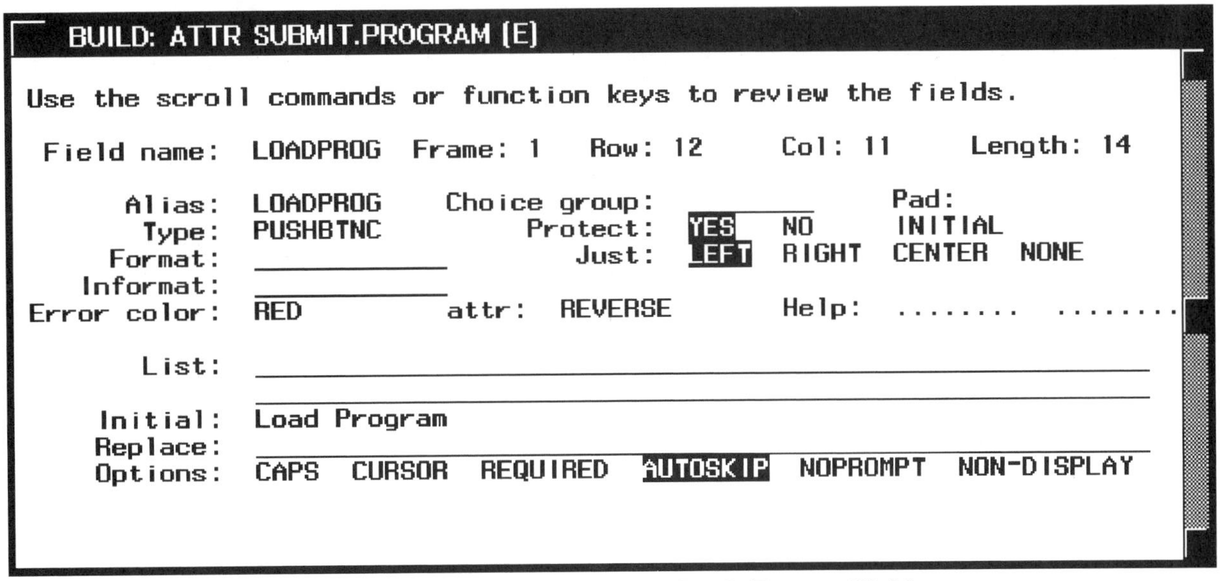

```
┌─────────────────────────────────────────────────────────────────────┐
│  BUILD: ATTR SUBMIT.PROGRAM [E]                                       │
│                                                                       │
│ Use the scroll commands or function keys to review the fields.        │
│                                                                       │
│  Field name:  LOADPROG  Frame: 1   Row: 12     Col: 11      Length: 14│
│                                                                       │
│      Alias:  LOADPROG    Choice group: ____    Pad:                   │
│       Type:  PUSHBTNC        Protect: YES   NO       INITIAL          │
│     Format:  _____         Just: LEFT  RIGHT  CENTER   NONE      │
│   Informat:                                                           │
│ Error color: RED          attr:  REVERSE       Help:  ........ .......│
│                                                                       │
│       List:  _____         │
│                                                                       │
│    Initial:  Load Program                                             │
│    Replace:  _____        │
│    Options:  CAPS   CURSOR   REQUIRED  AUTOSKIP  NOPROMPT  NON-DISPLAY │
│                                                                       │
└─────────────────────────────────────────────────────────────────────┘
```

Figure 4.4: Attributes For Push-Button Fields

Note that I protect the fields that define the actions to carry out. Protecting fields like this in a non mouse-based system is not a good idea because it prevents the user from TABBING to the field. In general, it is probably a better idea to leave push-button fields unprotected.

When users select the 'LOAD PROGRAM' or 'NEW PROGRAM' options, they are immediately routed to the screen in Figure 4.5. This is the SCL PREVIEW window and features the standard SAS software text editor. Users can code and edit SQL queries as they desire here.

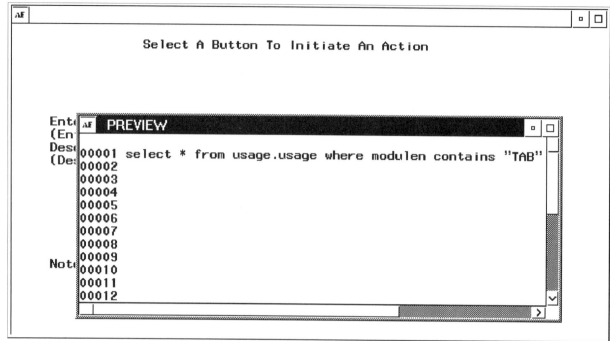

Figure 4.5:   The PREVIEW Window Used For SQL Code Entry

Note that I deliberately removed the command line to ensure that users do not drop out of the application's control.

Case Study 2   Free Flow Text Entry

The JARS application needs to link a database of free flow text with FSEDIT observations. My needs are quite specific; as well as not allowing changes to the text, I need to place a header and trailer record in the text each time a user adds to it.

The following program segment demonstrates how to achieve the task. Discussion follows the listing of the entry.

```
length temp $ 35 ;

init:
  rc = preview('clear') ;
  if preview('edit') eq -1 then rc=preview('clear') ;
  else do ;
    rc = preview('save','sasuser.temp.temp.source') ;
    temp = '===> START    ' || symgetc('sysjobid') ;
    rc = preview('clear') ;
```

```
        submit ;
          &temp
        endsubmit ;
        rc = preview('save','sasuser.diary.project.source',' ',
              'append') ;
        rc = preview('clear') ;
        temp = '===> END      ' || symgetc('sysjobid') ;
        rc = preview('copy','sasuser.temp.temp.source') ;
        submit ;
          &temp
        endsubmit ;
        rc = preview('save','sasuser.diary.PROJECT.source',
              'Diary For PROJECT Update '||symgetc('sysjobid'),' ','append') ;
        rc = preview('clear') ;
      end ;
  return ;
```

The first point to note is that this is an SCL entry and thus it is irrelevant whether the code is in INIT/MAIN or TERM. One of the three sections must exist, but which is used is up to the programmer as an SCL entry just executes code in the order it appears.

The first two lines of the INIT section remove anything currently in the preview buffer, then allow the user to enter text into that empty window. Since the window has no existing text, the requirement to prevent deletion or change of text is satisfied.

If the user leaves the screen using CANCEL rather than using END, the return code to SCL is -1. In that situation, empty the PREVIEW window and exit without saving the text.

Saving the text and including a header is all accomplished in the ELSE part of the code. While not used in the above program, you may need to issue a LOCK command to take exclusive access of the catalog entry immediately on entering the ELSE clause if multiple users could update the file.

The first step illustrated is to save the PREVIEW window contents to a temporary storage location. This is done to make use of the PREVIEW window to store a header record. Initialize a field to the header data, empty the PREVIEW window of the text just entered, and use the SUBMIT command with no optional arguments to place the header contents in the preview buffer.

This step is immediately followed by an APPEND of the PREVIEW window contents (namely, the header) to the end of the source member being updated. At this stage the objective of writing a header record to the text file, indicating exactly who is adding data, has been accomplished.

It is now necessary to recover the new text from the temporary storage area. First, empty the PREVIEW window of the header data, then use the COPY argument to recover the entered data. Now use SUBMIT again to place a trailer record at the end of the data now in the PREVIEW window. At this stage, appending the PREVIEW window onto the source entry completes the task.

This procedure may sound complex, but in fact, it is a simple manipulation of the PREVIEW window contents, using the very useful set of arguments to the PREVIEW function. Once the concept of what is being done is understood, the above is simple to follow.

The PREVIEW window is cleared at the end of the code; if this is not done, the contents are submitted at the end of the task stream.

One point to note: a lot of effort was spent setting up the header record. Why not just write a header before the user starts using the PREVIEW window? This can be done as follows:

```
length temp $ 35 ;

init:
  rc = preview('clear') ;
  temp = '===> START    ' || symgetc('sysjobid') ;
  submit ;
    &temp
  endsubmit ;
  rc = preview('save','sasuser.diary.project.source',
       'Diary For PROJECT Update '||symgetc('sysjobid'),'append') ;
  rc = preview('clear') ;
  if preview('edit') eq -1 then rc=preview('clear') ;
  else do ;
    temp = '===> END      ' || symgetc('sysjobid') ;
    submit ;
      &temp
    endsubmit ;
    rc = preview('save','sasuser.diary.PROJECT.source',' ','append') ;
  end ;
return ;
```

There is a fundamental logic flaw here. The header record is always written, but the user may cancel the entry and thus write no text to the SOURCE entry. But a header would still be written. Alternatively, put the header into the editor before the user starts editing and allow the user to add to the end of the header. But this strategy compromises the integrity of the header; in other words, it could be modified or deleted. The solution is a temporary storage area that will hold text that the user needs to save.

One difficulty with using headers and trailers to identify who is adding text is that if no text is entered and the user exits using END, the header and trailer are written to the catalog source member. It is possible to avoid this difficulty. You need to file the contents of the PREVIEW window to an external file, then use FOPEN and FREAD on that file. If end of file immediately appears, the PREVIEW window was empty and the contents, as well as headers and trailers, need not be written.

In the preceding program, the catalog member that is being written to has a fixed name. In the actual application that uses this code, the third part of the name ('project' above), is replaced by the name of the project read from the FSEDIT observation.

You can use the preceding code as it stands in either FSEDIT or SAS/AF applications. The PREVIEW window is available in FSEDIT in Release 6.07.

Case Study 3 Simultaneous Browsing And Editing

I am working on an application that will allow Databank to automate its costing, tracking, and reviewing of phases in our development life cycle. As does JARS, this application will require a project diary. The difference here is that two windows are required; one will browse the existing diary, and the other will edit a new, initially blank entry. It must be possible to swap between the two windows.

Before presenting any code, the screen in Figure 4.6 is what the application should produce. Note that in this screen there are two windows, one called DIARYVEW and one called DIARYEDT. Neither screen has a command line. The 'Options' text in the top left hand corner is a pull-down menu item (created using PROC PMENU) that allows you to swap options between screens, find text in the editor, or include an external file into the editor.

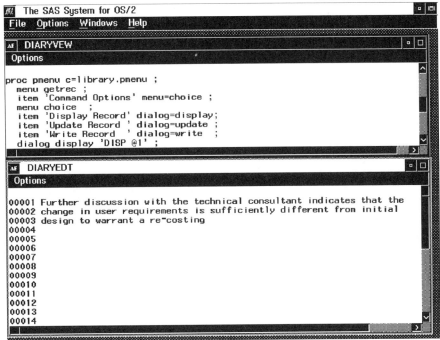

Figure 4.6:   Opening Multiple PREVIEW Windows

The task of getting DIARYVEW on screen is quite trivial. It is a simple use of the PREVIEW window in browse mode. Of much more complexity is the displaying of the edit window and moving between the windows. A further requirement that again, is relatively easy to achieve, is that the browse window cannot be exited until the edit window is exited.

Once the browse screen is displayed in SCL, control has been transferred from SCL to the PREVIEW window. You can't code SCL behind the text editor (but wouldn't it be useful?). The requirement is that the editor display be automatic, with no reliance on our users' entering a

---

command (the command line is being removed anyway). So it is necessary to persuade the PREVIEW window to trigger the edit automatically.

The only real option here is EXECCMD. It can be used to trigger a command that will be seen by the PREVIEW window. But what command will that be? The command cannot be a call to an SCL program because you can't use CALL DISPLAY from a command line. It could be to trigger a WDEV window command followed by a PREVIEW command (you can type PREVIEW on an AF entry's command line to get access to the PREVIEW window), but that complicates the saving of the text because the initiation of the PREVIEW window is outside SCL control. Indeed, I doubt that this approach would allow saving of the text under program control at all.

➡️ *There is a way to trigger an SCL program from a command line (or via EXECCMD when there is no command line). In Release 6.07 SAS Institute provides (but not yet on all platforms) the AFAPPLICATION display manager window command. This is similar to the AF command, except that it triggers a completely new AF application, running outside the control of the first.*

To cut a long story short, you can stack up an AFA command using EXECCMD, and that is seen by SAS appearing as a command in the DIARYVEW window. It executes as soon as the PREVIEW window is initialized for the browse and immediately starts a second AF application. That second application accesses the PREVIEW window in EDIT mode.

The AFA command starts a new task stream. Effectively two AF applications are running simultaneously, with neither having any dependence on the other. Coding here needs to be careful, I can't allow the browse screen to be closed and the user to return control to the SCL that called it unless the edit window closed first. If I did allow that, I could end up in the dangerous situation of the first application allowing the browse/edit option to be called again, thus starting a third application. The situation gets convoluted and integrity cannot be guaranteed.

➡️ *When you exit a task stream started with AFA to go back to a previous AF stream, the command buffer is purged. Thus it is impossible to use EXECCMD to send a command from an ending AFA stream back to its caller. However, SUBMIT COMMAND CONTINUE can be used as it does not purge the command buffer.*

The following program accomplishes the task and maintains integrity of the files by not permitting the first application to end before the second ends.

Discussion follows the code.

```
entry catname $ 40 ;

init:
  call preview('clear') ;
  if cexist(catname) then do ;

/* fill preview window with the existing text in the catalog */

    call preview('copy',catname) ;

/* set up size of browse screen */

    call wregion(1,1,12,80) ;

/* define a pmenu in next window */

    call execcmd('setpmenu sasuser.preview.previewb.pmenu;pmenu on;') ;

/* create command to trigger the EDIT screen when the BROWSE is
   displayed */

    call execcmd('afa c=sasuser.preview.edit.scl' ||
                 ' catname = "' || catname || '" startlne=13 ' ||
                 ' aws=no') ;

/* start up the browse screen, and disallow exit from here if the
   user is still editing */

browse:
    call preview('browse','DIARYVEW') ;
    if symget('editactv') = 'Y' then goto browse ;

/* always empty the preview buffer at the end of use */

    call preview('clear') ;
  end ;
  else  /* no catalog currently exists */

/* just call the edit screen, it will sort out the window size &
   other details. Note we need to use SUBMIT COMMAND as EXECCMDI and
   EXECCMD cannot function here   */

    submit command continue ;
      afa c=sasuser.preview.edit.scl
          catname = &catname
          startlne=1
          aws=no
    endsubmit ;

  return ;
```

The first point to notice about this entry is that there are two parts to it. These correspond to whether the catalog entry passed in already exists or not. If it does already exist, the two part screen consisting of the browse at the top and the edit at the bottom is set up; otherwise the edit part utilizes the entire screen.

The entry is straightforward until the second EXECCMD is struck. That second EXECCMD is being stacked up to issue a command that will be seen by the PREVIEW window opened in browse mode. The command that is issued is the AFA command.

The AFA command is documented in SAS Technical Report P-216, *SAS/AF Software, SAS/FSP Software, and SAS Screen Control Language: Changes And Enhancements, Release 6.07.*

The **catname** field is the name of the catalog that the text is to be saved to. It will be passed from the program that calls BROWSE.SCL. The second parameter, **startlne**, will be used by the WREGION routine in EDIT.SCL to determine where to start the edit screen.

AFA allows a second AF application to be started. The application is actually initiated from the command line of the PREVIEW window. Note the means of passing parameters; both **catname** and **startlne** are parameters for the AFA command. They are simply added to the end of the command, and the EDIT.SCL entry that is called will retrieve them. When parameters are stacked up like this, they are added to a local list, the command list, from where they will be retrieved in EDIT.SCL.

The AWS=NO option is necessary on some platforms, namely those that offer native windowing. Without that, the second AF application is not visible while the first is on screen, and the first is not visible while the second is on screen.

The PREVIEW window is started in browse mode. Note that it is in a loop that cannot be exited until the macro variable **editactv** is set to indicate that EDIT.SCL is finished. That is the mechanism that prevents the browse screen from being exited while the edit screen is still active in the other AF application.

Clear the preview buffer after completion, even of the BROWSE. No matter what option you use on the CALL PREVIEW, the buffer is still full and whatever is in there WILL be submitted to SAS for processing at the end of the task stream. So clearing it prevents a lot of syntax errors and confusion.

The final part of the entry is to be used when the catalog to be edited does not yet exist. No browse is required in that case, so still use AFA (so that the list retrieval set up in EDIT.SCL can be used), but set the **startlne** field to the top of the screen. The SUBMIT COMMAND statement is used because it allows commands to be executed even when no display screen is present (both EXECCMD and EXECCMDI require a display window).

```
init:
  call symput('editactv','Y') ;

/* called from AFA which supplies parameters in local command list */

  cmdlist = getniteml(envlist('L'),'_CMDLIST_') ;
  catname = getnitemc(cmdlist,'catname') ;
  startlne= getnitemn(cmdlist,'startlne') ;

  call execcmd('setpmenu sasuser.preview.previewe.pmenu;pmenu on;') ;

  call wregion(startlne,1,25,80) ;

/* always switch on NUMBERS in edit mode */

  call execcmd(';num on;') ;

/* do the edit, if they cancel from it then ditch anything entered,
   otherwise put it somewhere safe and exit */

  if preview('edit','DIARYEDT') eq -1 then call preview('clear') ;
  else do ;

/* you may want to modify next two lines to allow extra text such as
   headers to be inserted */

    call preview('save',catname,'','append') ;
    call preview('clear') ;
  end ;
  submit command continue ;
    qend ;
    end ;
  endsubmit ;
  call symput('editactv','N') ;
return ;
```

First, be aware that this is the entry called by the AFA command; in other words, it is the second AF application.

The very first task here is to set the macro variable **editactv**, which indicates that the editor is currently being used. This is used by the application in the first AF stream to prevent it from ending early.

The next three lines extract the parameters passed to the second application from the local list where they are stored by SAS. The screen size is set up, and it is ensured that line numbers will be active in the editor, which will be the next window displayed.

Near the end of the code, a SUBMIT COMMAND CONTINUE block is ending the current task stream with the QEND command and stacking up an END command to execute in the next displayed window. That window is the DIARYVEW window (the PREVIEW editor in browse mode).

The remainder of the code is just simple manipulation of the PREVIEW window discussed earlier. Note though that PREVIEW is one of the SCL functions which can be used either as a function (RC=PREVIEW) or as a call routine (CALL PREVIEW).

It is worth pointing out that all these case studies have provided just a shell to get at the real requirement, the need to use a text editor under application control. These case studies are an excellent example of looking between the lines. It is not obvious at first glance just why developers have access to the PREVIEW window -- but how many other software systems do you know of that permit total access to a sophisticated text editor under application control? Not many!

Entry: EXAMPLE.SCL

```
init:

  call display('sasuser.preview.browse.scl',
    'sasuser.diary.F02626.source') ;

return ;
```

This is just an example of how you might call the BROWSE.SCL program. You could call the entry from an FSEDIT observation, using some field on the database as an identifier, or indeed anywhere else in SCL. You must have a catalog name to save the text in.

Entry: System Pull-Down Menus and Function Keys

```
proc pmenu catalog=sasuser.preview ;
 menu previewb ;
 item 'Options' menu = browse ; /* pmenu for a browse */
 item ' ' ;
 menu browse ;
 item 'Return To Text  ' selection=enter ;
 item 'Search For Text ' dialog=findstr ;
 item 'Swap To Edit    ' selection=swape ;
 item 'End Browse/Edit ' selection=endit ;
 item 'Cancel Browse/Edit ' selection=cancel ;
 selection swape 'next diaryedt' ;
 selection endit 'End'           ;
 selection cancel 'Cancel' ;
 selection enter ' ' ;
 dialog findstr 'f @1' ;
   text #1 @1 'Enter The String (In Quotes) To Search For ' ;
   text #2 @2 'Note: Maximum Length Is 40 Characters ' ;
   text #4 @4 len=40 ;
 run ;
 quit ;

proc pmenu catalog=sasuser.preview ;
  menu previewe ;
  item 'Options' menu = edit ; /* pmenu for an edit */
  item ' ' ;
  menu edit ;
  item 'Return To Text  ' selection=enter ;
```

```
item 'Search For Text ' dialog=findstr ;
item 'Swap To Browse  ' selection=swapb ;
item 'End Browse/Edit ' selection=endit ;
item 'Cancel Browse/Edit ' selection=cancel ;
item 'Include Ext File' dialog=extlfle  ;
dialog findstr 'f @1' ;
   text #1 @1 'Enter The String (In Quotes) To Search For ' ;
   text #2 @2 'Note: Maximum Length Is 40 Characters ' ;
   text #4 @4 len=40 ;
dialog extlfle 'include @1' ;
   text #1 @1 'Enter The Filename (In Quotes) To Be Loaded ' ;
   text #4 @4 len=60 ;
selection swapb 'next diaryvew' ;
selection endit 'End'            ;
selection cancel 'Cancel' ;
selection enter ' ' ;
run ;
quit ;
```

In order to allow the application to maintain control over the user, the PREVIEW window command line is replaced by a pmenu and function keys. The menu is tailored so that separate options exist in the browse and edit windows. The menu provides the means to do the swapping between windows (although on some platforms a mouse click achieves the same aim). Note that the only editor commands that are used are FIND and INCLUDE, both being triggered by pmenu options. Add others as you require, or use the command line if you wish.

The function keys are set up to allow access to other functions of the editor that require no dialogue. These are

PF1 - Help	PF2 - Cancel	PF3 - End
PF4 - Top	PF5 - Bottom	PF6 - Zoom
PF7 - Backward	PF8 - Forward	PF9 - Rfind
PF10 - Vscroll Half	PF11 - VScroll Page	PF12 - Vscroll Cursor

This case study is the code used in production at Databank to add text entry capabilities to applications. In practice under MVS it works well, but the pmenu structure has proved difficult for users to adjust to. If many more command-line commands were needed, pmenus would get unwieldy, but our user base requires only the basic editing functions supplied (the UNDO editor feature is to be added!).

Chapter 5: Extended Tables

Contents

Comparison of Selection Lists, Extended Tables, and FSVIEW

➡ *An extended table is a means of programming windows that to the user look like the SCL built-in selection lists. That is to say, these windows are a means to implement scrollable tables.*

It is an application-specific decision as to which of the three types of constructs (selection list/FSVIEW/extended table) are used. This section considers guidelines for which methodology can be used in specific situations.

The SCL DATALISTx windows (I refer to the DATALISTC and DATALISTN functions as DATALISTx, as the discussion is applicable to both) are a very efficient means of displaying data from a data set and allowing a user to fill an SCL variable with values of variables from that data set. These SCL windows cannot be used when it is desired to update observations since they are designed simply to show a number of variables and allow a user to select values. DATALISTx windows can be a quick way of extracting multiple fields from an observation. In Release 6.07, the field values for a selected observation are placed in the local environment list. This means you do not have to code database accesses yourself after a selection is made.

FSVIEW and customized extended tables differ from the supplied selection lists in that an observation can be selected for further processing. FSVIEW is designed to allow updating of observations on a SAS database, while extended tables also allow that, as well as giving the ability to create customized selection lists.

Although selection lists such as DATALISTx allow multiple selections in the window, these are not passed back to the field that was assigned to the function result. In general, only the last selection is returned. However, in Release 6.07 and later releases, all selection list windows return all selections to an SCL list. Experience has shown that it is much easier to manipulate the list to find all selected values than to code custom extended tables that return all selections in one field.

FSVIEW is discussed later in this text. For the time being, it is enough to say that the SCL interface to FSVIEW can be difficult to use for any extensive SCL coding. FSVIEW does not present its SCL interface as if it were an extended table, although the screen looks like an extended table. Experience has taught that developing applications to manipulate data sets in an FSVIEW-like manner is often easier accomplished in a custom extended table. A later chapter will explore the SCL interface with FSVIEW.

Execution of Sections In An Extended Table

Executable code in extended tables always starts with the INIT section as for any SCL program, followed by the GETROW section to build the screen that the user initially sees. The order of processing in extended tables does not necessarily follow that of other SAS/AF screens thereafter.

Section execution is now dependent on just what the user of the application does. The chart in Table 1 is a summary under various conditions.

Dynamic Table

	Setrow(.,'0')						Setrow(.,'1')					
	Always			No Always			Always			No Always		
	Ent	Scr	End	Ent	Scr	End	Ent	Scr	End	Ent	Scr	End
Putrow	*1	*1	*1	*1	*1	*1	*1	*1	*1	*1	*1	*1
Getrow (1)	3	2		*3	2		3	2		3	2	
Main	2	*3	2	*2	*3	*2	2	3	2	*2	*3	*2
Getrow (2)		4			4			4			4	
Term			3			3			3			3

Non Dynamic Table

	Setrow(.,'0')						Setrow(.,'1')					
	Always			No Always			Always			No Always		
	Ent	Scr	End	Ent	Scr	End	Ent	Scr	End	Ent	Scr	End
Putrow	*1	*1	*1	*1	*1	*1	*1	*1	*1	*1	*1	*1
Getrow (1)	3	3		*3	3		3	3		3	3	
Main	*2	*2	2	*2	*2	*2	2	2	2	*2	*2	*2
Getrow (2)												
Term			3			3			3			3

Table 1

The table is read down columns. Suppose you want to find the order of processing for, say, a dynamic table not being used as a selection list (in other words, the selection list parameter of SETROW is 0) with CONTROL ALWAYS switched on. Look under the headings "Dynamic Table," "Setrow (.,'0')," and then "Always." Note there are three columns under each heading. These are, from left to right, the processing order when the user presses enter, scrolls the screen, or ends the screen. Thus a dynamic table that is not used as a selection list and has CONTROL ALWAYS switched on will carry out the processing in the order PUTROW/GETROW/MAIN/GETROW when the user scrolls the window.

Table 1 refers to an extended table that has no additional factors such as calls to EXECCMD, REFRESH, and so on. When other events triggered by such functions occur, the order of processing may appear different due to the way the other process might cause table rewrites.

The table in Table 1 is for the situation where a row has been selected or a field in the nonscrollable area has been modified (in which case PUTROW will not run, but the other processing occurs as above). The asterisks beside certain elements of the table mean that the section is not executed if no row is selected, and no field in the nonscrollable area has been modified. Thus, in that instance, from column 5, the order of execution is GETROW/GETROW.

Note that a push-button field is considered to be modified when you select it.

At first glance, the order of processing in some situations may seem strange. In particular, the running of GETROW immediately before MAIN and then after MAIN in some circumstances looks unusual. In fact, GETROW usually represents low overhead to the user. GETROW before and after MAIN runs only when scrolling, and then only on a dynamic table that requires the additional processing. The first GETROW is not even a complete GETROW; it does no more than work out _currow_ for the first row of the table after scrolling.

The SCL debugger is an excellent tool for seeing just how program flow occurs in extended tables (and other SCL programs). It was used to derive Table 1 and certainly answered some outstanding questions in my mind about the flow of programs with extended tables.

☹ *Not really a problem, but an awareness issue, is that a REFRESH in the TERM section of an extended table will cause GETROW to be executed. It is rather pointless as no change to the screen will be seen by the user.*

Customizing Pop-Up Windows Using Extended Tables

Extended tables can easily be used to emulate SAS software pop-up windows such as DATALISTC. You can thus use extended tables to create your own 'SAS software lookalike' list-style windows.

Case Study: External File Records In An Extended Table

SCL does an excellent job of supplying pop-up windows for many purposes. An occasion where you may wish to customize a pop-up window coded as an extended table is where the data source is in an external file rather than a SAS database. In that situation, no pop-up window is available. Furthermore, GETROW cannot read the external file, as it would be extremely difficult to maintain integrity as users attempt to scroll the screen.

When you are coding a pop-up window in this manner, irrespective of the input source, the PUTROW section has to be coded to handle the fact that users are selecting data to be passed back to the calling window. Generally the passing of data is accomplished by parameters.

In the following example, I have an external file with a FILEREF of PROBFILE. It contains two fields: the first is a list of currently opened problem numbers in a problem management system, and the second is a description of the problem. Our SAS/AF application needs to display a list of the two fields, allowing the user to select one problem number to be returned to the calling program in the field **pnum**.

Calling the extended table is simple. The following code accomplishes the call:

```
call display('ddname.catalog.getextl.program',pnum);
```

The called program (namely, the extended table entry GETEXTL.PROGRAM) is as follows under OS/2 (the screen is shown in Figure 5.1):

```
entry pnum $ 8 ;

length dummy $ 80 ;

init:
  control always ;
  textlist = makelist() ;
  rc = filename('probfile','e:\sasout\problem.txt') ;
  rc = fillist('fileref','probfile',textlist) ;
  rc = filename('probfile','') ;
  call setrow(listlen(textlist),1) ;
return ;

term:
  rc = dellist(textlist) ;
return ;

getrow:
  dummy = getitemc(textlist,_currow_) ;
  problem = substr(dummy,1,8) ;
  descrip = substr(dummy,10)   ;
return ;

putrow:
  pnum = problem ;
return ;
```

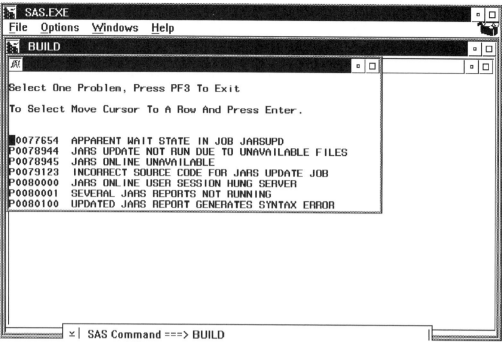

Figure 5.1:   Extended Table Used As A Selection List

In the above program, a list is used to store the data from the external file for subsequent
processing by GETROW. The list is used because it has minimal programming overhead and is
very fast. Note the use of the LISTLEN function to define the size of the extended table. This
allows a table to change size each time it is called without incurring the extra checking overhead
of a dynamic extended table.

The PUTROW section just assigns the currently selected problem number to the variable passed
as **pnum** for returning to the calling SCL program.

The extended table looks to the user like an SCL pop-up window. This is a powerful feature of
SCL since SAS software gives us many windows to do tasks, but also gives us the ability to code
our own tasks to look and feel exactly like the SAS windows. At risk of repeating myself, for the
end user this feature minimizes learning and maximizes productivity.

Error Handling In The GETROW Section

GETROW rarely fails. However, if you wish to code error handling for GETROW, it can be
done.

Before you attempt to code any error handling, you must be aware that you **cannot** prevent
GETROW from executing as many times as there are lines on the screen. Error handling can only
prevent GETROW from doing as much work as it would when no errors occurred.

You cannot carry out tasks such as resizing the extended table in GETROW to prevent GETROW from executing.

Error handling is most likely to be needed when you are using GETROW to read from an external file or SAS database. In that situation, the following strategy can be used:

1. Check the return code from the file read. If a successful read, then continue.

2. If an unsuccessful read, carry out the following tasks:

    A. set a variable called **fatal** to 'YES'

    B. at the start of GETROW, code the line

    ```
    if fatal eq 'YES' then return ;
    ```

    The line at the start of GETROW causes GETROW to execute only the condition each time through the section. It will not continue to set up the table for the user.

    C. you may wish to initialize other fields with the error number and description.

3. In the main section, check if **fatal** has the value 'YES' and carry out normal error handling, that is, messages to indicate the problem to the user.

The following program illustrates error handling in the GETROW section:

```
entry dsid0 2 prd kw $ ;

length fatal $ 3 ;

init:

<<< code in INIT >>>

fatal = 'NO ' ;
return ;

main:
/* check that GETROW succeeded, abend out if not, otherwise update
   the fields in the non-scrollable area */

  if fatal eq 'YES' then do ;
/* GETROW failed, issue a generic error message and CAN session */
...  at this point code a suitable message to display to the user ...
    put 'SYSTEM ABEND IN GETROW OF SHWTABLE -- DUMP INFO' ;
    put _all_ ;
    tmp=put(sysrc(),6.) ; put tmp= ;
    tmp=sysmsg()         ; put tmp= ;
```

```
      put '---------------------------------------------------' ;
      call execcmdi('endsas') ;
      return ;
    end ;

/* don't do anything if user wants out of application */
  if _status_ in ('E' 'H' 'C') then return ;

<<< Remaining code in MAIN >>>

return ;

term:

<<< any necessary TERM code >>>

return ;

getrow:
  if _status_ in ('E' 'H' 'C') then return ;

/* if fatal is YES, indicating a fatal end occurred in GETROW, push
   an END command and return. This does not stop GETROW from being
   processed the number of times it normally would, but causes
   MAIN to be immediately invoked when getrow is done, triggering
   the abend mechanism */
  if fatal = 'YES' then do ;
    call execcmd('end') ;
    return ;
  end ;

/* read an observation */
  rc = fetchobs(dsid0,_currow_) ;

/* check return code and carry out appropriate processing        */
  select  ;
    when (rc=0 | rc=%sysrc(_SWEOF)) ;               /* ok, good read   */
    otherwise do ;                                  /* bad read, abend */
      fatal = 'YES' ;
      return ;
    end ;
  end ;   /* end of select */
return ;

putrow:

<<< putrow code in here >>>

return ;
```

Note that in the GETROW section a check is done to look for the user's having pressed END. Normally GETROW does not execute when END has been pressed; however, if some action in TERM causes a screen rewrite, it will trigger GETROW processing.

When an error condition in GETROW is struck, the above code treats that as a fatal error and halts the entire SAS session. This may not be appropriate. The CALL EXECCMDI('endsas') statement can be replaced with code that is meaningful in your application context.

It will be rare indeed that error processing will be needed in the GETROW section. The example above is presented in the interests of completeness. All too frequently in my experience, SAS software is overlooked as a serious contender for large scale applications partly because of a perceived inability to handle boundary error conditions adequately. Being able to code for the totally unexpected is possible in SCL; it may just take a little creative thinking.

Adding Blank Rows For Data Entry

If your application design permits the additional entry of data to new blank rows via an extended table, you can adapt the GETROW section to place a blank entry at the end of the table.

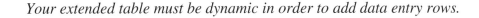 *Your extended table must be dynamic in order to add data entry rows.*

To add a blank row for data entry, ensure that GETROW gets called with the screen fields blank. The easiest way to do this is to append a blank observation to the table source in either PUTROW or MAIN.

Having A Blank Row Available On Initial Screen Display

Suppose you are reading data from a SAS data set and you wish to add a blank row at the end of the data read from the data set.

In the INIT section, use the following code to ensure that a blank observation is on the data set at the time that GETROW processes it.

```
init:
..
dsid = open(dsname,'u') ;
rc = append(dsid,'noset') ;
..
```

Because a blank entry (that is, with all fields missing) has been added to the data set, GETROW will process that observation as a normal data set observation.

Note that the data set is opened in update mode. It makes no sense to apply this code to input mode as the objective is to add observations for data entry. Update mode is necessary to save those observations.

This application is somewhat limiting. Because the record was added in INIT, you cannot use this code to add another row when this one is used. However, you can utilize the PUTROW or MAIN sections to add another blank observation.

Adding A Blank Row From The Current Last Row

The intention here is to present a blank entry automatically when the user modifies the last row. (The cursor does not need to be physically on the last row; the user may alter the last row and then move to one above it.) The logic is simple in PUTROW. You need to carry out the following tasks:

- check if processing the last row of the table

- if so, add a blank row to the end of the input source.

If the input source is a data set, use the following statement in PUTROW:

```
if fetch(dsid) eq -1 then rc=append(dsid,'noset') ;
rc = unlock(dsid) ;
```

This writes a blank observation to the end only when a data set read returns end of file, that is, when the user has just processed the last observation.

One difficulty with this strategy is that I have yet to find a means of forcing the cursor to move to the new blank row. Even using the NEWL option of SETCR does not seem to do this in this situation, as apparently GETROW establishes the cursor placement, and the row did not exist at the time GETROW last executed.

Adding A Blank Row From Any Row

The preceding section addresses the situation where the user is already on the last row. If the user is on a different row and wants a blank entry, the situation is rather different.

First, if the entry source is a data set, the blank row cannot be inserted at the cursor position because currently it is possible only to append observations to a data set, but not to insert observations. This is not a problem with a list-based table because lists have insert capability. Whether you use a list or a data set (or any other table source) there is one constant factor. Users must explicitly indicate that they want to insert a row. To do this, I assign a custom command to a function key.

Assume the custom command is 'ADDREC' and the table is sourced from a data set. In the INIT section, ensure that CONTROL ALWAYS is on. This will force execution of the MAIN section, which is where the blank observation will be appended to the data set. You need the following code:

```
init:
  control always ;
  ...
  dsid = open(dsname,'u') ;
  ...
return ;

main:
   if word(1,'u') eq 'ADDREC' then do ;
      rc = append(dsid,'noset') ;
      call execcmd('bottom') ;
      return ;
   end ;
   ...
return ;
```

This program causes the observation to be written and the screen to scroll immediately so that the new row is displayed. Once again, it does not seem possible to position the cursor right on the new row. Indeed, it may be positioned a number of lines above the new row.

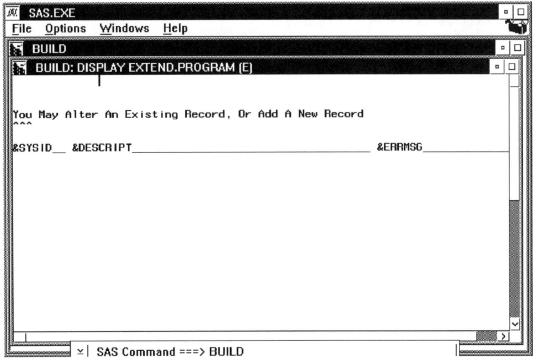

Figure 5.2: Extended Table Display Window

Consider the following situation. I want to update the data set SYSTEM.SYSID using the screen in Figure 5.2. It is necessary to display observations in the data set and in PUTROW to generate code to do the following:

- if changing an existing observation, use the UPDATE SCL function to write the modified observation back out.

- if entering data in the empty field at the end of the screen, write the new observation out and display another empty observation for adding data to. However, only do this if all fields are filled in.

SYSTEM.SYSID will have just two fields, **sysid** and **descript**. The only SCL check is that both fields are entered.

Accomplishing the second aim (that is, to write out the new observation and display another empty observation) is quite similar to accomplishing the first, with the difference being that I do not use the UPDATE function (as no observation yet exists on the data set), but rather use APPEND.

The following code accomplishes the task:

```
init:
  control always ;
  dsid=open('library.sysid','u') ;
  call set(dsid) ;
  call setrow(0,1,'N','Y') ;
  call setfkey('F9','ADDREC') ;
return ;

main:

/* if user entered ADD command then append a blank row at end */

  if word(1,'u') eq 'ADDREC' then do ;
    rc = append(dsid,'noset') ;
    call execcmd('bottom') ;
  end ;
return ;

term:
  call close(dsid) ;
return ;

getrow:

/* fetch the next row ... note FETCHOBS locks when opentype=U */

  if fetchobs(dsid,_currow_) eq -1 then call endtable();
  rc = unlock(dsid) ;
return ;

putrow:
```

```
/* update any modified row */
   if error(sysid) then do ;
     errmsg = 'ERROR' ;
     return ;
   end ;
   else errmsg = _blank_ ;

   if sysid eq . and descript eq _blank_ then return ;

   rc = fetchobs(dsid,_currow_,'noset') ;
   rc = update(dsid) ;
   rc = unlock(dsid) ;

/* deselect current row */

   rc = unselect(_currow_) ;

/* re-read and add a new row if we are on the last row */

   if fetch(dsid) eq -1 then rc=append(dsid,'noset')  ;
     else rc=unlock(dsid) ;
return ;
```

Note the use of the additional variable, **errmsg**. This allows a message to be tagged along with each row. Without this variable, if multiple rows are in error, it is possible to display a message for one row only. So you can see that a field may be assigned a value in PUTROW and that value is applied to the current row only.

Instead of using MODIFIED, it is always easiest to write a selected row back out provided that it satisfies the checks. If a row does not satisfy the checks, reject the entered data and display a message. Note that the use of the **errmsg** field is limited to a single message above. This is solely for illustrative purposes. I could have assigned one of a number of messages, depending on the error condition.

The **errmsg** field should be protected and have PAD set to blank.

The screen to do this, seen from the programmer's viewpoint, is in Figure 5.2. When the user sees this screen displayed, it contains a blank row at the end. This is for new **sysid** values to be entered after the user has processed the current last row. When the user fills that row, the observation is appended to the data set. The next execution of GETROW is based on the data set with that new entry, so it will appear on screen and a new blank entry will appear after it. From the user's perspective, the screen is in Figure 5.3.

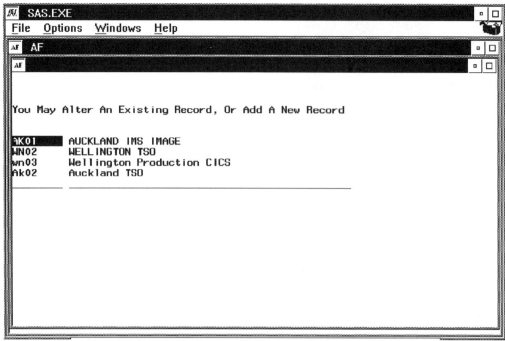

Figure 5.3:   Blank Row For Data Entry In An Extended Table

Row Layout In Extended Tables

Each row of the table can span more than one physical line. It is possible to set up a table that displays more data than can be fit on a line. You might consider the use of an entire screen as one extended table entry.

This tip is useful in many situations. For instance, suppose a data set exists which contains summarized data ready to feed to a report. The extended table can become the report. Thus SAS software automatically takes care of scrolling to new entries, and display is easily set up by code in the GETROW section.

This kind of extended table report has been used in the JARS system. Each week when new data are added, a summary job is run that creates a database containing, for each project, the following data:

- project id
- earliest date worked on
- latest date worked on

- hours and costs for this week
- hours and costs for year to date
- hours and costs for project to date

These data are presented as an extended table to allow easy scrolling through projects. A user may nominate specific projects or scan all projects. The screen to accomplish this, seen from the programmers viewpoint, is shown in Figure 5.4.

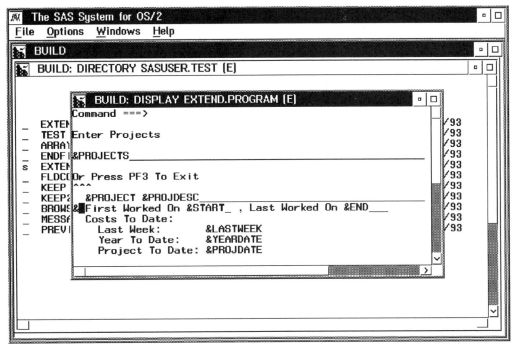

Figure 5.4:   Extended Table Row Covering Multiple Lines

Notice in Figure 5.4 that

- text can be entered in the nonscrollable area

- each logical row can span more than one physical line of the screen.

When users enter this option, they see the screen in Figure 5.5 where the summarized data for the first project are displayed. Pressing the FORWARD key will scroll to the second project.

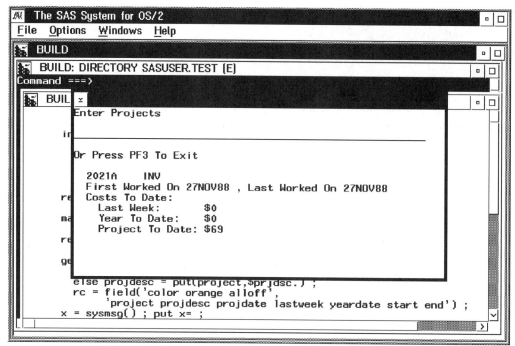

Figure 5.5:   Extended Table Used As A Report

Suppose now that the user types project ids into the top line as in Figure 5.6.

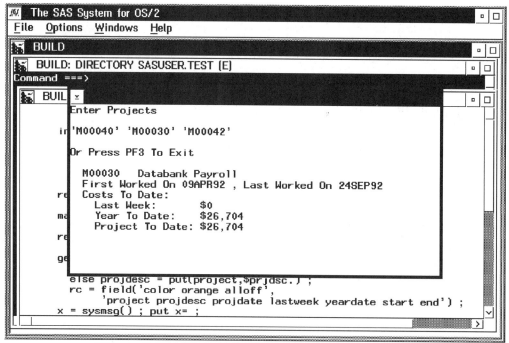

Figure 5.6:   Extended Table Used As A Report

Notice that the project ids have to be quoted both because the underlying SCL program is going to issue a WHERE clause using the IN operator and because having the projects prequoted by the user simplifies things somewhat. After pressing ENTER, the user sees a subset showing the first of the entered projects. Now when the user scrolls, the next of the entered projects appears. The user can only view the subset of projects he or she selected.

The code to accomplish all this is very simple. Essentially, it requires no more than to load an observation and issue a WHERE clause as necessary. The extended table takes care of all scrolling and keeping track of data set reads.

Before displaying the code, let me explain how this simple online report came about. It was driven by an urge to reduce use of both paper and computer resources. Often project leaders only require the bottom line -- how much a project is costing -- rather than everything about the project. The extended table will eventually allow a drill-down effect, the idea being that when users want more information they can enter, for example, 'D' on a field in the extended table beside a project of interest.

This action will drill down to another table containing the above data but stored at a department level for each project. A further drill down on a department will be available to refer to staff members. This will all be implemented via simple extended tables and is estimated to reduce costs of running current reports in JARS by a significant amount annually.

All the above will be implemented in the PUTROW section, which presently has no code. The following existing code drives the above extended table:

```
init:
  control always ;
  dsid = open('global.actsummy') ;
  call setrow(0,1,'N','Y') ;
  call set(dsid) ;
return ;

main:
  rc = where(dsid,'project in (' || projects || ')') ;return ;

getrow:
  if fetchobs(dsid,_currow_) ne 0 then call endtable() ;
  else projdesc = put(project,$prjdsc.) ;
return ;

term:
   call close(dsid) ;
return ;
```

Chapter 6: Using SCL With SAS/AF® Software

Contents

Overview

A number of elements of SCL either are SAS/AF specific or behave differently in SAS/AF and SAS/FSP. These arise out of design decisions at SAS Institute and are beyond our control. This chapter discusses some attributes of SCL that are more meaningful in an AF than in an FSP context.

Discussion in this chapter relates to

- creating application menus
- making reports dynamic
- using SAS/AF in noninteractive mode
- error handling.

Creating Menus With SAS/AF Software

This section discusses the many ways of coding the all important menus from which users will drive applications. SAS/AF offers many methods for creating menus, some of which are not obviously appropriate menuing tools. Discussion here centers around just what may be an appropriate method of menuing in specific situations and platforms. The following SAS/AF tools are discussed:

- the MENU entry type
- block menus using the BLOCK function
- extended tables
- choice groups
- SCL program entries

Note that frame technology is not discussed in this section. However, its usefulness as a graphical menuing environment should not be overlooked.

Using The MENU Entry Type

➡ *The MENU entry exists to provide a quick and easy-to-code menu system. Using this screen allows you to set up working front ends quickly and concentrate on application development.*

The MENU entry is used strictly for menuing, with no ability to do any programming in the screen. Advantages include the following:

- Consistency of 'look and feel'; each menu you develop has a list of options from which you make a selection using the option number or letter.

- Development is rapid.

- Extra text can be placed on the screen; however, it is static (meaning no AF screen fields).

- Branching into menu items is very fast.

- You can enter multiple menu items (for example, '=2.1' entered on the command line goes to option 2 in the current menu and then selects option 1 in the menu that option 2 provided).

Disadvantages include the following:

- Branching has to be done before any form of code is executed. This may not be suitable, especially if the application needs to restrict access to some menu items.

- It is not possible to place any application defined messages on the screen.

- Screen coloring and attribute definition are difficult, relying in general on escape codes and EDPARMS entries defined in SAS software.

Although it is somewhat limiting, the MENU entry should not be overlooked when considering menu systems for naive users, as it is a logical, clearly defined screen that is simple for the end user as well as the developer. Particularly in a nongraphical environment, the MENU entry may be appropriate. In a graphical environment, the MENU entry can appear somewhat archaic because its interface is different from the underlying operating system.

Using Block Menus

 For the user with a mouse, block menus are a continuation of the push-button system that is built into many parts of SAS software. They are simple to use and are intuitively obvious.

Block menus offer a consistent and simple menu interface. Advantages over other methods include the following:

- You need very little code to set the menu up.

- Block menus are defined by SAS software and will look and feel the same from screen to screen without developer intervention.

- They offer a consistent means of selecting menu options.

- They look professional under a graphical operating system.

- In situations where the application needs to restrict access to some menu items for some users, you can implement restrictions in the underlying program screen.

- They are suitable for either mouse or non mouse-based systems; effectively, all that you need to utilize these is a TAB key.

- Ability to sense users requesting help is built in, as opposed to the application's merely offering a menu selection for help.

Disadvantages include the following:

- Only 12 menu items can appear on a screen.

- No text other than a header block and a footer controlled by SAS software can be placed on the screen.

- Each menu item is restricted to 14 characters.

- It is difficult to place application messages on the screen.

- Function keys cannot be used.

Consider the following code from MARTS:

```
init:
 control always ;
 picked = 1;
 do until(picked = 0);
   picked = block('Rate System Menu','Main Menu -- PF3 To Exit',1,
                  'Update Rates','Resource Edit','',
                  'Customer Edit','','Charge Sys Ed ',
                  'SYSID Edit','Machine Edit','',
                  'Cust Grp Edit','','Reports') ;
   select(picked) ;
     when(1) do ....
     when(2) do ....
     when(4) do ....
     when(6) do ....
     when(7) do ....
     when(8) do ;
     when(10) do ;
     when(12) do ;
     otherwise ;
   end ;
end ;
return ;
```

In this example, not all 12 buttons are used, so some are left blank. SAS software does not attempt to place these on the screen; they are effectively ignored. However, the blank entries must appear in the block function call, or a compile error occurs. You do not have to leave any particular entries blank. In Figure 6.1, the blocks that were left blank were set up to show that you have a little control over how the final screen looks. If you left blocks 10,11, and 12 blank in the preceding SELECT/WHEN code, the screen would look quite different.

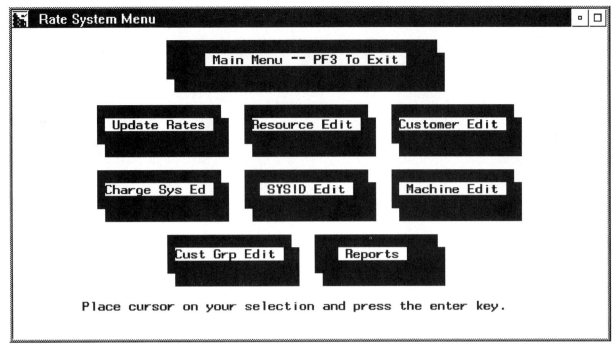

Figure 6.1: Example Block Menu

The screen is slightly difficult to use from a non-mouse user's perspective. Users without a mouse can select an item by either manually moving the cursor or using the TAB or new line key, then pressing ENTER. Despite the fact that block menus work well in either mouse or non-mouse systems, experience has shown this is not a popular form of menuing with some MVS users who find the block menus less intuitive than other forms of menuing.

Use of block menus is somewhat dependent on the operating environment and, to some extent, the user base.

Using Extended Tables

Extended tables have a unique feature for menuing: when coded carefully they can be added to without altering the code behind the menu. They are also effectively unlimited in the number of options that can be placed in them.

Extended tables can be used to display menus, and they offer some advantages over other methods. These include the following:

- When the extended table data source is a data set, the menu may be able to be added to without changing the program code.

- Extended tables allow menus to exist over multiple screens and allow users to search for specific menu items (by using the KEYFIELD COMMAND).

- Multiple menu items can be selected and processed in the PUTROW section of the SCL program entry without control passing back to the user between each selection.

- The nonscrollable area can be used for messages.

- Since you have to code the screen, a high level of user interaction is possible.

- You can set up your table in such a way that some options can be 'grayed' (made inaccessible) until some event occurs under application control to allow access to the option.

- If the extended source is a data set (in other words, the menu options are stored in a SAS data set), WHERE clauses can be used to prevent some options from appearing on screen.

The main disadvantage to extended tables is that they are not as professional looking as other methods in a graphical environment.

An example of using extended tables as a menu system comes from JARS. That application provides a set of reports that users can run. All the reports are in SAS macros (defined by the SASAUTOS fileref) named JARSRxxx, where the xxx is a unique report number between 000 and 999.

A list of report descriptions and numbers is in a data set. That data set contains a description field that includes a short description of the report. The description field becomes the extended table entry.

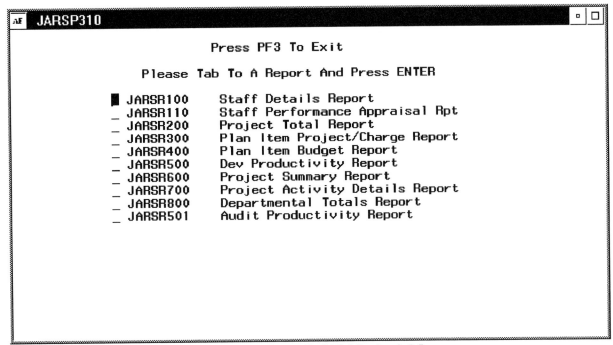

Figure 6.2: Extended Table As A Menu

When a user selects a report (see Figure 6.2 for a list of online JARS reports), the code in the SAS/AF program screen is identical for every report; all that changes is that the report number is attached to the literal 'JARSR' to form a report name. The macro containing the code is submitted to run the report.

The fact that the menu code structure doesn't change for any report is very important. It means that as a developer, when a new report is required you can concentrate on that report. This removes the overhead of having to alter menus to add the ability to select the new report.

Essentially the code to set up such a menu is as follows:

```
length repnum $ 3 ;

init:
  dsid00 = open('library.reports') ;
  call set(dsid00) ;
  call setrow(nobs(dsid00),1) ;
return ;

getrow:
  rc = fetchobs(dsid00,_currow_) ;
return ;

putrow:
  /* we have to reread here to fetch the correct report number */

  rc = fetchobs(dsid00,_currow_) ;

  runrept = '%JARSR' || repnum ;
```

```
       submit continue ;
         &runrept ;
       endsubmit ;
     return ;
```

The **repnum** variable is on the data set containing the report descriptions; this was opened as dsid00 in INIT with the CALL SET routine used to associate the data set variables with the SCL variables.

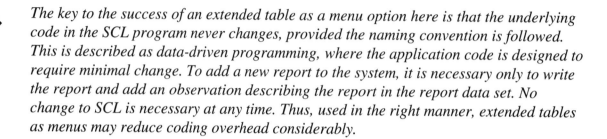

The key to the success of an extended table as a menu option here is that the underlying code in the SCL program never changes, provided the naming convention is followed. This is described as data-driven programming, where the application code is designed to require minimal change. To add a new report to the system, it is necessary only to write the report and add an observation describing the report in the report data set. No change to SCL is necessary at any time. Thus, used in the right manner, extended tables as menus may reduce coding overhead considerably.

A second example is an application that maintains a data set containing descriptions of the options in the main menu. Each observation in the data set also contains the name of the entry to branch to on selection, plus a variable that indicates whether a project has to be selected before the option can be accessed. The first option is to select a project. It sets a macro variable to Y when a project is selected. The GETROW section looks as follows:

```
if symget('projslct') ne 'Y' then rc = where(dsid,'wantprj ne "Y"') ;
else rc = where(dsid) ;
if fetchobs(dsid,_currow_) eq -1 then call endtable() ;
end ;
```

Here **wantprj** is a field on the data set (and the extended table) that indicates whether a project is required, and **&projslct** is a macro variable that indicates if a project is selected. When no project is selected, the user only sees menu options that do not require a project to have been selected.

There is also a variable on the screen (and the input data set) called **branch**. This defines where the option branches to if selected. The PUTROW section looks like this:

```
call display('ddname.jarscde.' || branch) ;
```

Those few lines of code define an entire menu, which never needs a code change. A new menu option simply is added to the data set and thereafter appears automatically on the screen.

Using Choice Groups

Choice groups are implemented as menus by using the CHOICE GROUP attribute of the SAS/AF field attribute window. Advantages of choice groups include the following:

- When used as push buttons under a graphical operating system, they impart a very professional look that often resembles the operating system.

- It is easy to place code in the selection screen to ensure users are allowed access to the menu item.

- In non mouse-based systems, it is possible to force users to think before they jump. A protected push button cannot be tabbed to, which means the user must be very deliberate about selecting such a menu item.

In some applications, it may be necessary to force users to be very definite about just what menu options they select. I have seen protected push buttons used under MVS to avoid having to code 'double check' type screens to ask users to verify that they really want to carry out some task. This is not a recommended option. If a menu selection is so critical as to require a verification from the user, then a verify screen should be coded rather than just making it difficult to choose the option.

- You can have a menu that grays some items, which means that you can prevent some classes of users from attempting to access those menu choices.

- Most of the screen is at the programmer's disposal.

- The menu can easily be programmed to allow the user to use option numbers. A readily apparent example of how this would work is the menu accessed by the FSEDIT MOD command.

The main disadvantage of choice groups is that under a non graphical, non mouse-based system such as MVS, usage is less intuitively obvious.

Choice groups as menu items are discussed in SAS Institute documentation with examples. Refer to *SAS/AF Software: Usage and Reference, Version 6, First Edition*.

Using SCL Program Entries

This is a highly flexible approach, and consequently may require extensive programming to achieve the menu. SCL program entries offer the following advantages:

- The entire screen is at the programmer's disposal, allowing maximum utilization for messages and menu items.

- A professional looking and intuitively obvious screen can be built, based around traditional 'pick a number' or 'press a function key' type approaches.

- This is the least platform-dependent option, as the screen can be coded to look like the operating system interface.

In Databank's JARS application, the main menu is a program screen, shown in Figure 6.3.

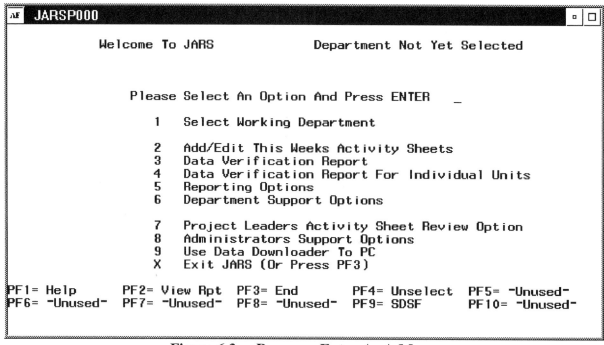

Figure 6.3:   Program Entry As A Menu

This program screen is used because at Databank, we wanted to

- allow code behind the scenes before a menu option is invoked

- allow various fields to exist on screen to reflect current status of certain events

- allow menu options selected by both number and function keys to control user selections

- have ability to switch highlighting on and off of fields as various events occur.

Notice that in addition to allowing a set of menu options, this screen also allows several other options through the use of function keys.

The SUNS application uses a program screen main menu that accesses all its options through push buttons. This approach is due to its having been developed on OS/2, which is a push button-oriented operating system. The screen is shown in Figure 6.4. This screen is a little unusual in that as well as having the main menu on the first screen, it also contains a number of fields that can be filled in before you trigger a menu option. Generally, the norm seems to be that menu screens allow entry of menu numbers, then branch to a screen that contains all code to do with that menu option.

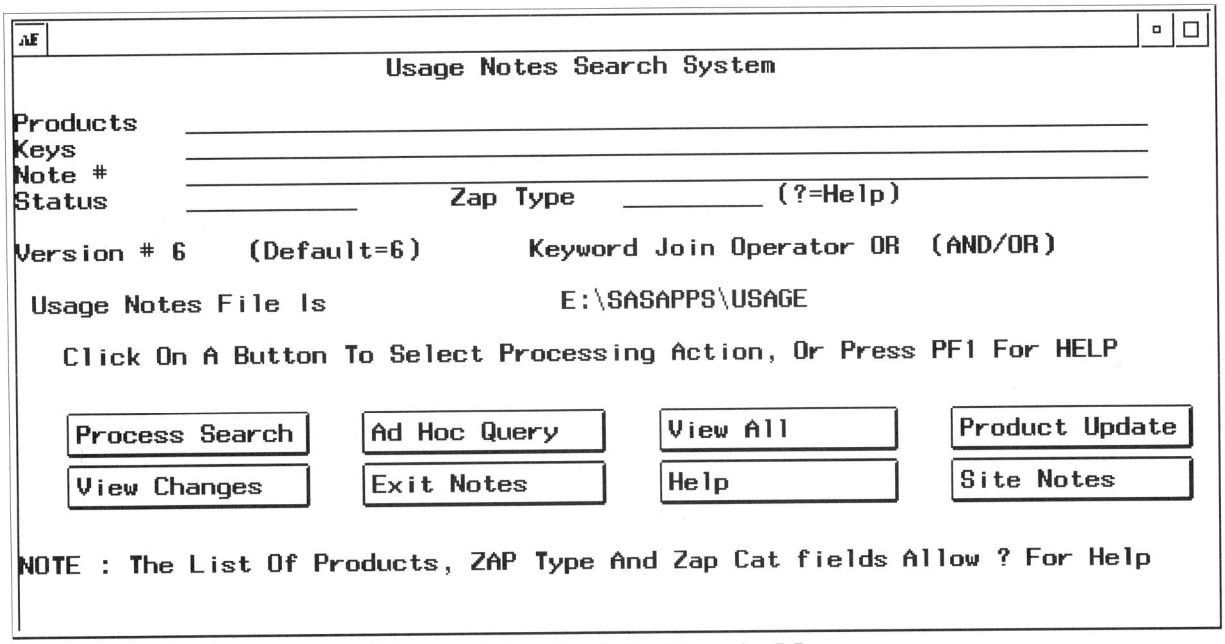

```
┌─────────────────────────────────────────────────────────────────────┬──┬──┐
│ ᴧᴲ                                                                    │ ▫│ ▢│
├──────────────────────────────────────────────────────────────────────┴──┴──┤
│                     Usage Notes Search System                                │
│                                                                              │
│ Products   _____ │
│ Keys       _____ │
│ Note #     _____                                                      │
│ Status     _____      Zap Type   _____  (?=Help)                 │
│                                                                              │
│ Version # 6   (Default=6)       Keyword Join Operator OR  (AND/OR)           │
│                                                                              │
│  Usage Notes File Is               E:\SASAPPS\USAGE                          │
│                                                                              │
│    Click On A Button To Select Processing Action, Or Press PF1 For HELP      │
│                                                                              │
│    ┌────────────────┐  ┌──────────────┐  ┌──────────────┐  ┌───────────────┐│
│    │ Process Search │  │ Ad Hoc Query │  │ View All     │  │Product Update ││
│    └────────────────┘  └──────────────┘  └──────────────┘  └───────────────┘│
│    ┌────────────────┐  ┌──────────────┐  ┌──────────────┐  ┌───────────────┐│
│    │ View Changes   │  │ Exit Notes   │  │ Help         │  │ Site Notes    ││
│    └────────────────┘  └──────────────┘  └──────────────┘  └───────────────┘│
│                                                                              │
│ NOTE : The List Of Products, ZAP Type And Zap Cat fields Allow ? For Help    │
│                                                                              │
└──────────────────────────────────────────────────────────────────────────────┘
```

Figure 6.4:   Push buttons As Menus

About 80% of processing in SUNS involves one menu option, so the fields that the user fills in for that option are on the first screen along with the other menu options, thus cutting down on the amount of menu selection that needs to be done.

Summary

One criterion for coding menus relates to what your site standards are. Another relates to the user knowledge base. Essentially, we build systems to be easy for the entire user base to use. Ease of use for one group of users may be very different from ease of use for another.

Decisions may come down to deciding whether your menuing style should reflect what users in the site feel comfortable with. In practice, this may mean utilizing SAS software's ability to design free form screens to make your SAS applications look and feel like an extension of what the user is used to, namely the underlying operating system.

Using SAS/AF To Produce Dynamic SAS Programs

Overview

In the context of this text, a dynamic SAS program is one in which the user does not have to change any code, yet it will allow the user to change parameters to receive a different report each time it is run.

A simple example is a monthly report that is run by the user and that will allow the user to select any month to report on. The user should not have to alter the program that produces the report; rather, online code should allow the user to enter the month of the report and then modify the report code itself.

SAS/AF is tailor-made for this sort of exercise. 'Fill in the blanks' type entries can be simply coded under SAS/AF. It is a fairly simple job to take existing programs and place them under SAS/AF control. The major decision to be made by the coder is which variables should be dynamic -- in other words, what 'blanks' the user fills in.

Creating A Fill-In-The-Blanks Screen

The tasks are straightforward. The following description assumes that a program exists but is not yet under SAS/AF control.

The first task is to decide what fields the user would need to be able to change each time the report is run. Related to this is to decide whether all these changeable variables are required to be entered, or whether entry of some variables should prevent entry of other variables. In the latter case, the SAS program may require some modification for it to function correctly when not all fields are present.

With that decision made, the next task is to design the screen, following site or application standards of course. The screen should contain a number of SAS/AF fields that correspond to the changeable program field entries.

The third decision is whether to run the code using the SCL SUBMIT command or to execute it in a separate SAS execution. The latter may require extra coding to set up.

Example -- The JARS Project List Report

This program allows a user to print information about projects on the JARS system. Requirements were that the program should allow the user to select all, one, or several projects. The user could also select a range of projects (using consecutive project numbers) or select projects under the control of specified departments. Any project worked on during a time period to be specified by the user could be selected if required. There was no requirement to keep the information that was entered for a later session.

Effectively, this is a situation that could be coded using macro variables. These could be changed before each run, thus customizing the report code each time it is executed. That situation easily converts to SAS/AF. The macro variables become SAS/AF screen variables and are entered by the user. Using SAS/AF means the user won't have to edit and change code.

The screen in Figure 6.5 is the one that the user will see when he or she elects to run this report:

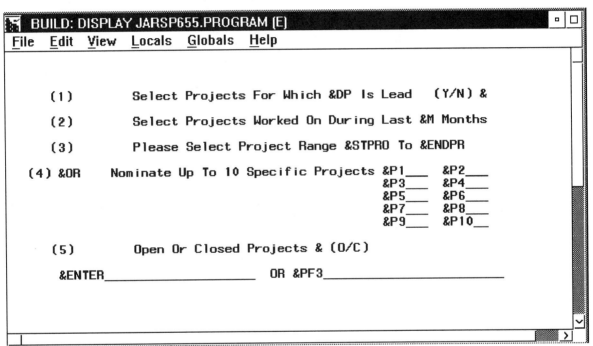

Figure 6.5:   Example Fill In The Blanks Screen

The report is run online as soon as the user enters the fields, provided that various other checks coded in the following SCL are satisfied. The following code is the entire program to accomplish the PROJECT LIST REPORT, presented here without the change and variable descriptor blocks:

```
array prj(10) $ 8 p1 p2 p3 p4 p5 p6 p7 p8 p9 p10 ;
array prjlit(10) $ 8 _temporary_ ('p1' 'p2' 'p3' 'p4' 'p5' 'p6' 'p7' 'p8'
'p9' 'p10') ;
```

```
array mess{*} $ 80 (
      'ERROR: JR655001 - Choose At Least One Of (1) or (2)'
      'ERROR: JR655002 - Select A Value Between 1 And 99 Months'
      'ERROR: JR655003 - Please Enter Start And End Of Range'
      'ERROR: JR655004 - Project Id '
      ' Does Not Exist '
      'ERROR: JR655005 - You May Not Specify A Range & Specifics'
      'ERROR: JR655006 - Status Must Be O or C'
    ) ;

length errorfld $ 8 ;

init:
 control always ;
 dp = symgetc('dp') ;
 rc = field('color yellow highlight','dp or') ;
 cursor leaddpt ;
 scrname = 'JARSP655' ;
 call wname(scrname) ;
return ;

main:
if _status_ eq 'E' then return ;

/* initialize field used to check if any obs available at various
stages */
norecs = 0 ;

call wname(scrname) ;
erroroff _all_ ;
cursor leaddpt ;

/************* Check Have Department Information **************/
 %checkent(leaddpt eq _blank_ and m eq _blank_ , message ,
   mess(1), ,op=,curfield=leaddpt,erroff=Y)

/************* check validity of months variable **************/
  if m ne _blank_ then do ;
    if length(m) eq 1 then m= '0' || m ;
    %checkent(m gt '99' | m lt '01',message,mess(2),,
        op=,curfield=m,erroff=Y )
  end ;

/************* check project range      ********************/
  %checkent(stpro eq _blank_ & endpr ne _blank_,
     message,mess(3),,op =,curfield=stpro,
     erroff=Y)

  %checkent(stpro ne _blank_ & endpr eq _blank_,
     message,mess(3),,op =,curfield=endpr,
     erroff=Y)

/************* check specific projects ********************/
  num = 0 ;
  do i=1 to dim(prj) ;
    if prj(i) ne _blank_ then do ;
      if putc(prj(i),'$valprj.') eq 'INV' then do ;
        rc = field('ERRORON',prjlit(i))   ;
        if errorfld eq ' ' then do ;
```

```
                errorfld=prjlit(i) ;
                message = mess(4) || prj(i) || mess(5) ;
             end ;
          end ;
          num = num + 1 ;
       end ;
    end ;


/************** check don't have both specific & range ********/
   %checkent(num and stpro ne _blank_, message, mess(6) ,
      ,op=,curfield=stpro,erroff=Y)

/************** check open or closed projects *****************/
   %checkent(statfld ne _blank_ & statfld not in ('O' 'C'),
      message,mess(7), ,op=,curfield=statfld,erroff=Y)

/* check if any errors in user parameters were noted and return with
appropriate error flags and messages if so */
   if errorfld ne ' ' then do ;
      rc = field('cursor',errorfld) ;
      call wname(scrname || ' ' || message) ;
      errorfld = ' ';
      return ;
   end ;


/************** option 1 has been selected *******************/
   if leaddpt eq 'Y' then do ;
      message = 'Note: Applying Criteria (1) ';
      call wname(scrname || ' ' || message) ;
      refresh ;
      submit continue ;
        proc sort data=library.projlist out=temp(keep=project) ;
           by project;
           where assgdept = "&dp" ;
        run ;
      endsubmit ;
   end ;
   else do ;
      submit continue ;
        proc sort data=library.projlist out=temp(keep=project);
           by project;
        run ;
      endsubmit ;
   end ;

/************** option 2 has been selected ******************/
   if m ne _blank_ then do ;
/* set enddte = first day of month m months ago */
      enddte = intnx('month',intnx('month',today(),-inputn(m,'8.0')),0) ;
      message = 'Note: Applying Criteria (2) ';
      call wname(scrname || ' ' || message) ;
      refresh ;
      submit continue ;
        proc sort data=global.activity out=temp2(keep=project)
              force nodupkey;
          by project ;
          where dept eq "&dp" & wedate gt &enddte ;
        run ;
      endsubmit ;
```

```
    if leaddpt eq 'Y' then do ;
      submit continue ;
        proc append data=temp2 base=temp force ; run ;
        proc sort data=temp force nodupkey ;
          by project;
        run ;
      endsubmit ;
    end ;
    else rc = copy('work.temp2','work.temp') ;
  end ;

  file = 'temp' ;
  link chkobs ;
  if norecs ne 0 then return ;

/*************** option 3 has been selected *******************/
  if stpro ne _blank_ then do ;
    message = 'Note: Applying Criteria (3) ';
    call wname(scrname || ' ' || message) ;
    refresh ;
     submit continue ;
        proc sort data=temp nodupkey force;
          by project;
          where project between "&stpro" and "&endpr" ;
        run ;
      endsubmit ;
  end ;

  link chkobs ;
  if norecs ne 0 then return ;

/*************** option 4 has been selected *******************/
  if num then do ;
    message = 'Note: Applying Criteria (4) ';
    call wname(scrname || ' ' || message) ;
    refresh ;
    submit continue ;
        proc sort data=temp nodupkey force ;
          by project;
          where project in("&p1","&p2","&p3","&p4","&p5","&p6","&p7",
                           "&p8","&p9","&p10") ;
        run ;
      endsubmit ;
  end ;

  link chkobs ;
  if norecs ne 0 then return ;

/*************** Now attach back with proj list ***************/
 message = 'Note: Creating Report File ';
 call wname(scrname || ' ' || message) ;
 refresh ;
 submit continue;
    data projlist ;
      merge library.projlist temp(in=keepds) ;
       by project;
       if keepds ;
    run ;
  endsubmit ;
```

```
/*************** option 5 has been selected ******************/
   if statfld ne _blank_ then do ;
      if statfld eq 'O' then status='status not in ("C","W")';
      else status = 'status in("C","W")';
      message = 'Note: Applying Criteria (5)';
      call wname(scrname || ' ' || message) ;
      refresh ;
      submit continue ;
        proc sort data=projlist nodupkey force ;
          by project;
          where &status ;
        run ;
      endsubmit ;
   end ;

   file = 'projlist' ;
   link chkobs ;
   if norecs ne 0 then return ;

/************* now do the report ***************************/
   call method('jarspdpt','jarsp655') ;

/**********************************************************/
   call wname(scrname) ;
   cursor leaddpt ;
   leaddpt = _blank_ ; stpro = _blank_ ; endpr = _blank_ ;
   do i=1 to dim(p) ;
     prj(i) = _blank_ ;
   end ;
   m = _blank_ ; statfld = _blank_ ;
return ;

term:
return ;

chkobs:
   dsid = open('work.' || file) ;
   if attrn(dsid,'ANY') eq 0 then do ;
     rc = close(dsid) ;
     message = 'Note : No Projects Meet Selection Criteria';
     call wname(scrname || ' ' || message) ;
     cursor stpro   ;
     norecs = 1 ;
     rc = preview('clear') ;
     return ;
   end ;
   rc = close(dsid) ;
return ;
```

The code to be submitted is not submitted as one large program, but as a series of smaller segments. This strategy allows me to check at various points whether the subsequent code is necessary and splits the program into submit code modules that correspond to each possible entry field the user can fill in. I am effectively joining the parameters with an AND condition in this case.

Note the macro %CHECKENT. This is discussed thoroughly in Chapter 8, "Some Useful SCL Programs;" for the meantime, it is enough to say that this macro addresses the fact that a large proportion of data checks in SCL have the same structure. %CHECKENT generates code that would otherwise have to be coded manually.

Two arrays are used: **prj** and **prjlit**. The first, **prj**, contains the values that the user has entered in the list of project id fields. The other array, **prjlit**, contains a literal that is the name of each field in **prj**. The use of arrays is necessary as some SCL functions (FIELD, for example) require the variable name passed as a literal. You cannot, as of Release 6.08, use the DATA step VNAME routine to accomplish this.

The program uses submitted code to carry out sorting of data sets, even though SCL has the SORT function available. Using submitted code is simpler here, given the complex WHERE clauses involved.

Running SCL Programs With SAS/AF In Noninteractive Mode

SCL programs can be run with SAS/AF in a batch (background) mode when no interaction with a user is required.

Reasons for wanting to run SCL in batch mode are many. For instance, there are some very rich file-handling capabilities in SCL that the DATA step does not provide. Suppose you wish to know if a file exists. In the DATA step, one way is to generate an error by issuing a FILENAME command and then checking for it failing. However, SCL has the FILEEXIST function built in.

To run SCL under a noninteractive mode requires that you run the procedure DISPLAY. Your SCL should be in a catalog entry of type SCL, since that entry type does not have a window associated with it. For example, you could code the following SCL program:

```
init:
  call symputc('exist',fileexist(symgetc('dsname'))) ;
return ;
```

It would be called as follows:

```
%let dsname = D07825.ALL.SOURCE          ;
proc display c=ddname.catname.entrynme.SCL ;

data _null_ ;
  if symget('exist') eq 0 then ...
```

This simple program allows your SAS session to run an SCL program without user intervention and return a macro variable back to SAS software that indicates whether the file exists.

There is a further use of PROC DISPLAY. Because it is part of the base SAS product, it can be used to run SAS/AF entries without having SAS/AF licensed. So you could have a developer's system on one machine and run the application on a different machine without having to license SAS/AF on the second machine. This has definite advantages for developing on a machine that is not the final target machine for the application. However, if your application calls any SAS/FSP procedures or routines, you must have SAS/FSP licensed.

 One point to be aware of with PROC DISPLAY is that because it is a procedure, submitted code will not run until the application has finished. This is a standard SAS software convention; you cannot run another DATA step or procedure while a procedure is executing.

Detection of Errors In SAS/AF Programs

Overview

This section discusses when the built-in error checking of SAS/AF should be used as opposed to writing SCL code to detect errors. This section addresses the situation in which an AF screen variable could be assigned an attribute such as DSNAME to verify that the entered field is a SAS data set name.

Here are questions that will help you decide whether to use SAS/AF attributes or SCL code:

- Do you need to have more control over the error messages reported, or would you rather leave them at SAS defaults?
- Is a command line in use?

The following discussion is presented by way of an example, showing what happens in various situations. I only discuss the DSNAME field type here, but the discussion is applicable to all type attributes.

Suppose you have a screen that allows a user to enter a SAS data set name into a field and wish to check that the entry is a valid data set name. Two methods of doing this are available: using the DSNAME type attribute in the SAS/AF attribute window or coding in SCL using the SASNAME function.

Using SAS/AF Type Attributes

This is the simplest method as it requires no coding. The SAS error message that is reported is concise and clear when just one field is in error. Figures 6.6 and 6.7 show the messages that are obtained when an invalid DSNAME is entered:

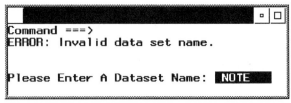

Figure 6.6:   Attribute Error Message

Note that the second screen (Figure 6.7) contains no command line (it was switched off in the GATTR screen). Even though the invalid field is highlighted, no error message appears because switching off the command line also removes the message line. Thus, if the command line is switched off, you should always code for field errors and present them on screen yourself.

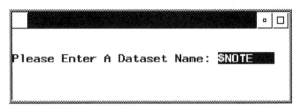

Figure 6.7: Effect Of Removing Command Line

Both the above entries have no SCL code behind them. Adding the following program allows you to determine whether SAS/AF placed the field in error and to make a more meaningful error message:

```
init:
  control error ;
return ;

main:
  if error(dsname) then
    call wname('Error: You Must Use A Valid SAS Dataset Name') ;
return ;

term:
return ;
```

The above code produces the screen in Figure 6.8 for the user.

Figure 6.8:   Customizing Error Message -- WNAME

Now when a command line is used, you have a new difficulty, namely that both the SAS/AF and the SCL messages are appearing, as is shown in Figure 6.9.

Figure 6.9: Displaying Both SAS And Custom Messages

You can easily eliminate this duplication by changing MAIN to read as follows:

```
if error(dsname) then do ;
  _msg_ = ' ';
  call wname('Error: You Must Use A Valid SAS Dataset Name') ;
end ;
```

Note that prior to Release 6.08, you could not always override _MSG_ in this manner.

SAS/AF attempts to place a sensible message for each error. For instance, if a numeric field has a LIST value of < 1 and the user enters .9, the message states that .9 is out of range. You can customize that to provide a more meaningful message indicating valid values. To do this, either do not use the LIST, or check the error status.

When multiple fields are in error, SAS/AF issues a message for the first field but highlights all fields in error. Thus, it is a fairly simple matter to train the user to look for all invalid fields.

Using Code Instead Of the SAS/AF Attribute

You can remove the DSNAME attribute from the variable attributes and consider coding to detect an invalid value. For the above situation, the following program is used:

```
init:
  control error;
return ;

main:
  erroroff _all_ ;
  call wname('') ;
  if _status_ eq 'E' then return ;
  if sasname(dsname) eq 0 then do ;
    call wname('Error: You Must Use A Valid SAS Dataset Name') ;
    erroron dsname ;
  end ;
return ;

term:
return ;
```

The screen that accompanies this program is effectively identical to the earlier example constructed by using the DSNAME type attribute and overriding the **_msg_** field.

Differences Between Type Attributes And Coding

There are a number of differences between the two techniques. First, they offer two different ways to accomplish the objective of not using the SAS default message.

Second, note that when not using the type attributes, it is up to you to switch on errors. However, the SCL can be coded to prevent any activity from occurring until the field is valid, so there is no reason to always switch errors on for the field in error. Use of **erroron** becomes a quick means of highlighting error fields, but it is not necessarily required for any other purpose.

The preceding example uses ERRORON and demonstrates another difference. When you explicitly switch errors on for a field, you should switch errors back off at the start of MAIN or as each field is checked.

 To see the impact of not remembering to switch errors off, try running the previous program without the ERROROFF _ALL_ and press PF3 after entering an invalid DSNAME. You can't exit the screen at all because ERRORON forces SCL to remain on this screen until errors are fixed and error attributes are removed. Since this is a programmed error condition, you must manually switch the error off.

The program uses WNAME to present all error messages in the same place, which is in the window border area. This means that there is no difficulty with messages not appearing when pull-down menus are in use. Note the dummy WNAME at the start of MAIN; it is necessary to use this to ensure that error messages from the last invocation of MAIN are removed before MAIN completes again.

A further difference concerns extended tables. When an extended table is being used, error handling is row specific. The concept of a scrollable field being globally in error does not exist; individual rows have fields placed in error. If the field is placed in error by SAS (in other words, if the error is an attribute error such as a character value being placed in a numeric field) prior to Release 6.08, the PUTROW section is not executed for that row. You cannot use PUTROW to issue an error message in this case until Release 6.08. In Release 6.08, PUTROW does execute for fields in error and can be used to return error messages.

If the row in error is the last one changed in the table, the MAIN section will know the fields are in error and can issue a message. However, if the row in error is not the last one processed and that last row is not in error, MAIN will not know about the error's having occurred.

GETROW is the best place to issue an error message in releases prior to 6.08. That section is always executed for each row in a table. When a row is in error, GETROW will not modify the row, but the ERROR function will detect a field in error on the row. Hence a message can be issued in GETROW. Note that GETROW will not overwrite a row in error, even if the source of the table data is a data set.

A final difference between coding and using type attributes is that in some situations it may be very difficult to code the tests. For instance, how do you provide a coded equivalent of the FMT type attribute? It is usually simpler to use the type attribute and check the error status as discussed earlier.

SCL has no mechanism for determining if any field in an entry is in error. You have to check each field individually.

Chapter 7: Using SCL With SAS/FSP® Software

Contents

Overview

The SAS/FSP product is quite different from SAS/AF in its interface with SCL and the way you code SCL. This chapter is devoted to SAS/FSP. Here I discuss topics related to the editing or browsing of data sets, as opposed to the entry of parameters and subsequent processing which is not necessarily data set oriented.

One of the objectives of SAS/FSP is to allow online access to observations in data sets. This may be on a single observation, using FSEDIT or FSBROWSE, or on a tabular view of an entire data set using FSVIEW.

The aim here is to show how to apply SCL to situations that arise due to the editing of database observations. An example situation is the storing and utilization of audit trails. It is not the purpose of this chapter to show how to access and subsequently enter SCL code to FSEDIT and FSBROWSE. However, for FSVIEW this topic is considered.

Before going any further, you should be aware that there is very little that SAS/FSP can do that SAS/AF cannot. FSLETTER is the standout exception, but most other functions can be emulated in SAS/AF. The difference is that using AF you need to write all the I/O and screen handling routines that SAS/FSP provides as an integral part of the product.

FSEDIT

Preventing Duplicate Keyfield Entries

When you have a data set that expects unique values for some field, you may need to have SCL code behind FSEDIT to ensure this happens. This section investigates how you might accomplish the task.

The most obvious way of creating unique values is to use an index on the field and make it unique. Then FSEDIT can keep track of duplicate keys itself. This method works, but in practice it is difficult to issue messages and assist users when duplicate entries are made. A major advantage is that it is not necessary to code any SCL at all to check for the duplicates.

The major problem is the timing of the index creation. It is logical that an index is updated when a new observation is saved. Thus, indexes are only checked after the TERM section. This means the user can enter data, press ENTER, get no error messages, and attempt to move to another observation, then receive an error message. This defeats one purpose of having SCL behind FSEDIT, namely to pick up error conditions at source immediately as they occur.

 It is not possible to check in TERM to see if an index create fails. The index is updated after completion of TERM. SAS software is responsible for returning control back to the procedure without moving to a new observation when the index is compromised. Because TERM knows nothing of the failed index update, you cannot find errors and issue messages.

In practice this problem is not as bad as it sounds. The user is still prevented from leaving the screen while duplicate observations exist, thus ensuring the integrity of the data set. More difficult to manage is the inability of FSEDIT to return any customized error messages.

The order of operation in FSEDIT rules that the FSEDIT SAVE is not done until TERM completes. Thus, it is impossible to detect any error conditions because the SCL is complete before the error condition is raised. The only form of error message is the default SAS message shown in Figure 7.1:

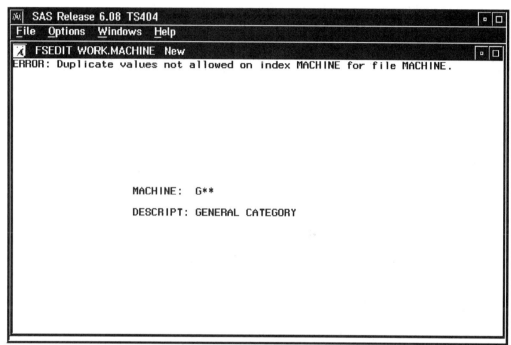

Figure 7.1:   Message When Attempting To Add A Duplicate Key To A Unique Index

Often the default SAS message will suffice. However, you may want to issue a more meaningful message. Quite simply put, you can't. The easiest means of identifying duplicate key values in FSEDIT is also the most difficult to customize in the user interface.

In many situations, you will find that the above suits both the programmer and the user. It is quick, and with a little training users can easily adjust to the fact that the error condition will not be raised until they try to exit the screen.

If your data set is not indexed, you have two options: either do or don't index it. In my applications, data sets that for some reason should not be permanently indexed can often have an index created immediately before entering FSEDIT, then dropped immediately on exit. You need to be a little wary if doing this because the time taken to create the index increases quite dramatically with the size of the data set.

If your user community or company standards prevent you from using the default message when a unique index is violated (either because the error is not raised at the same time as any other errors; or because the error message cannot be customized), there are other options.

One option is to use the LOCATEC function. To do this, you need to open (in SCL) the data set that FSEDIT is editing. The open is done in SCL in the FSEINIT section in input mode. It is closed later in FSETERM.

The main problem here is that when you press enter on an existing observation, LOCATEC may find that observation rather than a duplicate of it. So you need to ensure the current observation is not considered a duplicate. This is easily done by checking the observation number from the search with the current FSEDIT observation number and ignoring the LOCATEC outcome if they are the same.

Other than this, LOCATEC does three things: it provides a simple way to ensure that no duplicate keys occur, it bypasses using an index, and it identifies the error in MAIN, allowing a meaningful error message to be displayed.

The example following has an FSEDIT occurring on the library RATES.MACHINE. The code shown is the entire SCL that sits behind FSEDIT:

```
fseinit:
  dsid = open('rates.machine') ;
return ;

init:
 control always ;
 call wname(' ') ;
return ;
```

```
main:
  if _status_ eq 'E' then return ;         /* end, go back if no errors  */
  if not modified(machine) then return ; /* no change, no check needed */

  erroroff _all_ ;
  call wname(' ') ;
  if obsinfo('deleted') or word(1,'u') eq 'DELETE' then return ;

  if locatec(dsid,varnum(dsid,'machine'),machine) then do ;
    dupobs = curobs(dsid) ;
    if dupobs ne curobs() then do ;
      call wname('ERROR: That Value Of Machine Already Exists At
Observation '||
                 dupobs || '                ') ;
      erroron machine ;
    end ;
  end ;

return ;
term:
return ;

fseterm:
  call close(dsid) ;
return ;
```

☹ *There is a catch with the preceding code. If you enter FSEDIT with member-level locking, you cannot open the file again for read in the FSEINIT section. Thus the above code fails at run time when MAIN tries to read the DSID file. The only way around this is NOT to use member-level locking in the FSEDIT session.*

Note that when the data set has a different number of logical observations from physical observations, the previous program will still work. This is due to (and is the reason for) the use of the CUROBS function. That will always produce the physical observation number, while LOCATEC itself will return the logical. Thus the error message will report an incorrect observation number if CUROBS is not used. The code that would produce this incorrect code follows:

```
fseinit:
  dsid = open('rates.machine') ;
return ;

init:
 control always term ;
 call wname(' ') ;
return ;

main:
  if _status_ eq 'E' then return ;        /* end, go back if no errors
*/
  if not modified(machine) then return ; /* no change, no check needed
*/

  erroroff _all_ ;
  call wname(' ') ;
  if obsinfo('deleted') or word(1,'u') eq 'DELETE' then return ;

  obs=locatec(dsid,varnum(dsid,'machine'),machine) ;
  if obs ne curobs() then do ;
    call wname('ERROR: That Value Of Machine Already Exists At
Observation '||
                obs || '               ') ;
    erroron machine ;
  end ;

return ;

term:
return ;

fseterm:
  call close(dsid) ;
return ;
```

In summary, LOCATEC provides a quick and effective way to ensure that a database does not have duplicate observations when you are editing in FSEDIT. The only real shortcoming is the need to be careful to ensure that the physical observation number is reported in any error messages.

Another option is to replace LOCATEC with a WHERE clause. LOCATEC has some difficulties that especially have an impact as data set size increases. The default search algorithm is sequential; thus increasing data set size implies increasing processing overhead, as every observation will be processed. To use the optional binary search in LOCATEC implies a sorted data set, which is not always appropriate, especially when observations are being added to the end using FSEDIT (as it is impossible to sort the data set while in FSEDIT).

On the other hand, the WHERE clause will not process every observation and will never require a sorted data set to behave in a more efficient manner. Tests done reveal little difference between the methods until the observation being searched for is nearer to the end of the data set. Then LOCATEC goes slower, and WHERE shows no appreciable increase in overhead. There is a further advantage to using WHERE, namely that it will take advantage of any indexes involved in the search.

Here is the equivalent program to accomplish the above using WHERE:

```
fseinit:
  dsid = open('rates.machine') ;
return ;

init:
 control always term ;
 call wname(' ') ;
return ;

main:
  if _status_ eq 'E' then return ;        /* end, go back if no errors  */

/* if no change to the observation, then it is either in error or
   has never had an error, either way we do not have to do any
   work so just return */

  if not modified(machine) then return ;

  erroroff _all_ ;
  call wname(' ') ;
  if obsinfo('deleted') or word(1,'u') eq 'DELETE' then return ;

/* build a WHERE clause, see if any observations matched, ensure that
    if matches are not the current observation if not NEW, and return
    with appropriate message */

  rc = where(dsid,'machine eq "' || machine || '"') ;
  if fetch(dsid) ne -1 then do ;
    obs = curobs(dsid)   ;
    if obs ne curobs() then do ;
      call wname(
        'ERROR: That Value Of Machine Already Exists At Observation '||
                obs) ;
      erroron machine ;
    end ;
  end ;
```

```
   rc = where(dsid) ;

return ;

term:
return ;

fseterm:
   call close(dsid) ;
return ;
```

SAS Institute recommends use of LOCATEC on small databases where a sequential search will have little impact. This is definitely good advice. WHERE clauses and SCL searches are in general more efficient, despite the extra overhead of having to use FETCH or FETCHOBS to load an observation.

Printing Screens

If you have developed any FSEDIT applications with a number of screens, you will be aware of what a chore it is to print those screens. The only way is to access each screen physically and file or print it from there.

You can automate this process. Create a program to run interactively under SAS to access and print FSEDIT screens. Allow it to access every FSEDIT screen in a system. This can be done with ease, provided certain conditions are met. Here is how it is done.

Think for a moment about how you manually print an FSEDIT screen. First, you have to use the MOD command. Options 3 or 6 lead to the SCL; then you use either the FILE command to write the SCL to an external file or the PRINT command to write the SCL to a printer.

All this is equivalent to entering FSEDIT with the command

```
    MOD;6;FILE .... R;END;END
```

already on the command line. If you had a way of entering FSEDIT with that command line set up, and then added an extra END, you would be able to file SCL statements away without having to communicate with FSEDIT.

That ability exists through EXECCMD. Remember, EXECCMD stacks up commands for execution in the next displayed window. The idea is to write a program that issues the above commands using EXECCMD, enters FSEDIT, does the work, and exits, all without any user intervention.

The FSEDIT screen will execute any FSEINIT, INIT, MAIN, TERM, or FSETERM sections as if a user had accessed the screen from an application. Thus any files, variables, formats, and so on that the FSEDIT SCL expects must be available. Also, the first observation must not fail any checking, either attribute or SCL, that is done on the data set.

Given the above condition, you can now set up a program to run under SAS/AF that will call FSEDIT after stacking up the above commands. The program uses an SCL entry. It needs no window; thus it is unnecessary to make it a PROGRAM-type screen. The program follows:

```
init:
 call execcmd(
   "mod;6;file " || symgetc('outnme') || " r;end;end;end;") ;

 call fsedit(symgetc('filename') ,
             symgetc('screen')   ,
             'browse' ) ;
return ;
```

That is a remarkably simple program. Effectively it does no more than issue the commands that a developer would enter to print an FSEDIT SCL program to an external file. To call this, issue the following commands:

```
%let filename=RATES.RATETBLE ;
%let outnme=e:\sasapps\marts\ratetble.scn ;
%let screen=RATES.FSEDIT.RATETBLE.SCREEN ;
proc display c=catlg.printfse.printfse.scl; run ;

%let filename=RATES.MACHINE ;
%let outnme=e:\sasapps\marts\dups.scn ;
%let screen=RATES.FSEDIT.DUPS.SCREEN ;
proc display c=catlg.printfse.printfse.scl; run ;
```

The above program is drawn from the OS/2 platform running Release 6.08 of SAS software. When submitted from the program editor, it will copy the two SCL programs defined by the **screen** macro variable into the files represented by the **outnme** macro variable. In each case, you have to execute FSEDIT on a data set that is defined by the FILENAME macro variable.

This technique has been tested in Release 6.08 under Version 2.0 of OS/2 and Release 6.07 under MVS. I cannot guarantee its success under every platform or release. Hopefully SAS Institute will eventually cover this shortcoming in its SCL implementation with FSEDIT and provide a more flexible means of outputting SCL used in FSEDIT screens.

To make maximum use of this technique, I have a file for each application with the above macro definitions set up for each FSEDIT SCL in the application. When a printout is required, the above is run, copying all the FSEDIT files to external files (at my site, an up-to-date online copy of these screens is maintained outside of FSEDIT so developers can print if required. Thus we always use the FILE option).

One source of difficulty with the above has been noticed. That is that in Release 6.07 and later releases, SAS software produces a window after you have selected MOD to check whether FSETERM should be run. This only happens if an FSETERM section is present. It doesn't seem possible to skip over that, so some manual intervention may still be necessary. However, if the source code stream containing the macro variables is up to date, this is still a very simple and quick way to print screens.

Deleting New Observations

When you add a new observation, a DELETE prior to a SAVE on that observation puts you onto the previous observation. If the new observation was previously saved, the DELETE leaves the user on the deleted observation, with the usual DELETED message note in the message area.

Being placed on a previous observation can be an annoyance, particularly in an application that does not allow you to access more than one observation at a time. The situation occurs in SUNS, for example, when users are adding an observation to site notes but have no command line or pmenu. When the option to add a new observation under site notes is selected, only that observation should be accessible.

The intention is that if users delete the observation, then they should not be placed on another observation, but rather should return to the calling program. To force this behavior to occur, try the following code in your FSEDIT MAIN section:

```
MAIN:
  if _status_ eq 'E' then return ;
  cmd = word(1,'u') ;
  if cmd eq 'DELETE' and obsinfo('new') then do ;
     call execcmd('end') ;
     return ;
  end ;
```

The code works here because the intention is that users are only allowed to edit or view a single entry; thus a DELETE is equivalent to wanting to exit the option. Pushing the END via EXECCMD causes the observation to be DELETED; then FSEDIT processes the END command and forces users back to the menu.

Using the OBSINFO function allows the same SCL to be used on the data set when it is permissible to access more than one observation and a DELETE is done on an existing observation. In that situation, the default behavior of being placed on the last observation is perfectly acceptable.

Allowing FSEDIT SCL To Control Both Edit And Browse Sessions

It is a simple matter to invoke the FSEDIT routine in SCL to browse a data set. Just use the BROWSE parameter. However, this apparently simple operation may cause you to want to modify your SCL considerably to bypass operations intended for EDIT.

The question that arises is how can an SCL program be modified to detect whether an FSEDIT session has opened a data set for EDIT or BROWSE?

To accomplish this aim requires some work. You will need to code a macro variable before you enter FSEDIT. That variable (called, say **edstat**) should take on values of E if you intend to edit the file or B if you intend to browse the file. The following code will accomplish this:

```
call symputc('edstat','B') ;
call fsedit('work.x','... screen name ...','','browse') ;
```

or

```
call symputc('edstat','E') ;
call fsedit('work.x','... screen name ...') ;
```

You need to ensure that you always remember to set up the macro variable, and of course to set it up correctly.

Now use this macro variable in your SCL program behind the FSEDIT/BROWSE screen. Suppose you want no SCL run if the access is BROWSE. Use the following:

```
init:
  if symgetc('edstat') eq 'B' then return ;
  ... init section for edit ...
return ;

main:
  if symgetc('edstat') eq 'B' then return ;
  ... main section for edit ...
return ;

term:
  if symgetc('edstat') eq 'B' then return ;
  ... term section for edit ...
return ;
```

This programmed means of carrying out specific code dependent on whether you are editing or browsing works well, and it is independent of the means of calling FSEDIT. If you are calling via submitted code rather than the above SCL CALL, just set the macro variable either in SCL or in the submitted code itself.

Note that this strategy can also be used outside of SCL. If you intend running PROC FSBROWSE, maybe from the program editor, you can do so as follows:

```
%let edstat = B ;
proc fsbrowse data=work.x screen= ... screen name ... ; run ;
```

The SCL in the FSEDIT is always run, but only the check for **&edstat** being B is carried out unless the **&edstat** variable is set to other than B.

Adding Free-Form Text To FSEDIT Observations

One of the limitations with FSEDIT is that it is designed to allow editing of fields on a SAS data set, which makes it difficult to add free-form text that may be used to add further information about the observation.

Free-form text is useful in the JARS project register. Information about projects, such as the estimated cost, the estimated hours, the project leader, start dates, close dates, and a number of other simple fields, is stored. Project leaders can enter a 'running commentary' of project progress also in the form of free-form text.

On the FSEDIT observation, you would have to create a number of fields and display them if you wanted to add any free-form text. Unfortunately, when you are creating several long text fields for use in FSEDIT, several problems arise:

● No matter how many fields of 200-byte length are created, someone always needs more.

● Many observations will have no free-form text, so you are wasting storage space on those observations.

● There is no ability to use the SAS text editor with the fields.

I have sometimes seen text fields used on the data set and updated in FSEDIT. But the point here is to store potentially infinite amounts of text, and text fields on a database just cannot do that. While the SAS Notes database appears to use these fairly successfully, I have seen instances in other applications where the above problems arise as well as a further practical problem -- how to write a concise comment into the available lines when the comment itself demands that explanation be provided.

A simple technique can be used to get around this problem. When editing in FSEDIT, allow your system design to accommodate an external file to which free-form text can be added (external here means external to FSEDIT). Then use the methods discussed in Chapter 4 with the PREVIEW window to create a catalog member with the name tagged by a unique field on each observation.

➡️ *You could use the NOTEPAD window for entry of free-form text. I do not regard the NOTEPAD window as always being an adequate solution to this problem. While you could use this window to allow entry of large amounts of text, the saving of that text is totally up to the user. If the user neglects to save the text, it is difficult to recover from within the application, while with the techniques outlined above it is the application that always saves the text. To make maximum use of the NOTEPAD window from inside an application the user must remove any text already in the window; that is not the NOTEPAD window default, but EXECCMD can help with that by issuing a CLEAR command. I feel that NOTEPAD is a developer's tool and difficult to integrate into an application. However, if the user base is reasonably familiar with system editors, NOTEPAD may be adequate. But you will need to consider carefully how to save the text.*

➡️ *A simpler alternative than the PREVIEW window may be to use the CALL BUILD function and save the text to a HELP or CBT entry. You don't need to worry about clearing the editor afterwards or explicitly saving data, as CALL BUILD will have the catalog entry name at the time of calling and saves on exit. I have used this in an application where users could update the HELP screens. A short lesson on CBT meant that they were able to update the HELP screens effectively without having an impact on developers' time.*

Audit Trails

What Is An Audit Trail?

One of the fundamental questions that often arises with databases in any system (not just SAS software) is just what is being done with the database and by whom. Applications may have certain critical functions that demand that a trail be kept describing who carries these functions out.

Tracking usage like this is called an audit trail. It allows you to produce an audit report showing exactly who accessed the database and what they did. In many organizations, this is a vital part of company policy; in others it may be unimportant. Prior to SCL's availability, only very rudimentary trails showing who accessed a database could be kept.

Audit trails differ from journals in that an audit is only intended to be used as a means of finding what is done, whereas a journal can be used for recovery purposes.

Observations: The Technical Journal for SAS Software Users has had an ongoing discussion on how to achieve recoverability using journals. See Vol. 1, Num. 1 (Fourth Quarter 1991), Vol. 2, Num. 3 (Second Quarter 1993), and Vol. 2, Num 4 (Third Quarter 1993).

SCL can be coded for FSEDIT in such a way as to allow you to carry out specified processing whenever a user accesses, modifies, deletes, or even browses an observation. Thus it is possible to track what users do and produce reports at a later date.

When you are required to audit a data set, there is one fundamental question to answer before starting: What information will your audit trail store?

At a minimum, your audit should include information identifying the user editing the data set, the observation number, and the date it is edited. You should go further and look at each individual operation carried out if that operation alters the data set. Some situations may require that you audit any access, whether it be EDIT or BROWSE.

Under many operating systems, the **&sysjobid** macro variable identifies the user editing the database. On operating systems where that is not the case, (for example, Release 6.08 of SAS under Version 2.0 of OS/2 will not return a consistent value), you will need to require users to identify themselves before starting. If you can't identify the user editing the data set, an audit trail is of little use since the point is to know who is doing what with observations.

You can code your SCL in such a way to keep track of data set edits or both edits and browses. Often it is useful to be able to find out whether a particular individual has viewed an observation.

How To Write An Audit Trail

The object is to track what happens to the data set. In practice, there are two means of doing this:

● write the audit to a separate audit database

● store the audit information on each observation.

Storing The Audit Data In A Separate Database

This means that in addition to the data set being tracked, a separate data set is maintained to store the audit information. Each observation of that audit data set will contain fields created by the application, at specific points in the FSEDIT SCL.

Suppose you want to know who has accessed a data set and also whether an observation was browsed only (a browse may be defined as an edit operation with no changes made, or as a PROC FSBROWSE operation), deleted, or modified. If the observation was modified, you want to know which field was changed. Additionally, you need to store the date and time of the operation.

Your audit data set needs the following fields:

signon   -   the signon carrying out the task
operation   -   Browse, Edit, Delete
field   -   the changed field
date   -   date changed
time   -   time changed
keyfield   -   a field on the data set that can identify an observation being changed or edited

You need to structure your SCL to accomplish this. A separate observation is written for each operation or changed field. MAIN can easily cope with the Edit or Delete as follows:

```
fseinit:
  auddate = today() ;
  auduser = symget('sysjobid') ;
  dsid00  = open(<audit data set>,'U') ;
return ;

init:
  audkey  = put(curobs(),6.) || < unique observation identifier > ;
  audrec = '0' ;
return ;

main:
..
  cmd = word(1,'u') ;
  if cmd eq 'DELETE' then do ;
    oper = 'DELETE' ;
    field = ' ';
    link writeaud ;

    return ;
  end ;

  if modified('field') then do ; /* substitute field name */
    audfield = 'FIELD' ;
    oper = 'EDIT' ;
    link writeaud ;
  end ;
...

return ;
```

```
writeaud:
  audtime = time() ;
  rc = append(dsid00) ;
  audrec = '1' ;
return ;
```

You have to be able to answer the question of how to code the keyfield variable **audkey**. An audit trail is likely to be of little use if you can never match up an audit observation with a data set observation. If a field exists that uniquely identifies an observation (for example, a project identifier in a main project register), then that suffices as the keyfield. You may have to use observation numbers, but these are only of use if the data set will never be sorted into a different order.

If no such field exists and you cannot easily identify observations, question whether an audit trail is applicable. The application that can design data sets with no unique identifying data is rather rare; good data set design should usually include some means of uniquely identifying observations. (Note that the same issues arise when deciding how to save free-form text entries discussed earlier.)

Note how the preceding code sets up the static fields in FSEINIT. These fields will be the same on each audit observation written during this session by this user.

MAIN is where the DELETE or EDIT audit trails are written out. It is easy to detect a DELETE operation because the command line will have DELETE stacked up as the next word. When you detect a DELETE, enter data in the audit data set's operation field and write the observation to the audit data set. No value is entered for the FIELD here, as the DELETE operation is observation related, not field related.

To detect and track field changes, just use the MODIFIED function. You need to change the preceding code to replace 'field' with your variable name. This change causes the operation field to be set to EDIT and the audit data set field name to be set to the changed field name. Repeat this code as often as is necessary to accommodate all fields. You may want to set the code up so that the audit observation gets written only after any field checking is complete and fields are correct.

If you want also to track who looks at the observation, this can be accomplished in TERM. There is little point in doing this in INIT, as you would then always have to write a 'BROWSE' observation and that is not necessary if other operations such as DELETE or changing a field occur.

The code in TERM uses the **audrec** field in the above code. Specifically, set that field in MAIN only if an auditable event has occurred. If that has happened, there is no need to write a BROWSE observation. If the SCL reaches TERM and **audrec** is not set, then no auditable events have occurred and the only event that has happened is that the observation was viewed. Hence, in that situation, just write an audit observation in TERM to indicate a BROWSE. The code layout follows:

```
init:
...
control term ;
audrec = '0' ;
...
return ;

main:
....
return ;

term:
  if audrec = '0' then do ;
    oper = 'BROWSE' ;
    link writeaud ;
  end ;
return ;
```

In this program use CONTROL TERM to ensure that the TERM section of the FSEDIT/BROWSE SCL is executed irrespective of whether a field is changed or not. Then in TERM, just check to see if **audrec** has been altered since INIT ran. If it has not, then no MAIN section audit observations were written, which corresponds here to no DELETE and no field change. Thus, an effective BROWSE occurred, and you write an audit observation reflecting that.

Storing The Audit Data On The Database Being Audited

This option is limiting but can be useful. You can't store much useful information on the same observation. This method is very useful in the situation where an observation is created then never modified again, and BROWSE information is not necessary.

An example is Databank's JARS system ad hoc invoice data set. Here we store ad hoc costs on projects (in other words, costs not involved with staff time). For instance, if our staff have to travel to a different center, we may charge travel costs back to the client. That would be entered in this ad hoc charges data set.

There is no audit requirement except to know who entered the ad hoc observation, when it was entered, who requested it be entered, and who approved the entry. These become fields on the ad hoc data set, so the audit information is stored along with the data.

Note that the main criteria for being able to store an audit like this is that only one edit of an observation ever occurs, that is, the initial entry. Do not permit deletes, and do not allow any online user to modify entries. Thus a separate audit data set becomes unnecessary.

Batch Access To Auditable Databases

An inherent instability in audit trails behind the online window occurs when users, or developers/support staff, can update a data set in a non-online, or batch mode. In this situation the SCL behind the FSEDIT/BROWSE cannot be executed, so the automated audit trail does not operate.

Application design should determine if a data set can be online editable, batch editable, or both. Wherever possible, restrict this to online. Quite simply, you cannot guarantee integrity of the audit operation and thus the integrity of the data set when users or support teams can update in batch. However, it is often extremely difficult to prevent batch users from accessing data sets -- use the SAS password feature to assist here.

Note that batch here is used to mean any access that does not use the modified screen that contains the SCL. An online entry by a user who bypasses the modified screen is included here.

What To Do With An Audit Trail

Suppose you have an audit trail and there is a lot of information being stored about your data set. What do you do now?

There is little point to creating an audit if system designers have not made decisions about what to do with the audit. Applications use audit trails with several objectives in mind. These include

● knowing someone has viewed an observation and at what time.

● knowing who altered data sets, and when. For instance, one function of JARS is to monitor ad hoc expenses on projects; entry of expenses into that data set requires auditing.

● knowing about attempted illegal accesses to data sets or observations on data sets.

You should note that an audit trail usually just writes an observation to a data set stating what has happened. It is not necessary that SAS/FSP write this observation. If a SAS/AF process checks legality of an attempted entry to FSEDIT and prevents the user from accessing via FSEDIT, then the AF process should write an observation to the audit data set.

Objective One: Who has viewed the data set and when?

This information is usually required by online systems where it is necessary to know if a certain person has viewed an observation. 'Viewing' may include an edit or just a browse.

Assuming there is a mechanism for determining if access is a browse or an edit, the FSEDIT SCL can write an observation whenever a user accesses a data set. This subject was discussed in a previous section of this chapter. To determine who has viewed the main data set, print the audit data set. If you are interested only in who has viewed specific observations, then use the **audkey** field to look for keys identifying those observations.

SUNS has an option in the SITENOTE FSEDIT screen to return the signons of users who have viewed the current observation. The code behind this option follows:

```
submit continue sql ;
  select * from library.siteedit where
    audkey eq &idnumber ;
endsubmit ;
```

This program produces a list of all entries on the audit data set, LIBRARY.SITEEDIT, that have a keyfield that matches the current FSEDIT observation's unique IDNUMBER field. This is a very simple report, intended to do no more than list every audit observation that exists for a given value of **audkey**.

In this instance, **audkey** was set up as the value of the field that defines a problem observation number. Each problem observation number can occur only once; in other words, each one is unique. Thus the SQL WHERE clause extracts only these audit observations associated with the SCL (or macro) variable **&idnumber**. However, **audkey** can be any field, or combination of fields, that will uniquely match audit observations back to data set observations.

Consider the following situation. You have a data set containing chargeable batch job information. Each batch job is uniquely identified by the fields **jobname**, **rdrts** (Reader Time Stamp, a time stamp cut on MVS systems when a job enters the system), and **jesjobno** (a job number assigned by the MVS Job Entry Subsystem (JES) to each job). The audit key would have to include all those fields and might use some concatenation of them. An example could be

```
audkey = put(jobname,$char8.) ||
         put(rdrts,datetime19.2) ||
         put(jesjobno,$char4.) ;
```

The point is that to devise an effective audit trail you must be able to uniquely identify observations, which may mean that creation of an audit key field gets a little more complex as above.

Objective Two: Who has altered the data set?

It may also be a corporate requirement to track effectively who updates a data set. The difficulty comes with systems that do not assign a unique signon to users, but that have multiple users. To minimize the impact here, I have developed systems under OS/2 in which the user is asked to provide an identifying 'signon' at the system startup stage and is not allowed access if the entered value (the signon) is not listed in a SAS data set that lists valid signons. These systems create a unique auditable signon, provided (as always) that users do not share signons.

Given that a signon exists, if the only objective of the audit is to check who accesses a database and when, the audit task comes down simply to writing the signon to the audit database.

Objective Three: Who has tried to access the data set without authority?

There are two types of illegal access to consider:

● trying to access a data set that you are not entitled to view

● trying to access an observation that you are not entitled to view.

The first case should not be an FSEDIT issue. If a user cannot access a data set in a library for some reason, then the check and rejection should occur before FSEDIT starts, which may mean in the underlying AF code (or it could be done in the FSEINIT section). The audit trail does not have to restrict itself to FSEDIT; it is simply a SAS data set that can be opened and written to from anywhere. So write an audit observation from AF if that is the mechanism for triggering FSEDIT.

The second case is a little more difficult to cope with. WHERE clauses restricting users to specified observations work well. To make use of a WHERE clause, you need to maintain a database that determines which observations each user can access and a field (or some fields that together make a key) on the data set being edited that map back to the access data set.

The best way to illustrate this case is an example. In JARS each user is assigned a department that he or she can work with or view data for. This information is stored on a SAS data set called LOGONS. A typical LOGONS observation might look like one of the following:

```
signon = 'D06877' ;
access = '7%'     ;
type   = 'like'   ;
```

or

```
signon = 'D06773' ;
access = '746'    ;
type   = 'eq'     ;
```

or

```
signon = 'D07825' ;
access = '("742" "746")' ;
type   = 'in' ;
```

You can set up accesses like this to permit any valid WHERE clause processing.

When user D06877 logs on to the application, a WHERE clause is set up in a macro variable using the following code:

```
dsid00 = open('library.logons') ;
call set(dsid00) ;
rc     = locatec(dsid00,varnum(dsid00,'signon'),symgetc('sysjobid'));
rc     = fetchobs(dsid00,curobs(dsid00));
call symputc('wherecl','dept ' || type || ' ' || access) ;
call close(dsid00) ;
```

And FSEDIT is called in the following manner:

```
wherecl = symgetc('wherecl') ;
call fsedit('work.activity(where=(' || wherecl || '))') ;
```

Thus, the user only sees the observations that he or she is permitted to access. In this instance, the variable WHERECL would have the value

```
dept like '7%'
```

Coding a check like this in fact stops the user from accessing observations he or she shouldn't see, so it nullifies the need to attempt to write audit observations if the user does try to access the observations. It is difficult to prevent users from accessing observations in FSEDIT itself; the simplest way seems to be a simple but effective security mechanism like the above.

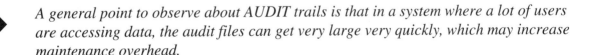 *A general point to observe about AUDIT trails is that in a system where a lot of users are accessing data, the audit files can get very large very quickly, which may increase maintenance overhead.*

FSVIEW

Overview

Using SCL with FSVIEW is completely different from using SCL with either AF or FSEDIT. The concepts of INIT, MAIN, and TERM do not exist; rather, SCL programming is achieved through use of formulas.

In FSVIEW a formula is a piece of code that must include assigning a value to a variable. That variable may be a data set variable or a window variable.

Assignment of values to a variable is not the only task that can be accomplished in FSVIEW SCL. You can carry out nearly the full range of SCL coding, but you need to take an approach different from the approaches that are typical in AF and FSEDIT.

SAS/FSP Software: Usage and Reference, Version 6, First Edition gives a hint as to how to code SCL in FSVIEW with an example showing how to ensure that data values are correct for fields not seen on the view window. In that example, a formula is created that checks whether a value is modified, then uses CALL DISPLAY to run an AF program to check an additional field.

The apparent awkwardness of this approach begs the question of why SCL should be used with FSVIEW in the first place. Look upon FSVIEW as a pseudo extended table with most of the work done for you in the data set I/O area, but without the flexibility of SCL coding that extended tables allow.

There are many advantages of using FSVIEW rather than FSEDIT, including that you get to see many observations and you don't need to be constantly using BACKWARD and FORWARD to access new observations. Advantages over AF include that you don't need to provide the I/O routines to maintain control of your data set.

Although FSVIEW seems somewhat primitive and intimidating in its mechanism for using SCL, once you understand the simple technique of calling AF programs to carry out SCL, the procedure becomes useful and usable. For all that, I find there are many difficulties with coding SCL behind FSVIEW; this subject is explored in the following sections.

When To Use FSVIEW

Applications that require an extended table approach may benefit from use of FSVIEW. By using FSVIEW, you use built-in functionality for accessing, editing, and saving database observations. By comparison, extended tables require you to build in this functionality. FSVIEW does not allow you to create and use a nonscrollable area, but doing so is simple and useful in extended tables.

FSVIEW has proved to be very useful in situations where it is necessary to display entire small databases (small in terms of variables). In that situation, FSEDIT is not useful with its single observation-oriented approach, while extended tables require additional coding to maintain.

FSVIEW is a database-oriented procedure, while extended tables need not display data from databases.

How To Use SCL With FSVIEW

Using SCL with FSVIEW presents many difficulties. These include the minimal number of lines available for formulas, the order that formulas execute in, problems with detecting new observations, and many more.

In practice, there are a number of ways that you can put comprehensive SCL code behind an FSVIEW window:

● Provide a separate formula for each piece of SCL code, remembering that you have only 4 lines per piece of code. There are several major disadvantages to this strategy:

   ● potentially many formulas will exist, making it difficult to test and code and to know the order they will be executed in

   ● only having 4 lines to code in makes coding impossible in some situations

   ● many formulas mean many extra fields defined in FSVIEW.

   Some situations definitely require formulas. When you only need to have a value defined for a variable, a simple formula does the trick.

● Call a macro containing SCL code to accomplish the entire task. Calling a macro containing all the SCL means that there is no overhead of calling another window because the SCL is defined to FSVIEW.

   That means that various restrictions occur; for instance, some of the useful SCL functions are not usable in FSVIEW (ERRORON, ERROROFF, CURSOR, PROTECT, for example). Furthermore, macros cause problems in that anytime you alter the macro, you need to remember to recompile the FSVIEW formula. Macros containing SCL code can be used, but the effort in getting them correct may be considerable.

● Call an AF SCL entry via CALL DISPLAY to accomplish the entire task. Code all your SCL in another AF entry. Use an SCL entry type if no window is necessary; otherwise use a program type. Pass variables to that AF screen (for example, via ENTRY) and do all error checking in that screen.

Coding in this situation passes variables for the observation from FSVIEW to the DISPLAY program; then any editing that is needed is done in AF rather than trying to pass messages back and correcting in FSVIEW. You have the full range of SCL available to you, and you don't need to know the order that formulas will be processed in.

- For each field to be checked, define a formula that is called for that field only. The major disadvantage here is that the code cannot easily do cross-checks with other fields. Generally, when a cross-check is done, you verify that each field is valid first, before checking the cross-reference. Hence it may be viable to use this method, and also a separate formula for cross-reference checks.

  This method works well when all the checks are on a variable-by-variable basis. It provides a means to do a form of labeled testing (in other words, it emulates the CONTROL LABEL feature of SCL).

The following discussion revolves around using a SAS/AF program to code the checks and calling that program from FSVIEW.

You require a formula that calls the display window. Two options are available to determine how to call the SCL:

- determine whether the SCL needs to be called in the formula and only call it if necessary

- always call the formula.

You can determine whether you need to call the formula provided you can fit a test and the CALL DISPLAY in the 4 available lines. A macro approach will help overcome the problem of space in the formula.

Suppose you have a screen that the user cannot add to, but can update. You want to call an SCL program via CALL DISPLAY only if a key field is altered.

Define a variable named **check** using the FSVIEW command DEF CHECK. This defines a formula for a variable named **check**. The **check** formula will check if the variable is altered. Then use DISPLAY to call the window if so. The formula is

```
check=modified(keyfield);
if check then call display('.... SCL program ....',
                           .... passed fields .... );
```

The display screen will carry out required error checking and validation. It will be responsible for forcing the user to correct entries if they are invalid. FSVIEW is not returned to until the entry is correct, at which point the called routine passes the corrected observations back to FSVIEW.

In FSVIEW the MODIFIED function does not return true on a new observation irrespective of whether fields have been altered.

The previous program works because no observations are being added. MODIFIED does not work on new observations. You *cannot* force the SCL to be carried out on new observations by changing the **check** formula to

```
check=modified(keyfield) or obsinfo('new') ;
if check then call display('.... SCL program ....',
                             .... passed fields .... );
```

because OBSINFO does not work for FSVIEW observations; it is for use with FSEDIT only. This is a difficulty with FSVIEW; you could feasibly add anything to a data set with totally invalid variable values. Unless you user goes back and changes an earlier new observation after FSVIEW has set up a new 'NEW' observation to add to, the SCL program in the CALL DISPLAY will not be executed on the observation.

The simplest alternative is to carry out the display unconditionally and allow all checking to done in the called routine, irrespective of whether a field is modified or not. It has a basic flaw: FSVIEW executes formulas at the time an observation is loaded. This includes loading a NEW observation. Hence the check is done before the user has a chance to enter any data. Thus the error screen pops up before anything has been entered.

To call the SCL program unconditionally, modify the formula above to read:

```
check= .;
call display('.... SCL program ....',
               .... passed fields .... );
```

This alternative does a lot of extra work, as it passes every observation to the display program irrespective of whether it was amended or not. (You must understand that when FSVIEW displays a table, it executes any formulas that are present for each observation that it displays. Thus an unconditional CALL DISPLAY in a formula means that every observation displayed gets passed to the DISPLAY program.) Furthermore, the difficulty caused by FSVIEW executing its formulas before the user has a chance to add any data to a new observation occurs again, so users immediately see a blank error screen.

This undesirable behavior with the blank edit screen can be controlled. Just check whether all fields are blank and return if so. For a new observation, all fields are initially blank. Thus, by checking any field, you can control the use of the unconditional call to prevent error messages from occurring on new observations. You can use the following code, for example, when multiple fields are to be checked.

```
check = . ;
  if keyfield ne ' ' then call display .... ;
```

or

```
check = . ;
  if field1 || field2 || field3 ne _blank_ then call display .... ;
```

Note that a new observation (always at the end of the screen in FSVIEW) causes the screen to be rewritten as FSVIEW determines whether it needs to scroll. Thus the formula activity is as if the screen is being displayed for the first time. Each observation being written to the screen executes the formula(s) and thus any SCL programs that are called. However, altering an existing observation does not force FSVIEW to rewrite the screen; it already knows that no scroll is required.

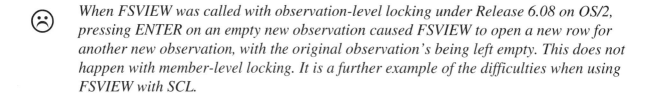 *When FSVIEW was called with observation-level locking under Release 6.08 on OS/2, pressing ENTER on an empty new observation caused FSVIEW to open a new row for another new observation, with the original observation's being left empty. This does not happen with member-level locking. It is a further example of the difficulties when using FSVIEW with SCL.*

When using the above methods with a formula, you will not generally want to display the **check** variable. Use the FSVIEW command DROP when you set up the formula to ensure that the user does not see **check**.

Case Study: A Simple Data Set Update

Now that some principles of how to apply SCL to FSVIEW fields are known, it is appropriate to try and apply those principles to a data set edit.

Suppose you have a data set called LIBRARY.SYSID. It contains fields **sysid**, **machine**, and **descript**.

FSVIEW will be used to update this file. When you are updating, the following conditions must be met:

- If any field is entered, the other two fields must also be entered.

- Both **sysid** and **machine** must be stored in uppercase.

- The value of **machine** must be a value of the variable **machine** for some observation in the file LIBRARY.MACHINE, which is a master list of machines.

- If you enter an equals sign ('=') in the machine field, it is a trigger to allow editing of the LIBRARY.MACHINE data set. Thus you may be editing an observation in LIBRARY.SYSID, determine that the observation being updated uses a value of **machine** not presently on the LIBRARY.MACHINE data set, and be allowed to edit that data set without exiting the edit of LIBRARY.SYSID. This is called a secondary update.

  When this option is used, the value entered is not to be passed straight back to the FSVIEW screen (there may be several values entered in the secondary update, so it is not possible to determine which one to pass back). The field will be left blank, with a message for you to fill it in.

- If you enter a '?' in the machine field, a list of valid machines pops up to assist you to enter a value.

Note that the requirements above immediately make the option of using a labeled type approach as discussed earlier difficult, as there is a cross-reference to cope with in requirement one. However, you will see that this approach combined with the third option becomes the most appropriate.

Assume the SCL check is in program RATES.AF.SYSID.PROGRAM. A possible formula in FSVIEW is

```
check=modified('sysid') or modified('descript') or
      modified('machine') ; if check then
call display('RATES.AF.SYSID.PROGRAM',sysid,descript,machine) ;
```

However, as explained previously, this does work on new observations. The unconditional call to the SCL program is not viable, due to its high overhead. Thus, you need a solution based on individual formulas for each field. This can be enhanced by using an SCL program for the more complex checks.

It is still necessary to find a way to ensure that the SCL gets run on any new observations when all fields are entered. This can be done but is somewhat messy. Here is what needs to be done:

- Before calling FSVIEW, create a macro variable **&origobs** containing the number of observations on the data set before editing. The code to do this is

```
dsid = open(<data set name>) ;
call symputc('origobs',put(nobs(dsid),6.)) ;
call close(dsid) ;
```

Now call FSVIEW in the usual manner.

- In FSVIEW, create a formula called **newobs**. The formula code is as follows:

```
newobs=curobs() ; if newobs > symgetc('origobs') then
call display(... < check program > ...)
```

This ensures that the **newobs** formula will only execute the SCL program when the number of the new observation exceeds the number of observations that were previously on the data set. Hence you do not see the SCL executed for every observation in the FSVIEW table.

A number of formulas will be used here. The first is the simplest, for **sysid**. This formula just reads

```
sysid=upcase(sysid) ;
```

This is very simple because **sysid** has no other checking, except the cross-check that a blank **sysid** is not permitted when another field is filled in. That check is easiest accomplished in a separate formula.

The **machine** formula is more complex. It has 4 tasks:

- uppercase the **machine** field
- check the validity of **machine** whenever the **machine** field is edited
- edit LIBRARY.MACHINES if **machine** starts with '='
- pop up an assisted entry window if **machine** starts with '?'

The formula is

```
machine=upcase(machine);
if modified(machine) then
   call display('rates.af.sclcheck.program',
   sysid,descript,machine) ;
if machine eq: '=' then call method('library.af.machine.scl',
   'machine1') ;
if machine eq: '?' then call method('library.af.machine.scl',
   'machine2') ;
```

Note that the formula is printed here in a more readable manner than FSVIEW provides; when editing in FSVIEW you will not be able to use the luxury of spare space at the end of each line. However, you could place the code in a macro to get a more readable (but external to FSVIEW) formula.

The first check in the **machine** formula is intended to ensure that the **machine** value exists in the LIBRARY.MACHINE database. (The SCLCHECK program is discussed further on; it does a large amount of checking on various conditions.) This check will be carried out only for existing observations that you alter because MODIFIED does not return true for new FSVIEW observations.

The use of SCL method blocks here is an acknowledgment that the two checks above need no window, but the code associated with the checks will not fit in the 4 FSVIEW formula lines. These checks could have as easily been set up as macros.

No formula is needed for **descript**; it has no checks nor uppercasing within itself. You need another formula to check that the fields are all entered if any one is entered. This is called **check1** and looks as follows:

```
check1=(sysid eq ' ' and descript || machine ne ' ') or
       (descript eq ' ' and sysid || machine ne ' ') or
       (machine  eq ' ' and sysid || descript ne ' ') ;
if check1 then call display('rates.af.sclcheck.program',
   sysid,descript,machine) ;
```

Thus this check is the cross-check that all fields are entered when any other field is entered. Here you do not execute a check within FSVIEW, but branch to a separate SCL program. That program has its own screen independent of FSVIEW for correcting the fields. That screen and the underlying program are discussed at the end of this section.

You still need to execute the SCLCHECK program when a new observation is edited and all fields are entered.Create another formula, **check2**, that uses the logic discussed earlier. Assuming **&origobs** was created, you carry out the SCL check as follows:

```
check2=curobs() ; if check2 > symgetc('origobs') then
call display('rates.af.sclcheck.program',
   sysid,descript,machine) ;
```

You have now accomplished means of doing all the checks. Now you only need to code the SCLCHECK.PROGRAM SCL entry.

The code and screen for that entry follows:

```
entry sysid $ 8 descript $ 40 machine $ 8 ;

init:
  control always ;

main:
  if sysid || descript || machine eq _blank_ then do ;
  /* although the file didn't have all fields blank when the
     user pressed ENTER in FSVIEW, they have obliterated all the field
     values in this screen, so we just return as the observation is no
longer
     invalid */

    _status_ = 'H' ;
    return ;
  end ;

  if _status_ eq 'H' then return ;

  call wname(' ') ;

  erroroff _all_ ;

/* ensure fields filled in */

  if sysid eq _blank_ then do ;
    call wname('Error: Please Enter SYSID') ;
    erroron sysid ;
    cursor sysid ;
    return ;
  end ;

  if descript eq _blank_ then do ;
    call wname('Error: Please Enter Description') ;
    erroron descript ;
    cursor descript ;
    return ;
  end ;

  if machine eq _blank_ then do ;
    call wname('Error: Please Enter Machine') ;
    erroron machine;
    cursor machine;
    return ;
  end ;

/* call the methods if user has entered an = or ? in this edit
   screen */

  if machine eq: '=' then call method('machine.scl','machine2',
    machine) ;

  if machine eq: '?' then call method('machine.scl','machine1',
    machine) ;
```

```
/* don't assume the user entered in UPPERCASE here */

  machine=upcase(machine) ;
  sysid  =upcase(sysid)   ;

/* ensure machine is valid */

  dsid = open('library.machine') ;
  rc = locatec(dsid,varnum(dsid,'machine'),machine);
  call close(dsid) ;
  if not rc then do ;
     call wname('Error: Invalid Machine Id - Enter ? For Help');
     erroron machine;
     cursor machine;
     return ;
  end ;

/* if got to here then no invalid data so we just exist the check program
*/

  _status_ = 'H' ;

return ;

term:
return ;
```

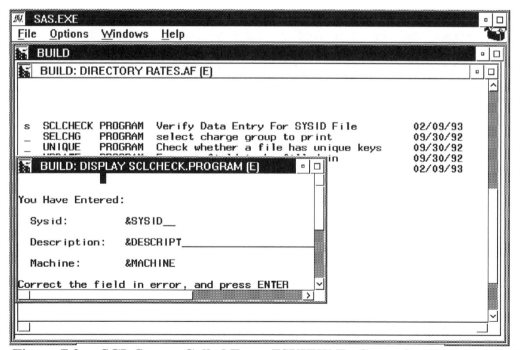

Figure 7.2: SCL Screen Called From FSVIEW To Carry Out Data Validation

Note that this entry illustrates that if you omit the RETURN at the end of INIT, the MAIN section can be treated as an extension of INIT. In this program, it is necessary to flag fields in error on entry to the screen and also when the user presses a key. By treating MAIN as an extension of INIT, you can carry out the checks in MAIN before the user sees the screen, thus placing error messages on screen immediately.

The above mechanism for using comprehensive SCL with FSVIEW is somewhat complex and awkward, and the need to ensure that the formulas are executed in the expected order often further complicates matters. The intention is to show that you can place comprehensive SCL behind FSVIEW tables; however, the effort expended in getting it right and creating a usable user interface may be better used in developing an extended table approach in SCL.

Additional Notes

When you code a formula in FSVIEW for a non data set variable, it actually creates a new window variable. That variable becomes part of the screen and is visible. By using the DROP command, you can remove the field from the screen. You may find that sometimes formulas execute in an unexpected order; use the FSVIEW MOVE command to realign fields. Formulas execute in the order that the fields appear on screen.

FSVIEW commands such as DROP and SHOW ID have their values stored right along with the formula. Thus there is no need for the user to have to reissue them. However, if you want to alter the stored values or carry out one of the other FSVIEW commands such as SORT without user intervention, you need to stack the commands up using EXECCMD before calling FSVIEW.

One of the most irritating aspects of FSVIEW is the inability to alter formulas easily. The 4-line restriction is very hard to work with, but even that is complicated by an inability to move or highlight parts of the text in the formula. If you want to insert text at the start, you will likely need to retype the whole formula if it spreads over all lines.

The **_blank_** variable is not available in an FSVIEW formula (or other SCL programs using SAS/FSP).

FSVIEW is used frequently now in my applications, but it is very rare that much SCL is placed behind it. Its major use has shifted from the original intention of doing a large amount of table-driven database editing, to creating a browse facility without SCL. Extended tables have usually turned out easier to set up and code, despite the overhead of having to code I/O routines.

If you do not have SAS/AF licensed, the only practical way to put comprehensive SCL behind an FSVIEW screen is to use macros and thus to restrict coding to just the elements of SCL allowed by SAS/FSP.

Calling FSLIST From SCL

Function Key Customization

It is quite a simple matter to call the FSLIST procedure from within SCL using the CALL FSLIST function. The only difficulty comes when you want to customize keys or remove the command line.

The difficulty with customizing keys is that FSLIST wants its key definitions in the SASUSER library in a catalog named SASUSER.PROFILE.FSLIST.KEYS. In many applications, this library may be temporary. For instance, in JARS users do not have a permanent SASUSER library since there is no reason to create and maintain such a library for each user. You cannot have an application SASUSER library, as SAS/AF software requires each user to have exclusive access to SASUSER .

If a temporary library is created for SASUSER, it is a simple matter to set up application function keys in SASUSER. Use the SCL COPY command. Set up your application-dependent function keys in your source code catalog.

In JARS, we have an entry in our main source code catalog called FSLIST.KEYS. When a user starts a JARS session, the following code is executed:

```
rc = copy('catlg.jarscde.fslist.keys',
          'sasuser.profile.fslist.keys','catalog') ;
```

The copy operation is very quick, and for our purposes far more effective than creating and maintaining a SASUSER file for each user.

There is nothing more to do for FSLIST to use these keys. The FSLIST routine will look in SASUSER for the key definitions and find them right where they have been copied. To maintain compatibility with the ISPF browse functions that FSLIST emulates, set the keys as follows, with remaining keys being blank.

F1	Help	F3	End	F5	rfind
F7	Backward	F8	Forward	F10	Left
F11	Right				

Removing the command line is slightly more difficult because it is necessary to issue a command to set up a dummy pmenu and switch it on. If an empty pmenu is not defined and the command line is switched off, FSLIST uses the standard set of system pmenus.

Removing the command line is accomplished by use of EXECCMD; just issue the following code:

```
call execcmd('setpmenu ... pmenu name ...;pmenu on') ;
call fslist ... ;
call execcmdi('pmenu off') ;
```

Use EXECCMD before FSLIST to stack up a command that is executed when the next window is displayed, and use EXECCMDI after FSLIST to switch off the pmenus immediately.

> *An alternative means of viewing external files is to use the PREVIEW function with the BROWSE option.*

Chapter 8: Some Useful SCL Programs

Contents

Overview

This chapter is a collection of macros and SCL programs that by themselves do not constitute applications, but that I have found useful as building blocks in other applications, or as tools and aids in system development.

SAS Allocations Window To Customize LIBNAME and FILENAME Commands

A most useful feature of the interactive SAS System is the ability it gives you to issue file allocations from within your session.

There are some disadvantages with this, though. Consider the following:

- You have to remember the file names, and SAS software does not (as of Release 6.08) give you the sophisticated file search capabilities of most operating systems. This is not a limitation of SAS, as it is generally accepted as an operating system feature (which isn't to say that it won't become a SAS software feature in the future, of course).

- If you place your allocations in an AUTOEXEC file, you will always get them allocated, which may not be desirable; moreover, explicit editing is required to remove them.

To get around these and other issues, a startup screen to allocate databases can be set up. The screen is run from your startup SASEXEC file.

The idea here is simple. Define a database that resides in each user's SASUSER database. That database, SASUSER.ALLOCS, contains the following fields:

```
/******************** SASUSER.ALLOCS *********************

dsname -- operating system name of data set to be allocated
type   -- whether a LIBNAME or a FILENAME
disp   -- how to open the file -- OLD, SHR, MOD or HOLD
ref    -- the FILE or LIB ref to attach to the allocation

*************************************************************/
```

Thus, each observation on the file will identify an operating system data set and give SAS software enough information to decide whether to allocate as a SAS library (LIBNAME) or an external file (FILENAME).

For maximum user interaction and ease of use, the allocation table is presented as a combined SAS/AF and SAS/FSP application. Effectively, the user only sees the SAS/FSP part of the application. This uses the FSVIEW procedure and is shown in Figure 8.1.

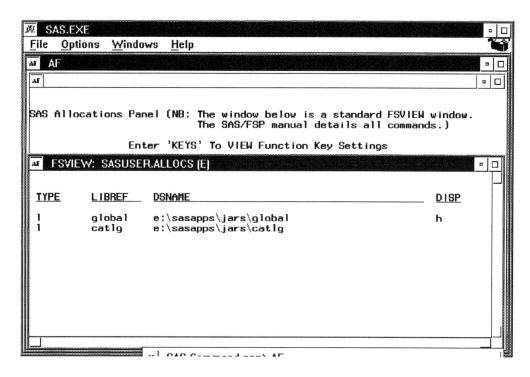

Figure 8.1:   Example File Allocation Screen

FSVIEW was chosen as the database control mechanism because it provides a simple tabular layout where database access is controlled by SAS software. In other words, you minimize coding. Additionally, very little testing of user input is required. Effectively, the only form of user input testing is to ensure uniqueness of filenames and librefs and to ensure existence of the database when it is to be allocated. The uniqueness tests are done using indexes, and SCL code is carried in SAS/AF when FSVIEW is exited.

If you do not have SAS/FSP, rewriting the FSVIEW part as an extended table will be a simple exercise.

Allocation is simple. When users indicate that they have finished with any editing of the table using FSVIEW, pressing F3 opens SASUSER.ALLOCS, checks the DISP field, and attempts to allocate any that are not DISP=H. Any unsuccessful attempt to open results in a message to the SASLOG files.

The coding is not trivial. However, as this is designed to be a developer's tool, less emphasis is placed on checking at entry time than might be expected with a less sophisticated user base. Thus FSVIEW becomes an appropriate edit mechanism, needing no code placed behind it.

The entire application is displayed below. Discussion of various attributes of the application follows.

In Figure 8.1, the user has entered just one data set name in the table to be allocated. As this allocation was done under OS/2, no DISP value is coded because that LIBNAME option is not available on that platform. The user would place an H in this field to keep the data set name on screen, but not to allocate in this session.

The following 3 SAS/AF catalog entries are associated with this screen:

ALLOC.KEYS   - key definitions:

```
F1 Help      F3 End       F5 Delete      F7 Backward
F8 Forward
```

ALLOC.HELP   - help screen:

```
HELP For SAS Allocations Panel

TYPE   : This variable is used to tell SAS whether the data set to be
         allocated is to be allocated via a LIBNAME (TYPE=L), or by a
         FILENAME (TYPE=F).

LIBREF: This is the LIBREF to be assigned, follow standard SAS libref
         conventions for your operating system

DSNAME: This is the DSNAME to be assigned to the LIBREF, follow standard
         naming conventions for your operating system as documented in the
         SAS Companion for your operating system.

DISP   : MVS: This can be OLD, SHR, MOD or H. Use H to leave a data set in
              the allocate table without having it allocated.
       : OS2: This can be blank or H. The concept of exclusive/shared access
              does not appear to exist in the LIBNAME on this OS. Use H to
              leave a data set in the allocate table without having it
              allocated.

Concatenations are not currently possible. Use the KEYS command at the
====> prompt to display function keys settings. The edit window uses
FSVIEW and all documented FSVIEW features (see SAS/FSP Software: Usage and
Reference) can be used. Do not use QUOTES around data set names, and always
use the fully qualified name.

Note that at any stage of your session, you can reinvoke the allocate
panel by typing the command AF C=SASUSER.ALLOCPAN.ALLOCS.PROGRAM on the
command line of any window.

<<< END OF HELP, PRESS  PF3  TO RETURN TO FSVIEW >>>
```

ALLOC.PROGRAM   - SCL program:

```
length libref $ 8 dsname $ 44 disp $ 3 type $ 1 ;

init:
```

```
/* start by turning off STATUS so that legend windows do not
   disappear when code is submitted -- This appears to work
   only under MVS from TS303 onwards */

rc = field('color yellow highlight' ,'saspanel keymess') ;

call execcmdi('zoom off;status off') ;
call wregion(3,40,3,40) ;
call putlegend(1,'Setup In Progress ...','','highlight') ;
call legend('','','','highlight') ;

/* set up the tables needed during the application. The tables
   here are operating system dependent, because the LIBNAME
   statement is NOT system independent */

if symgetc('sysscp') eq 'OS' then do ;
  submit continue ;
  proc format ;
        invalue $type (upcase) 'L','F' = _same_
                          other  = _error_ ;
        invalue $disp (upcase) 'OLD','SHR','MOD','H'=_same_
                          other  = _error_ ;
  run ;
  endsubmit ;
end ;
else if symgetc('sysscp') eq 'OS2' then do ;
  submit continue ;
  proc format ;
        invalue $type (upcase) 'L','F' = _same_
                          other  = _error_ ;
        invalue $disp (upcase) ' ','H'=_same_
                          other  = _error_ ;
  run ;
  endsubmit ;
end ;

/* check if the SAS database containing allocation exists and
   create if not. */

if not exist('sasuser.allocs') then do ;
  call wregion (1,40,3,40) ;
  call putlegend(1,'Creating SASUSER.ALLOCS','','highlight');
  call legend('','','','highlight') ;
  submit continue ;
  data sasuser.allocs ;
    length libref $ 8 dsname $ 44 disp $ 3 type $ 1 ;
    informat type $type. disp $disp. libref $char8. dsname
          $char44. ;
    format type $char1. disp $char3. libref $char8. dsname
          $char44. ;
    stop ;
  run ;
  endsubmit ;
  call endlegend() ;
end ;

/* check whether the unique indexes exist and create them if
   not. These indexes are used to ensure that the user does
   not enter a LIBREF more than once, and also prevents the
```

```
                user allocating a file more than once. If the second check
                is too strict, remove the lines that create the DSNAME index */

        dsid01 = open('sasuser.allocs','v') ;
        if isindex(dsid01,'libref') eq _blank_ then
          rc = icreate(dsid01,'libref','libref','unique') ;
        if isindex(dsid01,'dsname') eq _blank_ then
          rc = icreate(dsid01,'dsname','dsname','unique') ;
        rc = close(dsid01) ;

        /* pop up the fsview table for editing of entries */

        rc = copy('sasuser.allocpan.alloc.keys',
                  'sasuser.profile.fsview.keys ','catalog') ;
        call endlegend() ;
        call wregion(9,1,14,80) ;
        call execcmd(';;autoadd on;sethelp sasuser.allocpan.alloc.help;
                     show id type;autoadd on');
        call fsview('sasuser.allocs(cntllev=member)','edit') ;

        /* fetch the observations that the user wants allocated, ie those
           that do not have disp = H (Hold). Allocate the lib or file
           names, drop a message onscreen for any failures */

        dsid01=open('sasuser.allocs','i');
        call set(dsid01) ;
        do while (fetch(dsid01) ne %sysrc(_SWEOF)) ;
           if upcase(disp) ne "H" then do ;

    /* just allocate those that the user didn't marked as HOLD */

              if symgetc('sysscp') eq 'OS' then do ;
                select(upcase(type)) ; /* do the allocate */
                  when ('L') rc = libname(libref,dsname,'','disp='||disp) ;
                  when ('F') rc = filename(libref,dsname,'',disp) ;
                end ;
              end ;
              else if symgetc('sysscp') eq 'OS2' then do ;
                select(upcase(type)) ; /* do the allocate */
                  when ('L') rc = libname(libref,dsname) ;
                  when ('F') rc = filename(libref,dsname) ;
                end ;
              end ;

              if rc ne 0 then do ; /* assume allocate failed */
                sysmsg = sysmsg() ;
                select(upcase(type)) ;
                  when ('L') put 'LIBNAME -- ' libref ' ' dsname ' ' disp;
                  when ('F') put 'FILENAME -- ' libref ' ' dsname ' ' disp;
                end ;
                put 'ALLOCATION FAILED: RETURN CODE IS ' rc ;
                put 'SYSTEM MESSAGE IS: ' sysmsg ;
              end ;
              else do ; /* assume allocate succeeded */
                select(upcase(type)) ;
                  when ('L') put 'LIBNAME ' dsname ' Allocated As ' libref ;
                  when ('F') put 'FILENAME ' dsname ' Allocated As ' libref;
```

```
              end ;
              put 'DISP= ' disp ;
            end ;
       end;
    end ;
    rc = close(dsid01) ;

    _status_ = 'H' ;
return ;

main:
term:
return ;
```

The screen associated with the above program, seen from the programmer's viewpoint, is
presented in Figure 8.2.

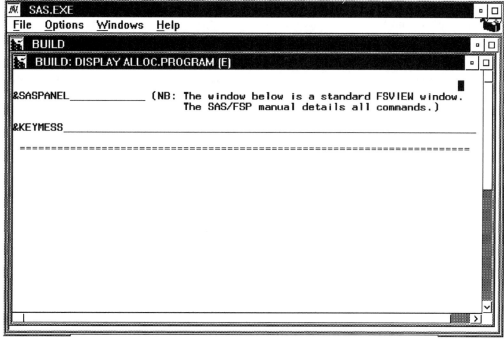

Figure 8.2: SCL Allocations Screen

In Figure 8.2, the fields **saspanel** and **keymess** are both protected, with INITIAL values of 'SAS
ALLOCATIONS PANEL' and 'ENTER KEYS TO VIEW FUNCTION KEY SETTINGS,'
respectively, set in the attributes window.

Note that all work is accomplished in INIT. At the completion of the task, setting _STATUS_ to
"H" terminates the screen. This is needed; otherwise, the SAS/AF screen would remain displayed
after completing the FSVIEW and cause the user to have to end manually. Since a display
window is required, a program screen is necessary here.

To start this screen up, place the following command in your SASEXEC file:

```
dm 'af c=sasuser.allocpan.alloc.program' af ;
```

The entire application resides in your individual SASUSER library, including the file that holds the data set information. That file, SASUSER.ALLOCS, is created automatically if it does not exist any time the AF program is run.

An AF Program To Assist Printing And Browsing Under MVS

This program was developed at Databank to give users of applications a mechanism in the application that would allow them to view or print reports that have been written to an external file.

This mechanism was necessary to prevent users of many applications from having to learn any aspect of the underlying development software. To shelter your own non-technical users from the SAS software print facility and also allow them to browse output before printing, use the screen in Figure 8.3 and carry out the processing described following the screen:

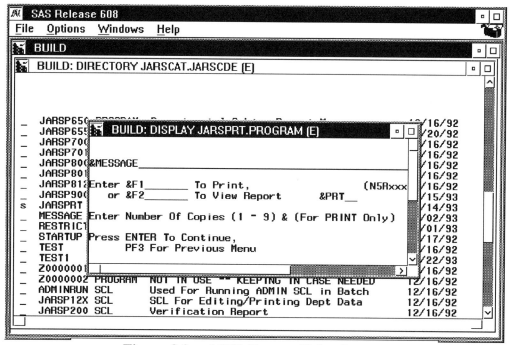

Figure 8.3:   MVS Browse/Print Screen

Note that

- output does not go to the OUTPUT window; instead, PROC PRINTTO, data step FILE statements, or SCL external file routines route output to an external file

- on completion of an online report, a window immediately pops up to allow the user to browse or print the report.

Here is the code behind the entry screen in Figure 8.3:

```
/* PRTREPT. Objective is to give user a screen which controls the
   browsing and printing of output files. */

array mess {*} $ 52 (
          'NOTE: Printing Report -- '
          'ERROR: Please Enter A Valid Printer Id'
          'ERROR: Invalid Number Of Copies'
          'NOTE: Printed Correct, Copies '
          ', At Printer  '
          ' '
          ) ;

entry libref $ 8 memname $ 25 optional=ftype $ 8 ;

init7:
  control always ;
/* initialise fields. The first three (Fx) are set up as screen
   fields so they can be highlit on screen*/
  ftype = upcase(ftype) ;
  if ftype eq _blank_ then ftype = 'PDS' ;
  f1 = 'Printer ID' ;
  f2 = 'Browse    ' ;
  prt    = _blank_      ;
  field5 = 1       ;
  message = mess{1} || memname ;
  rc = field('color yellow highlight','f1 f2 prt message');
  flname = pathname(libref) ;
  if ftype eq 'PDS' then fllibref=libref || '(' || memname || ')' ;
  else fllibref = libref ;
  cursor prt ;
return ;

main:
  message = mess{1} || memname ;
/* create a field with the full data set name, ie inc member*/
  if ftype eq 'PDS' then
    dummy = "'" || flname || '(' || memname || ")'" ;
  else dummy = "'" || flname || "'" ;
  if _status_ ne 'E' then do ;
  select(upcase(prt)) ;

  when('BROWSE') do ;
/* User wants to browse. Uses FSLIST to look at the file */
    call fslist(fllibref) ;
    prt = _blank_ ;
    cursor prt ;
```

```
            return ;
        end ;

        otherwise do ; /* assume print requested */
            if field5 lt '1' | field5 gt '9' then do ;/* bad copies */
              message = mess{3} ;
              cursor field5;
              return ;
            end ;
            else do ; /* print using TSO printoff */
              command = "printoff (" || dummy || ") copies(" ||
                field5 || ") dest(" || prt || ")" ;
              rc=system(command);
              if rc then /* printoff had an error */
                call display('catlg.sasafcde.message.program',
                              'ERROR: Print Off Did Not Work',' ',
                              '---->  Report Error To SAS Support',' '
                             ,'---->   Return Code ' || rc,
                              '---->   File ' || dummy) ;
              else
                message = mess{4} || field5 || mess{5} || prt ;
              cursor prt ;
              return ;
            end ;
        end ;
    end ; * select ;
    end ;
    return ;

term:
  return ;
```

Note the use of a special window in the program entry MESSAGE.PROGRAM for displaying long messages. This is further discussed in the section 'A Window For Displaying Error Conditions' later in this chapter.

Running Long NonInteractive Tasks In The Background

It is not unusual to write an online system that at some point has to carry out some very lengthy task such as a large report. Often it is not desirable to allow that to occur online, particularly if your users are inclined to sit at the terminal waiting for completion.

Discussion here addresses how to write such a task under MVS and OS/2 so that it executes as a background task. This allows the online user either to continue working on the online system or to log off and do some other productive work.

The basic premise here is that it is possible to carry out the task in the background. Some tasks may not fall into this category, so ensure that your application designer checks this. For example, sorting a large file in the background may not be a good idea if your SCL program wants to interact with that file.

The MVS part of this section assumes knowledge of batch jobs, JCL, and job card standards at your site. The non SAS code presented here will not be the same as that at your site, so check SAS procedure names with your system's programmers before attempting to use this code.

Using Background (Batch) Execution Under MVS

SAS under MVS offers two modes of operation. One is the interactive mode, in which users sit at a terminal and interact with the software; the other is noninteractive mode, in which users create a job stream for execution by a background process without further manual intervention.

That background process is called batch processing. In batch processing, you create an environment for SAS to run under and submit the SAS program to the batch system for execution under that environment. From the time of submission, the process is out of your hands; you have no influence over the job batch process except to be able to stop it prematurely.

The 3 parts to a batch process are

- Job cards: Job cards are records in your batch job that identify the job, the owner, the class it will run in, what level of system messages is required, where the job will run (if it is possible to route it to a different processor), which logical processor it will run on (if multiple images exist on a processor), and many other attributes.

- JCL: Job Control Language (JCL) is a means of identifying the files and programs that your batch stream will require. Your JCL will typically identify the program to run (NOTE: in JCL a program is not the code you wrote; rather it is the underlying software that will execute your program, for example, SASHOST), the files that the program requires, the files that your code requires, and the location of your code.

- Your SAS code.

Your objective is to build the SAS code online, then submit it for processing without user intervention. This implies that the online application must also build the job card and the JCL.

Building The Job Card

The easiest way to build a job card is to have the attributes stored already. The main attributes you need stored are a job name and an accounting code (and in some sites a programmer name may also be mandatory). Assume that the job name is the online signon plus extra letters to a maximum of 8 characters. For example, in the JARS application the job name is always set in the SCL to

```
jobname = symgetc('sysjobid') || 'JR' ;
```

as Databank signons are always 6 characters. The 'R' means JARS Report, as all JARS background submitted tasks are long running reports.

In JARS, an account code is stored for each user in a SAS data set as part of the JARS system. This forms the basis of a format called $UIDDEPT, which maps userid to account code. So in SCL, JARS uses the following code to build a jobcard:

```
user    = symgetc('sysjobid') ;
jobname = user || 'JR' ;
acctcode= put(user,$uiddept.) ;
jobcard1= "//" || jobname || "JOB (" || acctcode || ")" ||
          ",'JARS REPORTS',MSGCLASS=2,CLASS=L," ;
jobcard2= "// NOTIFY=" || user ;
```

Alternatively, you could find the account code by opening a file containing account codes and searching for the appropriate one.

The SCL variable **jobcard2** is used, as it is not possible to fit the whole jobname on one line. In the above, the MSGCLASS, CLASS, and NOTIFY JCL parameters will be site dependent. Assuming you can create $UIDDEPT as a mapping of signon to account code, the rest of the above can stay as is (it also assumes signon is 6 or less characters).

Building The JCL

With the jobcard(s) built, you now need to build the JCL that will be controlling the job. This is totally site dependent. You will need to consider whether to use existing procedures or in-stream JCL for file definitions. The following uses a prewritten procedure. That procedure (JARSRPT) sets up all required file definitions so they will not appear in the JCL.

JARSRPT is nothing more than the usual SAS catalogued procedure that you would use to run SAS jobs in batch, but with additional allocations that are specific to the JARS system. You can use your site's standard SAS JCL procedure here.

Use of the prewritten procedure makes the JCL very simple. Only two lines are required:

```
jobcard3= "//JARSRPT EXEC JARSRPT" ;
jobcard4= "//SYSIN   DD *" ;
```

These two lines will tell MVS that the JCL is in the procedure called JARSRPT (which means it must be in the default procedure search libraries) and that the source code (defined by LIBREF SYSIN) will be following the SYSIN DD * line.

The simplest possible way to build the JCL (and experience shows that simple is usually best) is to have the SAS code stored in an external macro. In JARS, all the reports are macros. Thus, to initiate a report it is necessary only to set up the macro name in the job stream. Using a macro is often better than %INCLUDE, as a macro allows us to use macro statements to omit parts of the source code if user-entered parameters do not need them.

Preparing The Job Stream For SUBMITTING

Given that all the JCL is now set up, and some means of inserting SAS code exists (maybe by a macro), you need to create a file as a temporary holding area for the JCL and SAS code. To do this, create a temporary file using the following code:

```
/* we need a temporary TSO file to hold code to submit */
  rc = filename('tempout','&tmpout','',
       'new space=(trk,10) lrecl=80 unit=disk');
```

Now you can populate that temporary file with our JCL and SAS code. The SCL to do this follows:

```
/* create JCL for the file to be submitted */
  fid = fopen('tempout','O') ;
  rc  = fput(fid,jobcard1) ; rc = fwrite(fid) ;
  rc  = fput(fid,jobcard2) ; rc = fwrite(fid) ;
  rc  = fput(fid,jobcard3) ; rc = fwrite(fid) ;
  rc  = fput(fid,jobcard4) ; rc = fwrite(fid) ;
  rc  = fput(fid,'%include source(common);'); rc = fwrite(fid) ;
  rc  = fclose(fid) ;
```

This example is from JARS. In that application, SAS code must always be called when a request to use JARS libraries is requested. That is the SAS code in the SOURCE(COMMON) member. Hence it is written straight to the external file for execution by the batch job.

Now the job card, JCL, and some prerequisite SAS code are all written out. All you need to do is write out the SAS code that you wish to have executed in the batch job. In general, this is application dependent. You may or may not have parameters that the user entered on screen. If you have no parameters and the SAS code exists as a macro in an automatic macro library, just add the following to the above code before the FCLOSE:

```
  rc  = fput(fid,'%<macro name>;'); rc = fwrite(fid) ;
```

Parameters entered on screen are a different proposition. In general, each application handles these according to the application design. In JARS, screen parameters aimed at becoming batch code are written to the external file as macro variables, and the SAS program that will be executed is coded to look for those macro variables.

Assuming the above code with the FPUT statement is in the screen that the user entered the parameters for the report in, that SCL code gets the batch stream into a submittable form. The following is not a JARS report, but it is sufficient to show the mechanisms required.

Suppose you had to enter a month on screen. It is stored in the SCL variable **month**. Use the following submitted code to write it to the temporary data set with fileref TEMPOUT:

```
  submit continue ;
  data _null_ ;
    file tempout mod;
    put '%let month = ' &month ';' ;
```

```
      put '%<macro name>' ;
      stop ;
   run ;
endsubmit ;
```

The TEMPOUT data set now contains everything that the batch job requires. To submit the job from within the SCL to the batch processor, you need the following code:

```
/* now submit the temp TSO file to batch */
  dsname = pathname('tempout') ;
  rc = system('submit(' || dsname || ')') ;
/* de allocate the temporary file and return */
  rc= filename('tempout','') ;
```

The above looks quite complex. In effect, the real complexity is ensuring that everything is done; the above mechanism for running in batch is simple when clearly understood. Be aware, though, that the way you place the SAS code into the TEMPOUT file is application dependent, and the above use of macros and DATA steps may not always be the best solution.

Starting Multiple SAS Executions Under OS/2

This section assumes no knowledge of anything except SAS. OS/2 is not burdened to any great extent with such intricacies as JCL and job cards, so it is much simpler than the MVS example. However (there is always a 'however'), as your OS/2 configuration gets more complex, so will background running. For instance, the discussion in this section assumes a single-user OS/2 system. Add on a network and the situation becomes somewhat different.

Assuming a single user system, you do not need to consider such intricacies as who is submitting a job (in other words, signons). However if your site uses signons to OS/2, it is simple to add this support on.

As a first attribute to check, ensure that both your system memory and swapper space will support multiple versions of SAS software executing.

You must maintain the integrity of the work files in each SAS session. Ensure that the background process triggered from within the main SAS session will use a different WORK space from the main session (and from any other sessions in use). This is done using the SAS-WORK option.

Assuming the code to be executed in the background has been written to an external file containing SAS code (as in the MVS example above), execute the following SAS statements from your SCL in your SAS session:

```
program = <file containing your SAS code> ;
rc=system('start sas ' || program || ' -work e:\saswork -icon');
```

or alternatively,

```
program = <file containing your SAS code> ;
rc=system('detach sas ' || program || ' -work e:\saswork -icon');
```

To the user, there is little noticeable difference in each of these methods (START versus DETACH); however, the START statement in OS/2 uses more resources than DETACH.

A Macro For Reducing Code In SCL Data Checks

Many input data checks in SCL follow this general layout and optionally issue a RETURN to prevent further processing:

- a comparison with a valid set of values
- errors switched on for a field(s) if invalid
- an error message

In order to reduce the amount of code in applications, I decided to reduce the above layout to a macro that could be called any time a check of input data was necessary. The macro has the following advantages over coding each check:

- reduces code
- provides identical layout for each check, making maintenance simpler
- simplifies error checking as only macro parameters can be at fault when code fails in testing
- eases the coding task

It was decided to use a macro rather than a method, as the macro parameters are resolved at SCL compile time and the code that results is compiled into the program. It is necessary to issue SCL comparison conditions via macro parameters, so a method could not easily be used.

An example of the sort of code that is replaceable by a macro follows. In this code there are three validity tests. (Note that this code is used in a case study on the CONTROL LABEL feature in Chapter 9 of this text.)

```
MAIN:
   /* ensure messages from last time through SCL
      are not still around */
   if errorfld eq ' ' then call wname(' ');

   /* check field1 */
   if field1=' ' then do ;
```

```
      if errorfld ge ' ' then do ;
        call wname('Enter A Value For FIELD1');
        errorfld = 'FIELD1' ;
      end ;
      erroron field1 ;
    end ;

  /* check FIELD2 */
  if field2=' ' then do ;
    if errorfld ne 'FIELD1' then do ;
      call wname('Enter A Value For FIELD2');
      errorfld = 'FIELD2' ;
    end ;
    erroron field2 ;
  end ;

  /* check FIELD3 */
  if field3=' ' then do ;
    if errorfld not in  ('FIELD1' 'FIELD2')
    then do ;
      call wname('Enter A Value For FIELD3');
      errorfld = 'FIELD3' ;
    end ;
    erroron field3 ;
  end ;

/* position cursor */
  if errorfld ne ' ' then rc = field('cursor',errorfld) ;
  else home ;
  errorfld = ' ';
return ;

field1:
   if putc(field1,'$field1.') eq '0' then do ;
    if errorfld = ' ' then do ;
      call wname('Invalid Value For FIELD1') ;
      errorfld = 'FIELD1' ;
    end ;
    erroron field1 ;
  end ;
  else erroroff field1 ;
return ;

field2:
  if putc(field2,'$field2.') eq '0' then do ;
    if errorfld = ' ' then do ;
      call wname('Invalid Value For FIELD2') ;
      errorfld = 'FIELD2' ;
    end ;
    erroron field2 ;
  end ;
  else erroroff field2 ;
return ;

field3:
  if putc(field3,'$field3.') eq '0' then do ;
    if errorfld = ' ' then do ;
      call wname('Invalid Value For FIELD3') ;
      errorfld = 'FIELD3' ;
```

```
        end ;
        erroron field3 ;
      end ;
    else erroroff field3 ;
  return ;
```

In the above code, the **errorfld** variable is used to flag which field is in error and also to determine whether to issue a message or not when another field is found in error. If a message is already issued, you usually do not want to overwrite it with a subsequent error message, so checking if a field is already in error using **errorfld** also allows you to decide whether to issue the message.

Note that after all possible errors are checked, the cursor position is set as the value of **errorfld**, and **errorfld** is blanked.

The preceding code follows the layout for replacement by a macro exactly. Each condition contains

- a comparison with a valid set of values
- errors switched on for a field(s) if invalid
- an error message

The code is easily translated to a macro as follows:

```
%macro checkent(field, /* field to use in comparison */
                field2,/* field(s) to place in error    */
                op1,   /* comparison operator */
                compare1, /* comparison values */
                op2,      /* ERRORFLD comparison */
                compare2, /* Field to compare with ERRORFLD */
                message,  /* message to issue */
                erroff=N, /* optional switch off errors */
                return=N  /* optional issue a return */
               );

  if &field &op1 &compare1 then do ;
    if errorfld &op2 &compare2 then do ;
      call wname(&message);
      errorfld = "&field2" ;
    end ;
    erroron &field2 ;
  end ;
  %if &erroff ne N %then %do ;
  else erroroff &field2 ;
  %end ;
  %if &return ne N %then %do ;
   return ;
  %end ;

%mend checkent ;
```

Now the SCL program can be replaced with macro calls:

```
MAIN:
  if errorfld eq ' ' then message = ' ';

  /* check field1 */
  %checkent(field1 , field1, = , ' ' , ge , ' ' ,
        'Enter A Value For FIELD1') ;

  /* check FIELD2 */
  %checkent(field2 ,field2, = , ' ', ne , 'FIELD1' ,
        'Enter A Value For FIELD2') ;

  /* check FIELD3 */
  %checkent(field3 , field3, = , ' ', not in ,
                ('FIELD1' 'FIELD2') ,
        'Enter A Value For FIELD3') ;

/* position cursor */
  if errorfld ne ' ' then rc = field('cursor',errorfld) ;
  else home ;
  errorfld = ' ';
return ;

field1:
  %checkent(putc(field1,'$field1.'), field1, = , '0' ,
        = , ' ','Invalid Entry For Field1',
        erroff = Y)
return ;

field2:
  %checkent(putc(field2,'$field2.'), field2, = , '0' ,
        = , ' ','Invalid Entry For Field2',
        erroff = Y)
return ;

field3:
  %checkent(putc(field3,'$field3.'), field3 , = , '0' ,
        = , ' ','Invalid Entry For Field3',
        erroff = Y)
return ;
```

What the macro has done here is reduced the size and verbosity of the SCL program, plus provided a flexible and easy means of carrying out any SCL test satisfying the above format.

Note how the macro can be used on all the comparisons above. Although the first parameter is documented as a field name, there is no reason why an expression should not be used. This is illustrated in the labeled sections, when a PUTC function is used to compare a computed value with a value.

Here are some other examples of how the above macro can reduce code:

(1)

```
if putc(field3,'$field3.') not in ('1','2','3') then do ;
  if errorfld = ' ' then do ;
    call wname('Invalid Value For FIELD3') ;
    errorfld = 'FIELD3' ;
  end ;
  erroron field3 ;
end ;
else erroroff field3 ;
```

reduces to

```
%checkent(putc(field3,'$field3.'),field3, not in , ('1','2','3') ,
         = , ' ','Invalid Entry For Field3',
         erroff = Y)
```

(2)

```
if putc(field3,'$field3.') ne putc(field1,'$field1.')
  then do ;
  if errorfld = ' ' then do ;
    call wname('Invalid Value For FIELD3') ;
    errorfld = 'FIELD3' ;
  end ;
  erroron field3 ;
end ;
```

reduces to

```
%checkent(putc(field3,'$field3.'),field3, ne ,
         putc(field1,'$field1.',
         = , ' ','Invalid Entry For Field3'
         )
```

(3)

```
if putc(field3,'$field3.') eq 'X' AND
  field1 not in ('A' 'B')
    then do ;
    if errorfld = ' ' then do ;
      call wname('Invalid Value For FIELD3') ;
      errorfld = 'FIELD3' ;
    end ;
    erroron field3 ;
    return ;
  end ;
```

reduces to

```
%checkent(putc(field3,'$field3.') eq 'X' and field1 not in ('A' 'B')
         ,field3, , ,
         = , ' ','Invalid Entry For Field3',
         return = Y
         )
```

These examples will suffice to indicate how the macro is used. You could not use a method as it would not be possible to include the checks defined by parameters 1, 3 and 4; they are SCL code that must be known at compile time. Note that example 3 extends the macro somewhat and shows how it can be used to generate code for complex expressions that at first glance may not be able to be included under the macro.

A Window For Displaying Error Conditions

Frequently, application design dictates how system messages should be identified and displayed to the user. This text has already discussed how to replace error messages issued by SAS with customized messages. This is generally done when the messages from SAS may be meaningless or too verbose for your user base.

Often, even though you attempt to give the user base short meaningful messages, some form of error may have occurred that requires you to issue a more verbose message. Perhaps you have discovered some form of internal error (for example, a missing system library) that you desire your user base to report for action by support staff.

It becomes quickly apparent that the SAS message area and other (up to) 80 byte fields are inadequate for reporting certain messages. If you want to issue long error messages, perhaps detailing action to take, it is simple to set up a screen for this purpose.

This screen is called MESSAGE.PROGRAM, shown in Figure 8.4 from the programmer's viewpoint. It has two functions:

- to tell a user what error condition has arisen, complete with details of what the user should do
- to stop the SAS session (you may want to alter this in your application)

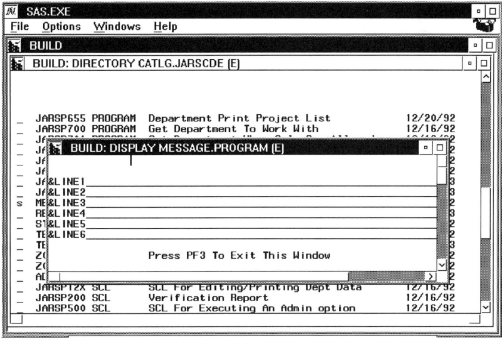

Figure 8.4: Screen For Displaying Multiple Messages

The SCL code and the screen are simple. How you use the screen (in Figure 8.4) is up to you; the messages to be placed onscreen are totally application dependent. On this screen, each of the six fields is centered and protected.

The code behind the entry is very small and simple. However, you can code as you desire to cause some action other than ENDSAS to occur:

```
entry line1 line2 line3 line4 line5 line6 $ ;
init:
  control always ;
return;

main:
  call execcmdi('endsas') ;
return ;

term:
return ;
```

An example of how this screen appears in use follows in Figure 8.5 A programmer has coded a check for a list create from a file failing. If such a failure is detected, the programmer assigns values to fields called LINE1 to LINE6, then calls the message program above. The program is designed to terminate SAS when the user presses ENTER, so the message contains information telling the user what to do and what to report to a support team.

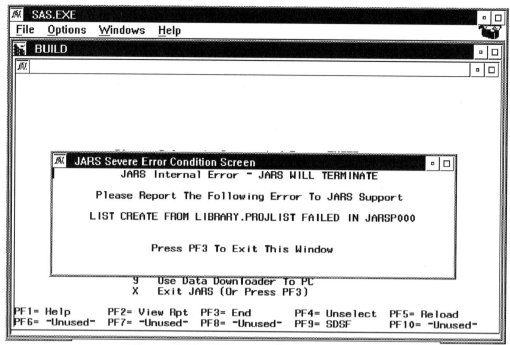

Figure 8.5:   Message Screen Example

Saving And Restoring Values of SAS Options

Many texts discuss the concept of 'pushing' and 'popping' data elements. A push copies the value of some data element to a temporary holding area, often called a stack. Usually, you push a value immediately before changing its value, with a view to later restoring (popping) the value. Essentially, you are saving a value that is required later, changing it, and using the changed value, then recovering the original value for continuing processing.

I have often wanted to change the value of a SAS option and then restore it later. This has usually meant using PROC OPTIONS to find the current status, changing the option, and later manually changing it back. SCL can automate this process and remove the need to use PROC OPTIONS.

Suppose you have a DATA step that you know in advance will produce more than 20 errors. By default, SAS software only prints 20 observations in error. If you want to print more errors, you can use the SAS options statement to increase the number. This is fairly easy because you already know that SAS will have the value 20 by default. But what about when you want to process some option that you do not know the value of in advance?

Consider the OBS option. If this has been set in an application, it may be quite difficult to determine what the value is at some point. You would have to use PROC OPTIONS, but that is often inappropriate because to change the option, you would have to halt the program, change the code, and then restart the program.

What is required is some means of finding the current value of an option, storing it, then changing it, carrying out processing with the changed option, and then restoring the option value -- without having to stop the application to run PROC OPTIONS at any stage.

This is an excellent example of how SCL can be used to add functionality to the base SAS System. One way you can accomplish the above task is to take the following steps:

1. create a list to hold the option value
2. pass the option name to an SCL program
3. read the current value of the option
4. store the option in the list
5. ensure the list will be available later in the session
6. change the option value
7. when finished with the option value, change it back.

You require 2 SCL programs and 2 macros. The macros are the users' interfaces with the SCL programs. When users want to push a value, they will code

```
%push_opt(option_name)
```

Users can then change the option, for example

```
options obs=78 ;
```

and carry out the processing they desire with that OBS value. Later in the program, when they want the pushed value of OBS back, they code

```
%pop_opt(option_name)
```

The macros push_opt and pop_opt are very simple. They merely initiate the SCL program. To do this, the macros do no more than the following

```
%macro push_opt(opt_name) ;
    proc display c=libref.catname.pushopt.scl batch; run ;
%mend push_opt ;
```

and

```
%macro pop_opt(opt_name) ;
   proc display c=libref.catname.popopt.scl batch; run ;
%mend pop_opt ;
```

You need to code the SCL programs in pushopt.scl and popopt.scl. The basic concepts are simple and accomplished by the following two programs.

PUSHOPT.SCL

```
init:

  opt_name = symgetc('opt_name') ;

  if exist('work.options.pushopt.slist') then do ;
    push_opt_list = makelist() ;
    rc = fillist('CATALOG','work.options.pushopt.slist',
                  push_opt_list) ;
    put 'Status Of Pushed Options At Start Of Push Operation' ;
    call putlist(push_opt_list) ;
  end ;
  else push_opt_list = makelist() ;

  /* assume character */
  c_optval = optgetc(opt_name) ;

  if sysmsg() eq _blank_ then do ;  /* good assumption */

   /* insert this item at the end of the list */
     push_opt_list = insertc(push_opt_list,c_optval,-1,opt_name);

   /* save the list back to the SLIST entry */
     rc = savelist('CATALOG','work.options.pushopt.slist',
                  push_opt_list) ;
     put 'Status Of Pushed Options At End Of Char Push Operation' ;
     call putlist(push_opt_list) ;

   /* finished -- delete the list and return */
     rc = dellist(push_opt_list) ;

     return ;
  end ;

  /* assume numeric */
  n_optval = optgetn(opt_name) ;

  if sysmsg() eq _blank_ then do ; /* good assumption */

   /* insert this item at the end of the list */
     push_opt_list = insertn(push_opt_list,n_optval,-1,opt_name);

   /* save the list back to the SLIST entry if option change ok */
     rc = savelist('CATALOG','work.options.pushopt.slist',
                  push_opt_list) ;
     put 'Status Of Pushed Options At End Of Numeric Push Operation' ;
     call putlist(push_opt_list) ;
```

```
            /* finished -- delete the list and return */
              rc = dellist(push_opt_list) ;

              return ;
          end ;

        /* option was not recognized */

        put 'ERROR: Invalid Option ' opt_name ' Was Passed To Push_Opt' ;
    return ;
```

POPOPT.SCL

```
    init:

      opt_name = symgetc('opt_name') ;

    /* make sure something has been pushed; otherwise we cannot pop
        anything */

      if exist('work.options.pushopt.slist') then do ;
        pop_opt_list = makelist() ;
        rc = fillist('CATALOG','work.options.pushopt.slist',
                    pop_opt_list) ;
        put 'Status Of Pushed Options At Start' ;
        call putlist(pop_opt_list) ;
      end ;
      else do ;
        put 'ERROR: Cannot POP Options As No Pushed Options Exist' ;
        return ;
      end ;

    /* find the option name in the list */
    /* note : start from the end as the list is a last in first out
                queue */
      position = nameditem(pop_opt_list,opt_name,1,-1) ;

    /* return if option not in pushed list */
      if position eq 0 then do ;
        put 'ERROR: Cannot POP An Option That has Not Been Pushed' ;
        return ;
      end ;

    /* fetch the list value */
    /* assume character */
      if itemtype(pop_opt_list,position) eq 'C' then do ;
        c_optval = getitemc(pop_opt_list,position) ;
        if optsetc(opt_name,c_optval) eq 0 then do ;
          link clearopt ;
          return ;
        end ;
      end ;

    /* must be numeric */
      else do ;
        n_optval = getitemn(pop_opt_list,position) ;
        if optsetn(opt_name,n_optval) eq 0 then do ;
          link clearopt ;
```

```
        return ;
      end ;
    end ;

  /* if got to here then for some reason nothing got set */
    put 'ERROR: Unspecified Error Popping Option ' _all_ ;

  return ;

  clearopt:

  /* clean up the list after restoring an option */
    rc = delitem(pop_opt_list,position) ;

  /* save the list back to the SLIST entry */
    rc = savelist('CATALOG','work.options.pushopt.slist',
                  pop_opt_list) ;
    put 'Status Of Pushed Options At End' ;
    call putlist(pop_opt_list) ;

  /* finished -- delete the list and return */
    rc = dellist(pop_opt_list) ;

  return ;
```

The use of the list structure here has some unexpected benefits. First, if you are used to stacks, you have most likely encountered LAST IN FIRST OUT (LIFO) stacks. This is a rigid structure that forces the most recent addition to the stack to have to be the next element removed (popped) from the stack. It is also a very common stack structure for push/pop type operations. Since the list structure allows searching for elements and deletion of elements, this type of construct is not forced upon us. You effectively have a structure in which no controls are placed on the in/out order. This would enable you to issue code like the following successfully:

```
%push_opt(obs)
options obs=400 ;
... SAS code ...
%push_opt(error) ;
options error=50 ;
... SAS code ...
%pop_opt(obs)
... SAS code ...
%pop_opt(error)
```

The list structure is not retained through the whole application in memory, but utilizes the WORK libref instead. Lists are retained in SAS software during an AF session, but this application actually stops the AF session (which is just the PUSH or POP SCL program). Hence you cannot store the list in memory throughout the SAS session and must rely on disk storage to store the list between macro calls.

Since PROC DISPLAY is used, and this application has no reliance upon windows, the macros can be called in batch. This is an interesting paradox: Screen Control Language has already in its short life span evolved past being a purely *screen* control language!

The push/pop macros have been verified in Release 6.08 under OS/2.

Making Views Easier To Create In SAS/ACCESS Software

A recent need to create a number of similar views resulted in this small utility. I needed a quick means of copying a view to another view in the same library. The views were all very similar, usually with just one or two variables different.

Initially, I used PROC COPY to move the desired view to the WORK library, then renamed the view in WORK to the desired name. Then I used PROC COPY again to move the newly named view back to the library I wanted the copy in.

This process is very unwieldy. The following macro is a much simpler way to copy views to another name in the same libref.

```
%macro cview(fromname , toname) ;

proc display c=sasuser.utility.cview.scl ; run ;

%mend ;
```

This executes the following SCL:

CVIEW.SCL

```
length x $200 ;

init:
  rc = copy(symget('fromname') , symget('toname') , 'view') ;
  if rc then do ;
    x = sysmsg() ;
    put 'VIEW Copy returned non zero return code - ' rc ;
    put 'Message Is: ' ;
    put x ;
  end ;
return ;
```

This simple program relies on the ability of the COPY function to copy a file to the *same* libref and simultaneously change the name. PROC COPY cannot do this; it has to copy to a different libref. This simplified our use of views, as an easily constructed macro call accomplished the task of copying the view.

Note that while the ACCESS window is open, this program will not work. You need to ensure the ACCESS window is closed to use this utility.

Chapter 9: Undocumented Features Of Some Commands And Functions

Contents

Overview

This chapter describes some little known features of SCL that have not been documented by SAS Institute (or that may have limited distribution via usage notes). In general, all the discussion in this chapter has been verified under Releases 6.07 and 6.08. Note though, the comments in here may relate to design issues that are the prerogative of SAS Institute and may change in future releases.

The CONTROL Statement

CONTROL LABEL

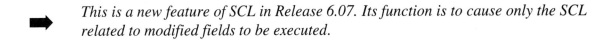

This is a new feature of SCL in Release 6.07. Its function is to cause only the SCL related to modified fields to be executed.

In Release 6.06 SCL in the main section was executed, and you had to use conditional statements to prevent sections from being executed. This was often desirable when a field was not modified.

Now in Release 6.07, by placing the statement CONTROL LABEL in the INIT section of an AF or FSP application using SCL, you cause SCL processing to undergo a major change in execution order.

The LABEL option causes SCL to first look for sections of code relating to modified window fields. These sections, identified by a label having the same name as the window variable, are executed only for modified fields that have no attribute errors. Execution occurs before MAIN. Compare this process to Release 6.06, where execution was always carried out in MAIN, and to bypass redundant code you had to explicitly seek nonmodified fields and branch around SCL code relating to them.

The big advantages of CONTROL LABEL are modularity, readability, and efficiency. Because programs can be built in modules that relate to fields, program structure is clear and code is only carried out when necessary.

There are some additional considerations you need to keep in mind when using labeled sections.

The order of processing is that all labeled sections get carried out in the order the fields appear on screen, but this rule only applies to labels that have the associated window field modified. Then MAIN is processed.

This means added difficulty in carrying out tasks that need to be carried out before field checks. Tasks such as initializing message fields or globally switching off field errors at the start of MAIN have no meaning because they may undo work done in a labeled section.

Some checking still has to be done in MAIN; for example, ensuring that a field is filled in and issuing an error if it is not must be done in MAIN. This is because the field has not been modified, so the labeled section cannot be executed.

If you have a number of labeled sections and one switches errors on for a field, you cannot bypass checking of all other fields. This differs from checking in MAIN, where you can issue a RETURN immediately if a field is in error, thus forcing the user to correct that field before continuing. Labeled sections will always be executed if the corresponding field was modified unless you place a CALL GOTO command in a labeled section. Coding CONTROL NOLABEL inside a labeled section switches off labels, but only **after** all labels have executed as required in this execution of the SCL.

Undocumented Feature

In Release 6.07, labeled sections of code under FSEDIT *will* be executed if a field is not modified, but the MAIN or some other section switches ERRORON for the window variable. Thus it is possible to carry out a cross-check on 2 fields, find an inconsistency, and switch errors on for both fields. When the user corrects one field, the labeled section for the other is executed, even though it was not modified.

Example Using CONTROL LABEL in FSEDIT

Suppose that a file is to be updated using FSEDIT. On screen and available for user update are 3 character fields. For simplicity's sake, let's call these **field1** to **field3**. All fields are blank on entry.

All fields must be filled in. Failure to do so should generate an error on the first empty field with an appropriate message. The other empty fields are to be highlighted.

All fields undergo further validation to ensure that the value entered is an element of the corresponding format $FIELDx. $FIELDx is structured so that valid values are set to '1' and invalid to '0' after applying the format. The PROC FORMAT code used to create each $FIELDx is similar to the following code:

```
proc format ;
  value $field1 'F00000','F00899' = '1'
                other             = '0' ;
run ;
```

The other fields follow a similar structure, although with different values. Thus for **field1**, the only valid values in the example are 'F00000' and 'F00899'.

The essence of the situation is to check each field in turn and switch ERRORON if the field is in error. On return the cursor should be positioned on the first field in error, and the message is for the first field in error.

Code Without CONTROL LABEL

When you do not use CONTROL LABEL, the following code is required:

```
MAIN:
  message = ' ' ;
  errorfld = ' ';
  /* check field1 */
  if field1=' ' then do ;
    if errorfld = ' ' then do ;
      message='Enter A Value For FIELD1';
      errorfld = 'FIELD1' ;
    end ;
    erroron field1 ;
  end ;
  if putc(field1,'$field1.') eq '0' then do ;
    if errorfld = ' ' then do ;
      message = 'Invalid Value For FIELD1' ;
      errorfld = 'FIELD1' ;
    end ;
    erroron field1 ;
  end ;

  /* check FIELD2 */
  if field2=' ' then do ;
    if errorfld = ' ' then do ;
      message='Enter A Value For FIELD2';
```

```
         errorfld = 'FIELD2' ;
       end ;
     erroron field2 ;
   end ;
   if putc(field2,'$field2.') eq '0' then do ;
     if errorfld = ' ' then do ;
       message = 'Invalid Value For FIELD2' ;
       errorfld = 'FIELD2' ;
     end ;
     erroron field2 ;
   end ;

   /* check FIELD3 */
   if field3=' ' then do ;
     if errorfld = ' ' then do ;
       message='Enter A Value For FIELD3';
       errorfld = 'FIELD3' ;
     end ;
     erroron field3 ;
   end ;
   if putc(field3,'$field3.') eq '0' then do ;
     if errorfld = ' ' then do ;
       message = 'Invalid Value For FIELD3' ;
       errorfld = 'FIELD3' ;
     end ;
     erroron field3 ;
   end ;
 /* position cursor */
   if errorfld ne ' ' then rc =
          field('cursor',errorfld) ;
   else home ;
 return ;
```

Note the use of the SCL variable **errorfld**. This variable does not appear on screen. It is required to hold the name of the first field that is in error. It is used for two reasons:

- because under FSEDIT the ERRORON statement also repositions the cursor
- to ensure that the message field only gets filled with the first error message.

If ERRORON is triggered for all fields in error, the cursor appears on the *last* field, whereas it is required on the first.

In the **errorfld** variable, store the name of the first field in error, and later use the FIELD function to place the cursor where required just before returning to the FSEDIT window. The value of **errorfld** will be the variable name that the cursor is placed on.

Code With CONTROL LABEL

The program changes considerably when CONTROL LABEL is used. The first attempt to code this is as follows:

```
MAIN:
  /* check field1 */
  if field1=' ' then do ;
    if errorfld = ' ' then do ;
      message='Enter A Value For FIELD1';
      errorfld = 'FIELD1' ;
    end ;
    erroron field1 ;
  end ;

  /* check FIELD2 */
  if field2=' ' then do ;
    if errorfld = ' ' then do ;
      message='Enter A Value For FIELD2';
      errorfld = 'FIELD2' ;
    end ;
    erroron field2 ;
  end ;
  /* check FIELD3 */
  if field3=' ' then do ;
    if errorfld = ' ' then do ;
      message='Enter A Value For FIELD3';
      errorfld = 'FIELD3' ;
    end ;
    erroron field3 ;
  end ;
/* position cursor */
  if errorfld eq ' ' then message = ' ';
  if errorfld ne ' ' then rc =
        field('cursor',errorfld) ;
  else home ;
return ;

field1:
    if putc(field1,'$field1.') eq '0' then do ;
    if errorfld = ' ' then do ;
      message = 'Invalid Value For FIELD1' ;
      errorfld = 'FIELD1' ;
    end ;
    erroron field1 ;
  end ;
  else erroroff field1 ;
return ;

field2:
  if putc(field2,'$field2.') eq '0' then do ;
    if errorfld = ' ' then do ;
      message = 'Invalid Value For FIELD2' ;
      errorfld = 'FIELD2' ;
    end ;
    erroron field2 ;
  end ;
```

```
      else erroroff field2 ;
  return ;

  field3:
    if putc(field3,'$field3.') eq '0' then do ;
      if errorfld = ' ' then do ;
        message = 'Invalid Value For FIELD3' ;
        errorfld = 'FIELD3' ;
      end ;
      erroron field3 ;
    end ;
    else erroroff field3 ;
  return ;
```

As the program stands, it will not operate exactly as the first program did. It is not necessarily the case that moving all code relating to modified fields from MAIN to a labeled section will provide the same functionality.

The first difference is that in the early code, you could place statements at the start of MAIN and have those statements carried out every time SCL checking ran. But using CONTROL LABEL, there is just nowhere to place these statements because it is not possible to tell at the time of coding which labeled section, if any, will be carried out.

Because you do not have information about the first section that will be executed, you cannot easily code initialization of the **errorfld** and **message** variables. They cannot be placed in the labeled section for **field1** because it is not possible to guarantee that the section will be executed. It is pointless to place these initializations in each labeled section because each section would undo the work done by another section.

The whole purpose of **errorfld** is to ensure that the cursor is positioned correctly and that the **message** field contains a message for the first field in error. It has finished its usefulness after the cursor placement; so it can be reset to blank when that is accomplished. Just place the statement

```
ERRORFLD = ' ';
```

immediately before the RETURN in MAIN.

Difficulties With Blank Fields

Consider the situation where **field1** is left blank and **field2** is entered incorrectly. In Release 6.06, this was not a problem as the processing in MAIN would have set **errorfld** to 'FIELD1' on the first check.

In Release 6.07, using labeled sections that first check from MAIN becomes potentially the fourth check as the labeled sections are executed first. There is no way to force MAIN to execute prior to the labeled sections if fields are modified.

If **field2** is filled out incorrectly and **field1** is left blank, the labeled section for **field2** will be the first code executed and will set **errorfld** to 'FIELD2'. The check in MAIN that **field1** is filled in is carried out later and the ERRORON flag set for **field1,** but the error message and the cursor placement will both be for **field2**. This violates the requirements that the first field in error be highlighted and the cursor placed on it with an appropriate message. The entry field **field1** is in error as it has been left blank.

It would appear that there is nothing you can do to avoid this situation without changing the logic. It is necessary to reconsider the entire way that the SCL is written. In short, do not expect that code developed without labeled sections (namely, code in Release 6.06) will convert to a situation that uses labeled sections (as in Release 6.07) and provide the identical functionality.

The rewritten code for MAIN is as follows. Here advantage is taken of the fact that **field1** messages are always to appear before **field2** and **field3**, and **field2** messages before **field3**. The code for MAIN follows; the labeled sections do not change:

```
MAIN:
  /* ensure messages from last time through SCL
     are not still hanging around */
  if errorfld eq ' ' then message = ' ';

  /* check field1 */
  if field1=' ' then do ;
    if errorfld ge ' ' then do ;
      message='Enter A Value For FIELD1';
      errorfld = 'FIELD1' ;
    end ;
    erroron field1 ;
  end ;

  /* check FIELD2 */
  if field2=' ' then do ;
    if errorfld ne 'FIELD1' then do ;
      message='Enter A Value For FIELD2';
      errorfld = 'FIELD2' ;
    end ;
    erroron field2 ;
  end ;

  /* check FIELD3 */
  if field3=' ' then do ;
    if errorfld not in  ('FIELD1' 'FIELD2')
    then do ;
      message='Enter A Value For FIELD3';
      errorfld = 'FIELD3' ;
    end ;
    erroron field3 ;
  end ;

/* position cursor */
  if errorfld ne ' ' then rc =
        field('cursor',errorfld) ;
  else home ;
  errorfld = ' ';
return ;
```

The logic has changed quite considerably here. A missing value in **field1** will overwrite the **message** and **errorfld** variables. This simulates the situation in the program without CONTROL LABEL. Further, if **field2** is missing, **message** and **errorfld** can be assigned values relating to **field2**, providing that **field1** is not already in error. The variables **message** and **errorfld** can be assigned values relating to **field3**, providing that neither **field1** nor **field2** is already in error.

The technique works well, but it really has the tradeoff that as the number of fields being checked in MAIN increases, so does the code. Think about how MAIN would look if our situation had 50, 100, 400, or more fields rather than 3. These issues can be got around by using array or list operations, but are messy and complex. The %CHECKENT macro (discussed in chapter 8) could also be used to cut down code, but would still be difficult to read.

Consider again the situation that **field1** is left blank and **field2** is filled in incorrectly. The above code now correctly highlights both fields, placing the cursor on **field1** and issuing a message appropriate to **field1**.

But further, because the labeled section is executed when ERRORON is in effect, the labeled section for **field2** will be executed next time the user presses ENTER, irrespective of whether the user has modified **field2**. That undocumented feature is really useful, as it ensures correct messages and cursor settings in the above situation. Without that, if **field2** was still invalid and the user did not type over it, the labeled section would not execute. The reason is that labeled sections only execute if the field is modified, and for this execution of the SCL **field2** is not modified.

The DATALISTx Functions

Using The DATALISTx Functions

Discussion in this section relates to the DATALISTN and DATALISTC functions. I have used DATALISTC in examples, but the discussion applies equally to DATALISTN except that DATALISTN is used on numeric variables.

Most display manager commands are available to the DATALISTC window. Thus if you have a long list to select from, you can use the usual backward and forward commands, plus you can use the FIND command to search for specific values.

It is possible to type over the entries in the DATALISTC window. This has no impact on the contents of the window; they are restored to their correct values when ENTER is pressed. Altering an entry, then pressing ENTER to select, causes the original value, not the altered value, to be passed back.

The DATALISTx functions should be used frequently in situations in which users may be required to select from a list of valid values. The functions cause a window to pop up containing specified variables (defined by the application programmer) of the observations in a data set. You can update a field in either AF or FSP by selecting a value from an observation.

Examples Using The Datalistx Functions

To illustrate how to use the DATALISTx functions, suppose you have a field named **dpt,** the value of which is to be a valid department. A database called TABLES.DEPTS contains the list of valid departments at the site, with variable **dept** containing department mnemonics and **deptdesc** containing department descriptions.

The following statements

```
classid = open('tables.depts') ;
dpt = datalistc(classid,'dept deptdesc') ;
rc = close(classid) ;
```

cause a window to pop up that contains all observations and the variables **dept** and **deptdesc** from TABLES.DEPTS. The application's user can move the cursor (arrow keys, tabs, and so on) to the desired value of **dept.**

Pressing ENTER causes that value to be moved into the field **dpt** in the AF or FSP program. Depending on how you called DATALISTC, the value is immediately moved back to the calling program or you can change the selection and use PF3 to end the DATALISTC screen.

You can control window placement by using the WREGION function immediately before calling DATALISTC. Function keys are the ones defined for the most recent AF screen (even if calling from FSEDIT, the keys are the last AF keys, not the current FSEDIT keys).

Letting The User Determine When To Use DATALISTx Functions

For maximum usefulness, the DATALISTC window can be invoked on specific request of the user. This can be done by allowing a key (?, for example) to be a help key and checking for that value in the field in SCL. Using ? is consistent with SAS software's own prompt for pop-up help windows. The SCL becomes

```
if dpt eq: '?' then do ;
  call wregion(10,8,10,50) ;
  classid = open('tables.depts') ;
  dpt =datalistc(classid,'dept deptdesc');
  rc = close(classid) ;
end ;
```

Note that pressing END in the DATALISTC window while the cursor is positioned on the command line causes the field **dpt** to be returned empty. To ensure that a value is always selected from DATALISTC, modify the above code to read

```
if dpt eq: '?' then do ;
  call wregion(10,8,10,50) ;
  classid = open('tables.depts') ;
```

```
      do while (dpt eq '' or index(dpt,'?') eq 1) ;
         dpt=datalistc(classid,'dept deptdesc');
      end ;
      rc = close(classid) ;
   end ;
```

If using ? in this manner, ensure that you change the default prompt character in the AF entry's GATTR screen. It is ? by default, and SAS/AF will pop up its own help screen if you do not change the default.

Comment On Using The OPEN Function

The preceding code on the DATALISTC function opens and closes the data file each time DATALISTC is used. You should not blindly go ahead and code open and close routines like this.

The decision about how to open and close files is a function of each application. The above code is used in a situation where the DATALISTC is rarely used, and experience has shown that more resources would be used in the long run by opening it at the application start. Opening it at the application start means you always open, but the above code ensures the file is only opened when necessary.

Had this DATALISTC been part of an application in which users would frequently access the DATALISTC, the file would have been opened once in the window INIT section and closed in TERM. Indeed it may even be necessary in some systems designs to open a frequently used file much earlier, for example when the SCL starts, and pass the data set id through using parameters to following programs.

The EXECCMD And EXECCMDI Functions

 EXECCMD takes an argument and passes that argument to the next displayed window as if it were a command entered on the command line of that window. The command(s) are not carried out until the SCL rewrites the current window or starts up a new window.

Note that at this point the SCL program has not finished, nor is control necessarily about to return to the user.

If an SCL program has CONTROL ALWAYS switched on, then any pressing of the ENTER key causes the MAIN section to be invoked. EXECCMD in some cases invokes the MAIN section code, as there is an implied ENTER at the end of commands. This seems to cause problems only when the EXECCMD argument is a procedure-specific command; global commands such as PMENU ON do not cause problems.

If the EXECCMD is in the MAIN section, then, depending on the argument, SCL can loop as it constantly reinvokes the EXECCMD. This only occurs when the EXECCMD issues a command that is to be operated on in the current window.

You can get round the looping problem with some extra coding. When EXECCMD is called, WORD(1) contains the value of the first EXECCMD argument. Thus, by checking WORD(1) immediately before calling EXECCMD, you can make the EXECCMD conditional. That will prevent the looping problem.

Case Studies Using EXECCMD

To illustrate the looping problem noted above, run the following program in FSEDIT. *Note that this program will put your FSEDIT session into a loop, so make sure you know how to use your system's ATTENTION/BREAK key.*

```
init:
 control always ;
return ;

main:
 put 'In the main section' ;
 call execcmd('save') ;
return ;

term:
return ;
```

You notice that the program goes into an infinite loop because the EXECCMD causes MAIN to be reinvoked and thus the EXECCMD is invoked again. If you are able to view the log, you will see many messages that read '**In the main section**'. You will most likely need to use your system's equivalent of the BREAK key to get out of this loop.

Now try the following program:

```
init:
 control always ;
return ;
```

```
main:
 put 'In the main section' ;
 if upcase(word(1)) ne 'SAVE' then
    call execcmd('save') ;
return ;

term:
return ;
```

When the MAIN section gets invoked, WORD(1) is not equal to 'SAVE' (unless 'SAVE' was typed on the command line, in which case the EXECCMD is not invoked). Triggering the EXECCMD causes the MAIN section to be reinvoked, at which point WORD(1) is equal to 'SAVE', thus causing the EXECCMD to be conditionally bypassed.

EXECCMDI

Often you can use the EXECCMDI function rather than EXECCMD. The EXECCMDI function executes the command immediately rather than when control passes back to a window. You can only use global SAS commands, rather than procedure specific commands, with EXECCMDI; thus the FSEDIT SAVE command as illustrated in the preceding program could not be used (no error or warning is issued; the command just does not get executed), but the PMENU OFF could.

EXECCMDI may flush the command line. For instance, consider the following code, used in SUNS to activate a legend so the user can dictate how long the legend window is on screen (the legend window is called MESSAGES):

```
call execcmdi('next messages','noexec');
```

If the user puts a command on the command line, and the EXECCMDI is carried out before the user's command is operated on, the command line is flushed and the user's command lost.

When Is EXECCMD Carried Out?

EXECCMD arguments are stacked up and carried out when control passes back to the application. This could happen when you are returning to the window in the current program or calling another program.

Hence EXECCMD can be used to pass commands through to the next window. An example is customizing a pmenu for FSLIST. To do this, issue the SETPMENU command in FSLIST. This requires the user to issue the command to set up the pmenu.

Alternatively, immediately before issuing an SCL CALL FSLIST command, issue an EXECCMD to set up the pmenu for FSLIST.

Suppose the pmenu is in the catalog entry pmenu of the catalog FSLIST with libref P. Use the following in SCL:

```
call execcmd('setpmenu p.fslist.pmenu.pmenu;pmenu on');
call fslist(.....) ;
```

The FSLIST procedure will have pmenus set up to use those defined in the FSLIST catalog rather than the defaults.

You can control when EXECCMD is executed to some extent by using the REFRESH command. The following changes pmenus in the midst of a program and continues with the new PMENUS defined:

```
call execcmd('setpmenu p.fslist.pmenu.pmenu');
refresh ;
```

However, in this instance you could have just as easily used EXECCMDI. Note that the REFRESH command will cause execution of an EXECCMD argument only in the current window as only that window is refreshed.

FSVIEW provides a further example of the usefulness of passing commands to the next window. Suppose you wish to set some id variables in a following FSVIEW window that does not have a formula defined. Issue the following commands in your SCL:

```
call execcmd('show id idvar') ;
call fsview(......) ;
```

As the EXECCMD runs when the window is changed, in other words, when FSVIEW takes control, the SHOW ID statement is applied to the FSVIEW window.

Some problems have been noted under both Releases 6.06 and 6.07. If you find that the EXECCMD appears not to set the ID variable in FSVIEW above, try preceding it with another command, for example, ADD.

```
call execcmd('add;show id idvar') ;
call fsview(......) ;
```

Or replace it alternatively with two dummy enters, as follows:

```
call execcmd(';;show id idvar') ;
call fsview(......) ;
```

The FILLIST Function

The 'TYPE' Argument

This function fills a list from an external file or from a SAS catalog. The documentation in *SAS Technical Report P-216* is slightly misleading, in that the term SAS FILE is used as a source of filling the list. While it is true that the catalog entry type resides in SAS FILES, so do other sorts of member types. Only the CATALOG entry type can be used as a source of text to fill the list with from a SAS FILE.

Return Codes

A successful fill has been noted returning a code of 65792 when reading from an external file. I could see nothing unusual about the file and am mentioning this purely to make you aware that nonzero return codes may have been successful executions of the function.

The FKEYNAME Function

This function does not return the function key names unless the function is called from a program entry that has a display screen. A program entry with a blank display screen will not reveal any error messages because this is not an error. Function keys have no meaning in an entry that has no display for the user to interact with; hence FKEYNAME returns a blank in that case. Therefore, you cannot have a user press a key, then call an SCL entry, and expect to find the key name available.

These comments relate also to the GETFKEY and SETFKEY commands.

The LENGTH Statement And Variable Type Assignment

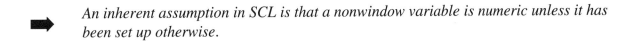 *An inherent assumption in SCL is that a nonwindow variable is numeric unless it has been set up otherwise.*

Thus the following code is insufficient in itself to tell SCL that the field is character:

```
if index(keyfield,'F02626') then do ; ...
```

But the code

```
length keyfield $ 70 ;
...
if index(keyfield,'F02626') then do ; ...
```

explicitly tells SCL that **keyfield** is a character variable.

There is an alternative, namely to assign a value to the field explicitly before using it in a character function. If you explicitly assign a character value to a field the first time it is used in the SCL, it is flagged as character at compile time. Thus the following code will also ensure that **keyfield** is character:

```
keyfield = ' ' ;
...
if index(keyfield,'F02626') then do ; ...
```

However, because **keyfield** will have a length of 200 in this case, this is not a good way to define character variables. Use a LENGTH statement.

Although this situation is similar to the DATA step, it is often overlooked. In particular, at compile time, no data set information is available for opened data sets. Any field used in the above manner that is assigned a value using CALL SET must be explicitly assigned a character value.

Note that careful checking of any messages in the MESSAGE screen after an SCL entry compile will indicate where SCL has defaulted a variable to NUMERIC and it is being used in a character function. In the above example, with the first occurrence of **keyfield** being in the INDEX function, the following message will be observed in the MESSAGE window:

```
WARNING: [Line x] Converting Numeric Variable KEYFIELD To Character
```

 WINDOW variables are assumed to be character and require that the ATTR window for the variable have TYPE set to NUM in order for SCL to consider them numeric.

This is even true of numeric variables on a database linked to window variables by CALL SET because SCL has no way of knowing at compile time just what a data set structure looks like.

Therefore, if you forget to alter the ATTR for a numeric variable on a display window to set the variable explicitly to NUM, the CALL SET will NOT link the variables, and at run time you will see a blank window variable. No default numeric-to-character conversion is done as in the DATA step. Furthermore, even though a variable with the display variable name exists in the data set being linked with CALL SET, no error or warning message is produced to point out a possible conflict. This has been known to cause a high debugging overhead, especially the first few times you forget to change the ATTR.

The LOCATEC/N Functions

These functions allow a database to be searched for an observation that has a specified value in a variable.

LOCATEC has 3 parameters. The first is the file id to be searched. The second is the number of the variable in that file to be compared with the value specified in the third parameter.

Using the variable number sounds difficult. However, once you discover that the VARNUM function exists, things become much easier. VARNUM returns a variable number in an opened database when given the variable name as a literal parameter. (If you don't use a literal, SCL tries to resolve the variable name you passed into a value and then use that value as the parameter.)

The third parameter can be a variable or a value. That is, for LOCATEC, pass a character variable to have LOCATEC search for its current value, or pass a text literal. For LOCATEN, pass a numeric variable or a number.

Using In The Presence Of Deleted Records Or WHERE Clauses

A difficulty you may encounter, until you are used to working with logical records is that the LOCATEC/N functions can return an unexpected observation number, even though they have found the correct observation. This is because LOCATEC/N use logical rather than physical records.

An example will serve to illustrate the situation. Suppose you have a SAS data set with one variable (numeric) called **x.** You invoke FSEDIT on the data set and enter the following SCL code:

```
fseinit:
  test = open('work.x') ;
return ;

init:
  control always ;
return ;
```

```
main:
  obs = curobs() ;
  rc = locaten(test,varnum(test,'x'),x) ;
  put obs= rc= ;
return ;

term:
return ;

fseterm:
  rc = close(test) ;
return ;
```

The expectation here is that when you enter a number of observations, the MAIN section will return OBS and RC equal when you return to a record after saving. Until a record is deleted, that is precisely what happens.

When a record is deleted, LOCATEx behaves somewhat differently from what is described above. If record 3 were deleted, the LOCATEx would work correctly on records 1 and 2 but would return rc=3 rather than 4 on record 4 and one less than expected on succeeding records.

To check the real observation number returned, use the CUROBS function. It always returns the physical observation number. Thus you call LOCATEx, then call CUROBS(<dsid>) to find which observation really got returned.

The problem occurs because SAS uses logical records when doing searches in the presence of DELETEd records. LOCATEx is generally used to identify a particular record for some further processing. Suppose you access the record using, say, FETCHOBS. You request the record indicated by the return code from LOCATEx.

The record indicated by LOCATEx will be the logical record. Using the return code from LOCATEx in the FETCHOBS will fetch the physical record corresponding to that return code. This may return incorrect records for processing.

The following code then will *not* necessarily fetch the desired record:

```
rc = locatec(dsid00,1,'X'); /* find first occurrence of X */
if rc then fetchobs(dsid00,rc) ; /* fetch the record */
else return ;
```

However, the following amended code will always fetch the correct record:

```
rc = locatec(dsid00,1,'X'); /* find first occurrence of X */
if rc then
   fetchobs(dsid00,curobs(dsid00)); /* fetch record */
else return ;
```

The LVARLEVEL Function

This function fills a list with the values of a variable in a data set. If the variable is formatted, the formatted values are loaded.

Although not documented, this function does a reverse fill. That is to say that the last record on the database becomes the first record in the list, and so on back. The first record in the database becomes the last record on the list.

Effectively, this command acts like a series of inserts at the top of the list. In applications where the physical position in the list is critical, this behavior may not be helpful. To get the list in the correct order, apply the REVLIST function as follows:

```
rc = revlist(listid) ;
```

The MODIFIED Function

Undocumented Features Of MODIFIED

It is certainly the case that the function returns TRUE when a field is modified. However, the following condition is also required:

MODIFIED returns true if the field has been changed since the last time the SCL was executed.

Thus it is not the case that altering a field always causes MODIFIED to return true the next time the MODIFIED function is executed. In particular, the following situations will not return true:

● the field is altered within an SCL program

● the field is altered, SCL is executed and returns before any call to the MODIFIED function is made, then SCL is executed again and calls the MODIFIED function

● the TERM section of an SCL program is executed and calls MODIFIED if the user has already caused the SCL to run by using a command other than END (this is effectively a special case of the last situation).

→ *Conversely, there are situations where MODIFIED will return true even when a field is not changed.*

This applies particularly to extended table processing; when the ENTER key is pressed on an extended table entry, MODIFIED will return true for any field on the record, even if the user has not changed the fields.

Potential usage of MODIFIED has often required a design change due to the situations just described. Be wary of assuming that MODIFIED always tells you if a field is altered; that is not the case in the 3 conditions listed earlier in this section.

Modified: A Case Study

The ramifications of the third situation above can be seen by the following case study from one of Databank's applications. We have a database that can be updated by multiple users using FSEDIT under SAS/SHARE. The database is a report trigger mechanism, each observation containing a field called NCOPIES that is initially set to zero.

To initiate a report, the user simply changes NCOPIES to a nonzero value. The TERM section triggers a report request if NCOPIES is nonzero, and NCOPIES is reset to zero when the report is run.

When only one user could access the database at a time (that is, before SAS/SHARE was available under Release 6.06), the following code was used in TERM to trigger a report:

```
term:
 if ncopies then call symputc('replist',symgetc('replist') || ' ' ||
repname);
 return ;
```

This was a simple piece of code that was based on the fact that as only one user could be accessing the database, any report requested would be for that user. When the user left the reports database, all requested reports were then run, the report names being stored in the macro variable REPLIST.

When SAS/SHARE became available, that code was no longer reliable because a user could enter a record that already had NCOPIES set by another user. So to trigger a report, the TERM section was changed to

```
term:
 if ncopies and modified('ncopies') then
   call symputc('replist',symgetc('replist') || ' ' || repname);
 return ;
```

The MODIFIED function was used to check if the user currently accessing the report profile actually requested the report. In testing, developers tested this by setting NCOPIES and then moving from the record, for example, by using BACKWARD, FORWARD, END, ADD, and so on.

In production, the users immediately reported that reports were not being printed. Watching users request a report, it became clear that they often changed NCOPIES, pressed ENTER to verify the screen (it contained a number of other fields), then moved from that screen. By the time the TERM section executed, the MODIFIED function no longer returned true and no reports were printed.

Getting around this problem required some extra coding in the INIT/MAIN sections. The FSEDIT SCL became

```
INIT:
 control always ;
 ....
 report = 'N' ;
 ....
RETURN ;

MAIN:
 if modified('ncopies') then report='Y' ;
 ....
RETURN ;


TERM:
 if ncopies and report='Y' then
    call symputc('replist',repname);
RETURN
```

What has been done here is to force the MODIFIED function to be called as soon as the MAIN section executes, thus setting a flag to indicate that the user has modified **ncopies**. If a user accesses a report that another user already set **ncopies** for, no report will be printed because MODIFIED applies only to the current user.

Note that in the above code, the setting up of the **replist** macro variable is done in TERM rather than MAIN because it is conceivable that the user could change **ncopies** back to zero before exiting. If you set **replist** in MAIN and this happened, you would need to provide extra code to remove the report name from **replist**.

Extended Table Considerations

Another potential difficulty with MODIFIED occurs with extended table processing. When the user selects a row of an extended table, MODIFIED is set to true for any field in the table row.

A design requirement in one of my screens was for the user to be able to alter a row sourced from a data set, press ENTER, and have the row saved only if fields in the row had been modified. It was a specific design requirement to cut down I/O by not resaving records when the user accesses a row and presses ENTER without changing any fields.

Because MODIFIED returns true for any field in a selected row of an extended table, it is not possible to use MODIFIED in this manner. Furthermore, the ISSEL function (used to determine if a named row of a table is selected) returns true when a row is selected, irrespective of whether the row has any fields changed.

The design requirement could not be met using an extended table in this situation. Ultimately, it was decided to use the extended table and accept that additional I/O might be generated. This is a particular problem on the OS/2 platform, where the ENTER key is often used to move from line to line in a linefeed manner.

The OBSINFO Function

The OBSINFO function is available in Release 6.07. It should be noted that in addition to the documented behavior when using the MODIFIED argument, OBSINFO('MODIFIED') returns true on a new record in FSEDIT even when no fields have been altered.

This behavior occurs because in FSEDIT this function argument is an indication of whether a record needs to be written back out to the data set being edited. SAS Institute's definition of 'needing to be written back out' is that a variable's values have changed, and it is an FSEDIT design decision that a new record (with all missing values) has in fact had all its field values changed.

The OPTGETx And OPTSETx Functions

➡ *Documentation for the OPTSETN function implies that the function can be used to set numeric options in the same way that the SAS OPTIONS statement operates. This is not the case.*

Any numeric SAS option that accepts a mnemonic (MAX, for example) will not accept that mnemonic with OPSETN.

For instance, consider the following using the OBS option:

```
rc = optsetn('obs',0) ;
< scl processing >
rc = optsetn('obs','max') ;
```

This code will not work. The SCL OPTSETN function accepts only numbers as the second parameter. Once you have changed OBS= using OPTSETN, you cannot reset it to MAX using OPTSETN.

To reset this option to allow processing, you could decide to set obs=<some very large number>. This can cause difficulties because when OBS is set to other than MAX, SAS operates in subset mode. It may be necessary to use options such as FORCE on calls either to PROC SORT or the SCL SORT function.

There are two workarounds. One uses submitted code to reset the option using SAS, as follows:

```
submit continue ;
  options obs=MAX ;
endsubmit ;
```

In Release 6.06, you cannot do this from FSEDIT, as submission of code is not permitted.

The other workaround is to store the value of OBS and restore it when finished with the reconfigured value. To do this, you require the OPTGETN function also.

```
pushobs = optgetn('obs') ;
rc00 = optsetn('obs',0) ;
.... processing ....
rc00 = optsetn('obs',pushobs) ;
```

This does reset OBS to the MAX value, and it is correctly headed 'MAX' in the options window.

Toggle Options

Some options in SAS are 'toggle' options. That is, they are either ON or OFF, as opposed to being assigned a value. An example is ERRORABEND/NOERRORABEND.

You cannot assign the value ERRORABEND to the SAS option ERRORABEND, nor can you assign the option NOERRORABEND. However, you can toggle the ON/OFF status of these toggle functions.

When you use cval=OPTGETC('errorabend'), you will not get a value assigned to CVAL. The reason is that in SCL, the toggle options actually return a numeric value of zero if on (ERRORABEND is 'ON'), or 1 if off (NOERRORABEND is 'OFF'). You need to use the OPTGETN function to return the numeric value, even though it appears that the option takes character values.

Thus to switch off MPRINT or SYMBOLGEN in an SCL application, you would code

```
rc = optsetn('mprint',1) ;
rc = optsetn('symbolgen',1) ;
```

➡️ *Various options have no impact in SCL. For instance NOFMTERR does NOT identify attempts to use a nonexistent format in the same manner that SAS software does. Instead, SCL abends if a format is not found and dumps the contents of the window data vector.*

The REFRESH Command

REFRESH causes the screen in FSEDIT or AF to be updated and redisplayed.

 The command is not documented in any of the SCL guides but is in *SAS Technical Report P-199, Using SAS Screen Control Language in Release 6.06*, as well as in *SAS Technical Report P-216.*

If you have a screen that carries out some task for a long time period, REFRESH is ideal for keeping the user informed of what is happening. A message can be assigned in the SCL, REFRESH can be called to display the message, and processing can continue without returning control to the user.

Also, when SCL is updating screen fields, REFRESH can be used to display each one as it is updated. As REFRESH rewrites the current display screen, it can be used to force an EXECCMD to execute its arguments.

Using REFRESH In Release 6.07

☹️ *REFRESH in Release 6.07 begins by removing all text from the command line. It is not put back.*

This means several potential problems. For instance, you can never issue a nonglobal command and have it executed, either by typing it in or by assigning it to a function key. The problem is that when the REFRESH function is executed it destroys the whole command line. This means that you can never leave an FSEDIT screen except by using the ATTENTION (BREAK or INTERRUPT) key.

There are, however, ways around this difficulty; a macro-based workaround is presented under the heading "Using REFRESH Successfully In FSEDIT" later in this chapter.

Using REFRESH With Extended Tables

REFRESH can cause some difficulty with extended tables if used irresponsibly. Because REFRESH rewrites the screen, it reinvokes the GETROW section. Note though that a REFRESH executed in the GETROW section itself is effectively ignored in Release 6.08.

Using REFRESH with extended tables can add to I/O overhead. Each call to REFRESH in the MAIN section or the TERM section causes GETROW to be carried out. Thus, if you have 3 calls to REFRESH in MAIN, GETROW is carried out 4 times, 1 for each REFRESH plus the one routinely done after leaving MAIN. A REFRESH in TERM generates the rather unnecessary step of updating the table.

To cut down I/O, try to avoid using REFRESH with extended tables, particularly those where the table is built from a database. Using LEGENDS to display information while the SCL is running will reduce the extra overhead.

Using REFRESH Successfully In FSEDIT

The following macro can help with the problem of REFRESH purging the command buffer. The macro does not allow the REFRESH to be executed if a command has been entered. Since it does not use _BLANK_, the macro is usable in both SAS/AF and SAS/FSP applications that use SCL.

```
%macro norefrsh ;

   if word(1) eq ' ' then do ;
      refresh ;
   end ;

%mend norefrsh ;
```

The obvious disadvantage with the NOREFRSH macro is that if you need the REFRESH, you will not be able to use it when a command is entered. To use this macro, just replace any references to the REFRESH statement with a macro call to NOREFRSH.

Release 6.07 and later releases allow the ALLCMDS option of CONTROL to prevent command-line commands from being executed. This applies only to LOCAL commands; global SAS commands cannot be trapped and discarded. REFRESH can also be used to bypass LOCAL commands.

However, REFRESH will not assist in preventing global commands from being executed. Suppose you wish to allow only the commands DISP, WRITE, UPDATE, and HELP. All other commands are to be discarded. Given that REFRESH flushes the command line, it might be expected that the following code would accomplish this:

```
cmd = word(1,'u') ;
if cmd in ('DISP' 'WRITE' 'UPDATE' 'HELP') then do ;
  .... process above commands ....
end ;
else refresh ;
```

Although REFRESH flushes the command line, global commands are executed *before* SCL begins. It is impossible to prevent GLOBAL commands from executing for this reason (except by removing the command line). The code will remove any LOCAL command from the command line before it is executed at the end of the SCL. Thus, for instance, you could prevent a user from entering the MOD command in FSEDIT.

The CALL SET Function

Confusion over just what this function does has been noted frequently. In fact, this is a simple and powerful routine that offers the ability to exchange values between data set and SCL variables.

The main point to consider is that CALL SET only exchanges data between like named and typed variables.

When a variable named **project** exists in an open data set, and an SCL program entry has a window variable named **project**, a record read from the data set is automatically moved into the window variable when CALL SET is used, provided the variable types are the same. However, if the window variable were called **projid**, it would be necessary to use the GETVARC or GETVARN routines to move the value into the window field.

This routine allows easy population of SCL variables without extra effort by the programmer. In some situations, you may wish to switch off that variable exchange. There are two options:

- close the data set that the CALL SET applies to, and then reopen it without a CALL SET (Note - this implies that the CALL SET should be in INIT; otherwise, it may get re-executed)

- if the only input mechanism is the FETCHOBS function, use the NOSET option on that function

CALL SET moves data between like-named variables whether they are window variables or not. If you wish to populate a nonwindow variable, use the LENGTH statement to define the variable before the CALL SET. If you do not use a LENGTH statement, the SET will not work (for instance, attempting to link the **keys** value from USAGE). USAGE with an SCL variable using the following code will not work because the CALL SET does not recognize the field:

```
init:
  dsid = open('usage.usage') ;
  call set(dsid) ;
  do i=1 to nobs(dsid) ;
    rc = fetchobs(dsid,i) ;
    if index(keys,'S0C4') then put i= keys= modulen= ;
  end ;
return ;

term:
  call close(dsid) ;
return ;
```

However, if you place this line immediately before INIT, the SET will succeed:

```
length keys $ 80 ;
```

The reason is that SCL defaults nonwindow variables to numeric, so the variable attributes are different from those in the data set.

The Display Manager STATUS OFF Command

This command has an impact upon the default legend processing in SCL when you submit code for execution by SAS software. The default when starting SAS software is to have STATUS ON. The immediate (and only documented) function is to display the messages on the task line that a DATA step or procedure is running (for example, **PROC PRINT running**).

☹ *When you issue a legend in SCL and then use SUBMIT CONTINUE, the legend disappears. In Release 6.07, issuing the display manager STATUS OFF command at the beginning of the application overrides that behavior with legends, allowing them to remain active at all times. This is the intended behavior and continues under Release 6.08.*

Chapter 10: Case Study -- Format Creation & Storage

Contents

Overview

This chapter presents a complete working application that can be used for managing format tables. To put the application in perspective, the history of how the application evolved and notes about how it may evolve in future are presented.

This application is a version of one currently running in production at Databank Systems. I have changed the text style somewhat here, especially in the use of the word 'we' to refer generically to Databank Systems SAS programmers.

Duplication Of Format Tables

When a suite of programs was passed from one development team to another, it was noted that many user-defined formats were hard coded in the program code, and that often those formats were duplicated; in other words, they were coded in multiple programs. The formats were not static, and they had to be altered from time to time.

Further investigation company wide showed that many applications used formats, yet most defined the formats either in the program code or in application-specific data sets. Many formats occurred multiple times, wasting both development effort and space. Very rarely were formats coded either in external included code or in SASLIB/LIBRARY data sets.

It was recognized immediately that the formats used in the applications fell into two categories:

- multi-usable, that is, many applications or programs could use the formats
- program specific, that is, the formats were truly only usable for a single program

An example of a multiusable format was one that mapped bank id numbers onto a textual bank description. This occurred repeatedly, both in the suite just acquired and in other systems.

Our developers identified the problem as their not having any central control over the creation, storage, and maintenance of formats. It was decided to create such a central storage area, where anybody who required a particular format could log on, check if it was available, and use an existing format if so. They could also add a format to the system, making it available for other users.

Requirements For Centralized Format Storage

Analysis of the problem and collection of user requirements for a centralized format system revealed the following requirements from potential users (many of whom are developers -- we are creating a developer's support tool here):

- All change to formats had to occur via an online application.

  It was decided that an SCL front end that permitted the creation and storage of formats would be built. Format tables would be stored in SAS data sets, which a user would be able to access via extended tables or FSVIEW. No ability to delete the data set(s) would be available from within the SCL application.

  The need to allow users update access to update the formats in the online system left a difficulty, namely that at an operating system level it is necessary to give users read/write access to allow them to use the data sets under SAS. This means that they have access outside of SAS and could conceivably modify the system data sets if they knew how.

In practice, this is a problem that occurs frequently. This application gets around the problem the same way that many do: it ignores it and hopes that the user base will never attempt to access its files outside of the SAS application software. The option is available to use SAS software's data set password features, so that the databases are accessible through the online system only if the password is known.

- Only VALUE and INVALUE statements are required.

  This requirement made application design reasonably simple. No format that was a candidate for this system used PICTURE formats, only VALUE and INVALUE.

- The library containing the formats for inclusion into SAS should be laid out as SAS code containing the formats in an external file, rather than using SAS catalogs and Version 6 CNTLIN features. Many users wanted to check quickly what is available in a format table from outside of SAS software.

  CNTLIN data sets are simple, effective, and more secure than code in external libraries, but the overwhelming preference was to use external libraries. We were concerned that the created external files would be copied into source code, thus re-creating the same situation that originally led to this system's being required.

  Although it was a requirement to use external files, the requirement was readdressed. The ease of use of Version 6 catalogs defined to the LIBRARY libref was stressed, and eventually users agreed to use Version 6 catalogs for the storage of formats, via CNTLIN. Using CNTLIN prevented users from being able to look quickly at a format. This was considered unavoidable, and it was stressed to users that the application should be responsible for all functions.

- Each format created had to have a unique format name.

  The unique format name was critical. This requirement was not a user requirement; it was a developer's (of this format system) requirement. It was necessary to force this in order to keep the system simple. Without this requirement, we would have needed to use multiple libraries for storing the formats, adding another level of complexity.

  We decided to create a central data set of demographic information about formats defined to the system and have a format name field on that data set. This data set, labeled the Format Descriptor Area (FDA), also included

  - Format Storage Area (FSA) name
  - Format name
  - The owner of the format (usually whoever entered the format)
  - A password to prevent other users from changing the format
  - A description of each defined format

- A description of the 'START' field
- A description of the 'END' field
- A description of the 'LABEL' field
- Maximum length of each field above
- A label for HLO processing
- The date the format was first created
- The signon of the person entering the FDA record

- Users only required the basics of PROC FORMAT, namely a VALUE statement, value clauses (including the ability to specify ranges), labels, and an OTHER category. It was decided to add to this the ability to specify _ERROR_ and _SAME_ options.

  Since the users of this system would be SAS literate, it was considered feasible that the users rather than the application would be responsible for ensuring that formats were entered correctly. However, the application would be able to inform a user when a format creation failed.

- When using the format system, users wanted to store text information about the format.

  The requirement would allow our users to keep data online about the format, for example, which jobs are using a format, or perhaps where a format's data are taken from, or who a contact support person is. To create text information, we would use the ideas discussed in this text earlier, linking a free-flow text file with a database observation through the PREVIEW window.

  I realized that a field was needed that identified the format as a valid SAS data set name. This would allow us to use a SAS data set name to store formats and also to identify a text entry in a catalog. Format names were not applicable, as they are not necessarily valid data set names. Hence I defined the term Format Storage Area (FSA) to mean a valid SAS name that would be used for storing the format in a SAS data set and also as an identifier for storing free-flow text.

- Any format created by a user had to have the capacity to be locked out of being changed by other users unless specific access was granted. This was to ensure that another user couldn't change an 'almost what I want' format to something unusable to the original user's applications.

  It was decided to put this function in the hands of the user. The user would be able to enter into the FDA record a password that would be masked on entry. Unless other users knew the password, they would not be allowed to access the format. Initial creators of a format could leave the FDA password field blank, which implied anyone could access the format. A blank password would have to be confirmed at time of creating the FDA.

- The system had to be intuitively obvious and easy to use. Users wanted a menu-driven system that would find major mistakes for them before the formats were created, implying an interactive system with a high degree of user interaction.

Some users wanted the PROC FORMAT code to be rebuilt immediately after changing or creating a format. However, some wanted to be able to timestamp a particular format value so that it would not get used until that time.

The above requirements are challenging. The design for the system is not presented here as it is very lengthy. Instead, a comment following each of the SCL entries in the system describes how the objectives were achieved (some were not!).

Code For Formats System

The application shown here was originally implemented under MVS using Release 6.07 and then substantially upgraded to run under OS/2 running Release 6.08. The code and screens presented here are from Release 6.08. It has not yet been possible to port the application back to Release 6.08 under MVS, so no comment about the ability of the application to function on that platform is made.

This section lists all the programs in the formats system. Each program is presented with discussion following. For each entry, the corresponding screen is shown twice, once from the programmer's viewpoint and then from the user's.

ENTRY: CHKPASS.PROGRAM   Get A Password From User

This entry is intended to be called by other entries whenever a password is required. The password system in this application is simple. The password is stored in the FDA, and it is read by this entry at run time. The user entry is compared with the password in the FDA.

The user simply enters the password into the window in Figure 10.1. The 3 possible return codes are

0   The password was entered correctly
1   The user entered the wrong password 3 times
2   The user terminated the password entry without completing the entry of the password

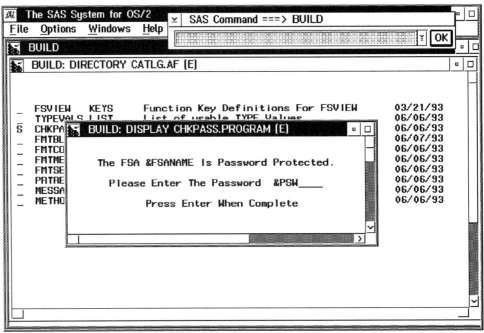

Figure 10.1: Password Entry Screen

It is up to the calling program to determine how to handle each of these return codes; the return code is passed back via parameter VALPSW.

The screen in Figure 10.1 is the screen as the programmer sets it up. In this screen, the **fsanam** field is protected. The **psw** field is where the cursor is placed, and the field is a nondisplay field.

When users access this screen, they initially see the window in Figure 10.2. If they then enter an invalid password, the WNAME area is filled with the appropriate message.

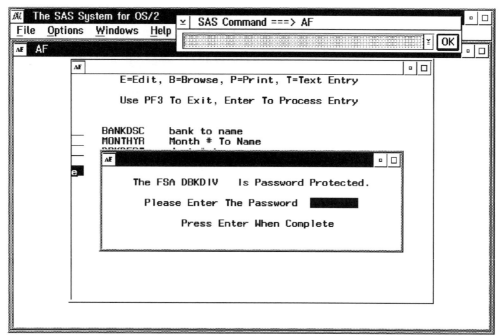

Figure 10.2:   User's View Of Password Screen

**** SOURCE *****

```
entry fsaname $ 8 valpsw $ 1 owner $ 8 fmtnam $ 8;

/* this screen is intended to prompt a user to enter a password
   if one is required. It is assumed that the caller has already
   verified that the fsaname is an existing file

   VALPSW = '0' -- password check successful
   VALPSW = '1' -- password check failed
   VALPSW = '2' -- user backed out using END without completing entry

*/

init:

/* initialise */

  control always ;
  rc = field('color yellow reverse','psw') ;
  valpsw = '1' ; /* assume bad password */
  tries = 0 ;
  psw = _blank_ ;
  owner = 'UNKNOWN' ;
```

```
/* open the fda to prepare for checks, extract password/owner */

    dsid00 = open('ratesf.fda') ;
    rc = where(dsid00,'fsaname eq "' || fsaname || '"') ;
    rc = fetch(dsid00) ;
    pass  = getvarc(dsid00,varnum(dsid00,'psw')) ;
    owner = getvarc(dsid00,varnum(dsid00,'owner')) ;
    fmtnam= getvarc(dsid00,varnum(dsid00,'fmtnam')) ;
    call close(dsid00) ;

return ;

main:

   if _status_ eq 'E' then do ;

/* user requested an exit. tell the caller via the valpsw parm
   that the user was unable to complete the password entry */

     valpsw = '2' ;
     return ;
   end ;

   if psw ne pass then do ;

/* user has entered an incorrect password. Increase the number of
   tries so far,and exit if they have hit 3 invalid entries */

     tries+1 ;
     if tries eq 3 then do ;
       _status_ = 'H' ;
       return ;
     end ;

     /* bad password entered, pop up note in window name area */

     call wname('ERROR: Incorrect Password, Attempt ' ||
                 put(tries,1.) || ' Of 3') ;
     cursor psw ;
     return ;
   end ;

/* getting to here should only be possible if the password was
   entered correctly. Set the return code appropriately and go
   back to the caller */

   valpsw = '0' ;
   _status_ = 'H' ;
return ;
```

Note the explicit setting of _STATUS_ to 'H' to exit from this program entry when the user has entered a correct password. If the normal exit used END, it would conflict with the code at the start of MAIN that sets the return code to an invalid code when the user ends.

This approach to passwording has inherent problems. As usual, the question of how to prevent users who are SAS literate from accessing a data set (in this case the FDA) outside of the application arises. The simple answer is the usual answer -- we can password protect the data set and let SAS handle the prevention of access, or we can ignore the possibility of the problem.

For this application, the data set is not password protected. It simply was not considered necessary given that the users here are developers, and this application is a development tool. Whether to protect data sets is an application design decision.

ENTRY: FMTBLD.PROGRAM Enter A New Format Table Structure

This entry is the means by which a user defines a new format to be created. The user defines the name of the format and then defines what the **start, end**, and **label** fields will mean in the CNTLIN data set. This entry is stored in the FDA, the format descriptor area.

We created the program entry screen in Figure 10.3. This entry contains all the information necessary to build the database that will store the format values. The intention of this entry is that it defines one new format storage area each time it is called.

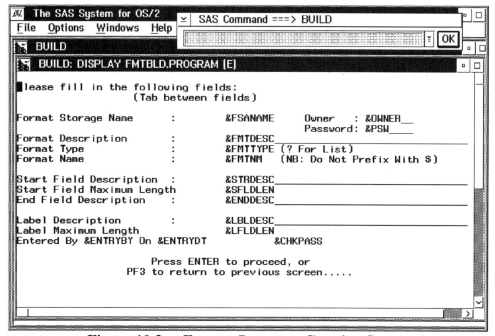

Figure 10.3:   Format Structure Creation Screen

At the main menu, the user selects the option to use this screen, defines one format descriptor area, and is then placed back at the main menu. This approach is again a design decision; it was assumed that when the application first went in, a lot of formats would be developed, but later users would rarely want to create more than one new format in a single session.

The field attributes are as follows where the defaults are not shown. Note that all fields have AUTOSKIP options on in addition to the following list. All fields are character unless stated otherwise.

Attribute	FSANAME	PSW	FMTTYPE	FMTNM	SFLDLEN
Options	CURSOR CAPS	CAPS NONDISPLAY	CAPS	CAPS	
Format			$1.		
Informat			$1.		
List			=TYPEVALS		<116
Alias				FMTNAM	
Type					NUM
Initial					8

Attribute	LFLDLEN	ENTRYBY	ENTRYDT	CHKPASS
Options		CAPS		CAPS NONDISPLAY
List	<1 40			
Type	NUM		NUM	
Initial	8			
Protect		YES	YES	YES
Format			DATE7.	

Note that the **chkpass** field is initially set to PROTECT and NONDISPLAY. This means that the user is not aware of this field's presence on the screen. Later, under program control, this field is reactivated for the user to verify the format storage area password.

```
      length rc1 $ 1;

      init:
         control always;
         messlist = symgetn('messlist') ;
         entryby = "&sysjobid" ;
         entrydt = "&sysdate"d ;
      return;

      main:
         call wname("");    /* Clear window name in border.           */
         erroroff _all_;    /* Clear error flags for all window fields.*/
         goterror = 0;      /* Initialize error flag.                 */
         rc1 = '0' ;

      /* test if user has pressed PF3 to exit or typed END*/
         if _status_ = 'E' then return;

      /* now validate each of fields */

      /* check that the storage area is a valid SAS data set name */

         if sasname(fsaname) = 0 then do;
           call wname(getnitemc(messlist,'badname ')) ;
           erroron fsaname;
           goterror = 1;
         end;

      /* check the FSA does not already exist */

         if fsaname ne _blank_ then do ;
           call method('catlg.af.methods.scl','chkuniq',
                       'ratesf.fda',
                       'fsaname',
                        fsaname,
                        rc1) ;

         if rc1 eq '9' then do ;
            message = getnitemc(messlist,'logmess1') ;
            put message ;
            put _all_ ;
            return ;
         end ;

         if rc1 eq '1' then do ;
            if goterror eq 0 then
               call wname(getnitemc(messlist,'fsaexsts')) ;
            erroron fsaname ;
            goterror = 1 ;
         end ;
       end ;

      /* check that the descriptive fields are entered */

         if fmtdesc eq _blank_ OR
            strdesc eq _blank_ OR
```

```
          enddesc eq _blank_ OR
          fmttype eq _blank_ OR
          fmtnam  eq _blank_ OR
          owner   eq _blank_ OR
          lbldesc eq _blank_ OR
          sfldlen eq .        OR
          lfldlen eq .
       then do ;
         if goterror eq 0 then
            call wname(getnitemc(messlist,'badflds ')) ;
         erroron fmtdesc strdesc owner enddesc lbldesc
                 sfldlen lfldlen fmttype fmtnam ;
         goterror = 1;
       end ;

/* check the format name is a valid SASNAME */

       if sasname(fmtnam) eq 0 then do;
         if goterror = 0 then
            call wname(getnitemc(messlist,'badfmt1 ')) ;
         erroron fmtnam;
         goterror = 1;
       end;

/* strengthen the above check to ensure that the format name does
   not end with a numeric */

       if substr(compress(reverse(fmtnam)),1,1)
          in ("0" "1" "2" "3" "4" "5" "6" "7" "8" "9") then do ;
         if goterror = 0 then
            call wname(getnitemc(messlist,'BADFMT2 ')) ;
         erroron fmtnam;
         goterror = 1;
       end;

/* ensure that the format name does not currently exist */

       if fmtnam ne _blank_ then do ;
         call method('catlg.af.methods.scl','chkuniq',
                     'ratesf.fda',
                     'fmtnam',
                     fmtnam,
                     rc1) ;

         if rc1 eq '9' then do ;
            message = getnitemc(messlist,'LOGMESS2') ;
            put message ;
            put _all_ ;
            return ;
         end ;

         if rc1 eq '1' then do ;
            if goterror eq 0 then
               call wname(getnitemc(messlist,'FMTEXSTS')) ;
            erroron fmtnam ;
            goterror = 1 ;
         end ;
       end ;
```

```
      if fmttype in ('I','P','N') and sfldlen > 8 then do ;
          if goterror eq 0 then
              call wname(getnitemc(messlist,'MAXERROR')) ;
          erroron sfldlen ;
          goterror = 1 ;
      end ;

      if fmttype in ('I','P','N') and sfldlen < 3 then do ;
          if goterror eq 0 then
              call wname(getnitemc(messlist,'MINERROR')) ;
          erroron sfldlen ;
          goterror = 1 ;
      end ;

/* if an error occurred send it back to the user */

      if goterror eq 1 then return ;

/* if user did not enter a password make them confirm that none
   is required */

      if psw eq _blank_ then
         call display('catlg.af.fmtconf.program',psw) ;

/* user has validated password but got it wrong,make them re-enter
   the password and after pressing ENTER they can again re-validate
   the password */

      if chkpass ne _blank_ AND chkpass ne psw then do ;
         call wname(getnitemc(messlist,'psscheck')) ;
         chkpass = _blank_ ;
         cursor psw ;
         protect chkpass ;
         rc = field('color blue alloff','chkpass') ;
         return ;
      end ;

/* verify the password if entered */

      if psw ne _blank_ and chkpass eq _blank_ then do ;
         call wname(getnitemc(messlist,'pssagain'))  ;
         cursor chkpass ;
         unprotect chkpass ;
         rc = field('color yellow reverse','chkpass') ;
         return ;
      end ;

/* add this fsa to the fda */

      dsid00 = open('ratesf.fda','u') ;
      efldlen = sfldlen ;
      call set(dsid00) ;
      if append(dsid00) then do ;
        call close(dsid00) ;
        txt = sysmsg() ;
        call wname(getnitemc(messlist,'IOERROR')) ;
```

```
            put _all_ ;
            return ;
         end ;
      call close(dsid00) ;

/* create the new FSA database */

      if fmttype in ('C','J') then vartype = 'C' ; else vartype = 'N' ;

      dsid00 = open('ratesf.'||fsaname||'(label='||fmtdesc||')','N');
      rc00   = newvar(dsid00,'start',vartype,sfldlen,strdesc) ;
      rc00   = newvar(dsid00,'end',vartype,sfldlen,enddesc) ;

/* note --label field is numeric for a numeric informat, we want it
   to stay character otherwise in this application */

      if fmttype ne 'I' then
         rc00   = newvar(dsid00,'label','C',lfldlen,lbldesc) ;
      else
         rc00   = newvar(dsid00,'label','N',8,lbldesc) ;
      rc00   = newvar(dsid00,'fmtname','C',8,'Format Name') ;
      rc00   = newvar(dsid00,'hlo','C',1,'High/Low/Other') ;
      rc00   = newvar(dsid00,'type','C',1,'Type Of Format') ;
      call close(dsid00) ;

/* as this screen is intended to load just one format structure,
   we now generate an END */

      _status_ = 'H' ;
   return;
```

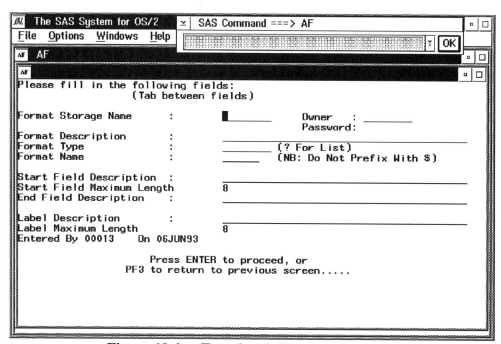

Figure 10.4:   Entering A Format Structure

When users access this screen, they initially see the blank entry screen in Figure 10.4. After filling out this screen and pressing **enter** to save the FDA entry, they have two possibilities: either enter a password or not.

If a password is entered, the **chkpass** field is UNPROTECTED in SCL and pops up for users to verify the password. Otherwise, they are requested to verify that no password was intended. This is shown in Figure 10.5:

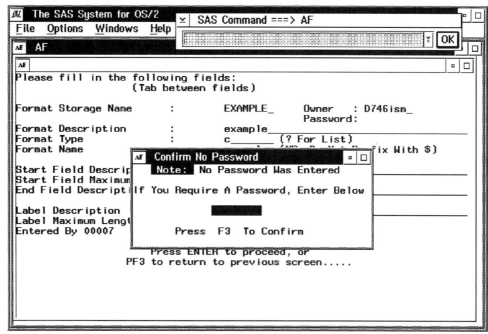

Figure 10.5:   Verify No Password On An FDA Entry

The intention of the 'Confirm No Password' screen is to remind users that a password is possible. Often a password will not be required. This application generates formats for use in both production and nonproduction systems. It is often the case that for a nonproduction job, the format is not password protected, but it usually is for production applications.

The password system is certainly not totally adequate. Although it meets user requirements, an immediate necessary enhancement is the option to access the FDA again to add a password later. Alternatively, it may be necessary to force use of passwords.

ENTRY: FMTCONF.PROGRAM   Confirm No Password When FSA Entered

The entry screen here does no more than request that some data be entered in a field. The screen from the programmer's viewpoint is in Figure 10.6 and from the user's viewpoint in Figure 10.5 above. In this screen, the single field, **psw,** has the CAPS, CURSOR, and NONDISPLAY attributes only set. All other attributes are left at defaults.

```
entry psw $ 8 ;

init:
main:
term:
return ;
```

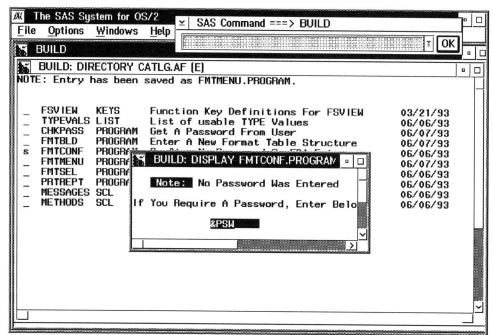

Figure 10.6:   Verify No Password On FDA Screen

From the code viewpoint, this screen does nothing. It pops up if the user does not enter a password when creating an FDA entry. If the user exits this entry immediately with the password field left blank, then no password is attached to the FSA; otherwise the FSA password becomes the value entered in this screen.

ENTRY: FMTMENU.PROGRAM   Main Menu For Formats Entry

This is the first entry seen by a user. As it is the system entry mechanism, some additional work is done before the user gains control. This includes initializing the message system and ensuring that FSLIST has usable function keys (remember this system was originally written for MVS).

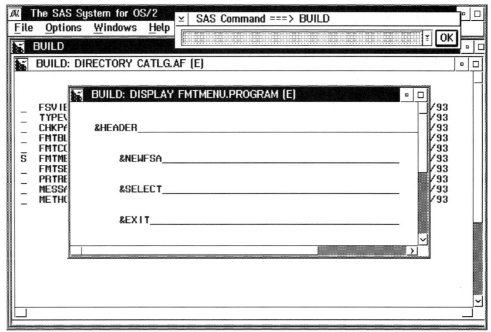

Figure 10.7:   Format System Main Menu

We defined the screen in Figure 10.7. The fields on the screen have the following attributes:

Attribute	HEADER	NEWFSA	SELECT	EXIT
Options	AUTOSKIP	AUTOSKIP	AUTOSKIP	AUTOSKIP
Type		PUSHBTNC	PUSHBTNC	PUSHBTNC
Protect	YES	YES	YES	YES
Just	CENTER			

Additionally, the following INITIAL attributes apply:

HEADER	Tab To An Option And Press Enter, Or Click With Mouse
NEWFSA	Add A New Format To The System
SELECT	Edit/Browse/Print A Format, Or Add Text
EXIT	Exit The System

***** *SOURCE* *****

```
length valpsw $ 1 owner $ 8 fsaexist $ 3 fmtnme $ 8 ;

init:
 control label ;
 rc = field('color yellow reverse','header') ;
```

```
   /* set up FLIST keys (same as FSVIEW in this instance) */

   rc = copy('catlg.af.fsview.keys','sasuser.profile.fslist.keys',
             'catalog') ;

   /* initialize message subsystem */
    call display('catlg.af.messages.scl') ;
   return ;

   select:

   /* user clicked on SELECT button -- They want to select a format to work
   with.
      Check if any are defined, if not issue an error message and return to
   user
      Otherwise allow access via extended table */

     dsid01 = open('ratesf.fda') ;
     rc = attrn(dsid01,'ANY') ;
     call close(dsid01) ;
     if rc ne 1 then do ;   /* no formats -- exit */
       %errmess(getnitemc(symgetn('messlist'),'NOTABLES'))
       return ;
     end ;
     /* ok, go to extended table */
     call display('catlg.af.fmtsel.program') ;
   return ;

   newfsa:

     /* let them add a new storage area definition to the FDA */
     call display('catlg.af.fmtbld.program') ;
   return ;

   exit:

     /* no more, leave system, return to startup program */
     _status_ = 'H' ;
   return ;
```

ENTRY: FMTSEL.PROGRAM   *Selection List To Choose A Format*

This program entry defines an extended table listing all the existing formats. From this screen, the user can select a format to either modify, browse, print, or alternatively update the diary entry.

The user is shown the format name and description on the extended table. A field is provided to enter the type of operation desired: E=Edit, B=Browse, P=Print, and T=text.

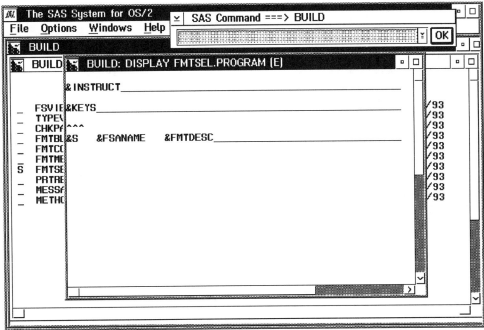

Figure 10.8:   Carry Out An Operation On A Format

The screen that we defined is shown in Figure 10.8. The relevant field attributes are:

Attribute	INSTRUCT	KEYS	S	FSANAME	FMTDESC
Options	AUTOSKIP	AUTOSKIP	AUTOSKIP CAPS CURSOR	AUTOSKIP CAPS	AUTOSKIP
Protect	YES	YES		YES	YES
Just	CENTER	CENTER			

In addition, the following INITIAL values apply:

INSTRUCT   E=Edit, B=Browse, P=Print, T=Text Entry
KEYS   Use PF3 To Exit, ENTER To Process Entry

Editing of a format entry is by FSVIEW. This application requires little use of SCL at the time data are entered (because it is largely left up to users to ensure correctness), so FSVIEW is appropriate. There are two sets of FSVIEW formulas defined, one for numeric **start/end** values and one for character. This program entry is responsible for determining which to use.

The screen allows for a dynamic FSVIEW window in the sense that EXECCMD is used to customize the formula each time FSVIEW is called. Each format can have its own field lengths for **start/end** and **label,** and EXECCMD uses these by passing through a FORMAT <VARNAME> <VAR FORMAT> command to the next window, namely the FSVIEW.

*****SOURCE *****

```
length valpsw $ 1 owner $ 8 fsaexist $ 3 fmtnme $ 8 fmttype $ 1;

init:
  control always term ;
  call setcr('stay','return') ;

  dsid01=open('ratesf.fda');
  call setrow(0,1,'N','Y');
  call set(dsid01) ;
  rc = field('color yellow highlight','instruct keys') ;
  rc = field('color green alloff','fsaname fmtdesc') ;
  messlist = symgetn('messlist') ;
return;

term:
  call close(dsid01);
return;

putrow:
  call wname('') ;

/* check selection field. If they entered a blank then just send
   them back. If they entered one of BEPT then process the request
   otherwise, issue an error message and return to the user */

  rc = unselect(_currow_) ;
  if s eq _blank_ then return ;
  if s not in ('B','E','P','T') then do;
    call wname(getnitemc(messlist,'BEPONLY ')) ;
    return;
  end;

  select (s) ;
    when ('B') do ;
      call symputc('wantpass','N') ;
      link chkall ;
      if errstat eq '1' then return ;
    call method('catlg.af.methods.scl','browse',fmtnme,fmttype,
                messlist,nobs);
    end ;

    when ('E') do ;
      call symputc('wantpass','Y') ;
      link chkall ;
      if errstat eq '1' then return ;
      call method('catlg.af.methods.scl','editit',fsaname,fmttype,
                  fmtnme) ;
    end ;

    when ('P') do ;
      call symputc('wantpass','N') ;
      link chkall ;
      call method('catlg.af.methods.scl','prntfmt',messlist,
                  fmtnme) ;
      rc = system('print ' || dequote(symgetc('prtfile')));
    end ;
```

```
      when ('T') do ;

         /* text entry, we want a password here */
         call symputc('wantpass','Y') ;
         if cexist('ratesf.diary') eq 0 then do ;
           call wname(getnitemc(messlist,'CATGONE ')) ;
           return ;
         end ;

         /* make sure everything is ok */
         link chkall ;
         if errstat eq '1' then return ;

         /* define the source entry to save the text in */
         textname = 'ratesf.diary.' || fsaname || '.source' ;

         /* if we already have some text then load it */
         if cexist(textname) eq 1 then call preview('copy',textname);

         /* as we cannot put custom messages on the preview screen, display
            a legend to give a little help */
         call wregion(20,1,4,80) ;
         call putlegend(1,
           center('Type KEYS For Function Key Definitions',80));
         call legend('Note:') ;

         /* set up the region for the preview window and set up commands
            to pass to preview */
         call wregion(1,1,19,80) ;
         call execcmd('num on;pmenu off') ;

         /* and allow access to the text */
         if preview('edit') ne -1 then rc = preview('save',textname);
         rc = preview('clear') ;
         call execcmd('pmenu on') ;
         call endlegend() ;
      end ;
   end ;
   s = _blank_ ;
return;

getrow:

   /* simple, always just read the next available observation */
   if fetchobs(dsid01,_currow_) eq -1 then call endtable();
return;

chkall:
/* ensure the fsaname exists */
  errstat = '0' ;
  if not exist('ratesf.' || fsaname) then do ;
    call wname(getnitemc(messlist,'NOFSA') || fsaname) ;
    fsaname = _blank_ ;
    errstat = '1' ;
    return ;
  end ;
```

```
/* get the number of obs in the table */

 dsid00 = open('ratesf.' || fsaname) ;
 nobs = nobs(dsid00) ;
 call close(dsid00) ;

/* make sure they are allowed to access this format */

 dsid00 = open('ratesf.fda(where=(fsaname eq "' || fsaname || '"))') ;
 rc = fetch(dsid00) ;
 pass = getvarc(dsid00,varnum(dsid00,'psw')) ;
 fmtnme = getvarc(dsid00,varnum(dsid00,'fmtnam')) ;
 fmttype= getvarc(dsid00,varnum(dsid00,'fmttype')) ;
 call close(dsid00) ;

 if symgetc('wantpass') eq 'Y' then do ;
  if pass ne _blank_ then do ;
    call display('catlg.af.chkpass.program',fsaname,valpsw,
                  owner,fmtnme) ;
    if valpsw eq '1' then do ;
      %errmess(getnitemc(messlist,'SECVIOL1'),
               getnitemc(messlist,'SECVIOL2') || owner)
      errstat = '1' ;
      return ;
    end ;
    if valpsw eq '2' then do ;
      %errmess(getnitemc(messlist,'PSSABRT1'),
               getnitemc(messlist,'PSSABRT2'))
      errstat = '1' ;
      return ;
    end ;
  end ;
 end ;
return ;
```

When the user chooses the SELECT push button from the main menu, the screen in Figure 10.9 is displayed. This is the user's view of the screen shown earlier in Figure 10.8.

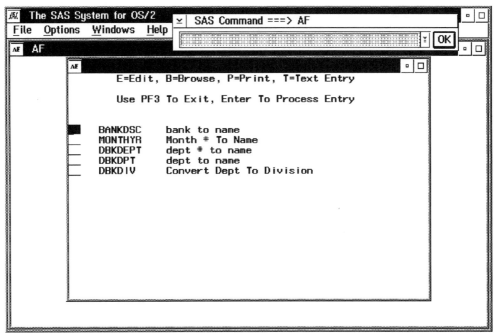

Figure 10.9:   Carry Out An Operation On A Format

There are four possible options from the screen in Figure 10.9.

Edit Option

This option allows the application's user to add or delete values from the selected format. The edit uses FSVIEW. In this situation, FSVIEW is used as minimal SCL is required behind the tabular edit structure. Extended tables would certainly have worked here, but with more coding.

On selecting the Edit option, the user is placed in the screen shown in Figure 10.10. In the screen shown, the format named DBKDIV is being edited. The TYPE is 'J', indicating a character informat.

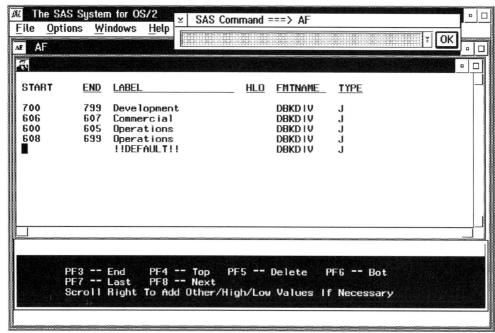

Figure 10.10:   FSVIEW Screen For Adding Format Items

The screen is standard for editing this application in the sense that the user will always see the **start**, **end**, **label**, **hlo**, **fmtname**, and **type** fields to edit. However, because of the EXECCMD argument that is passed through from FMTSEL.PROGRAM, the physical layout of the screen is always slightly different.

On each new observation, a default label of !!DEFAULT!! (or -999999 for a numeric informat) appears. The user can use this to store an observation on the format data set, but not have it included in the format. When the format is created in the MAKEFMT method, observations with a label of !!DEFAULT!! or -999999 are excluded from format processing.

A number of simple formulas are associated with the FSVIEW. The following set exists for use with character-based formats. These formulas reside in the FSVIEWC catalog:

```
END= end ; if end = ' ' and start ne ' ' then end=start ;

HLO= hlo ; if hlo ne ' ' and start||end ne ' ' then hlo = ' ';

START= start ; if start eq ' ' and end ne ' ' then start=
       end ;

FMTNAME=  symgetc('fmtname') ;

TYPE= symgetc('fmttype')

LABEL= label;if label= ' ' then label = '!!DEFAULT!!';
```

Effectively, when a **start/end** range is identical (it is in fact not a range but a single value), the above formulas for **start** and **end** will deduce one from the value of the other. The **hlo** formula prevents an **hlo** value from being assigned when a **start** or **end** is also assigned. The **fmtname** and **type** fields are assignments based on the macro variables created before FSVIEW starts. Because these are straight-out assignments, the user cannot change these values. They can be typed over on screen but are immediately reset when the formula is executed when the user presses ENTER. The **label** formula assigns the default label of !!DEFAULT!!.

A numeric format results in a very similar set of formulas. These are

```
HLO= hlo; if hlo ne ' ' and (start ne . or end ne .) then hlo = ' ' ;

START= start ; if start eq . and end ne . then start=end;

END= end ; if end eq . and start ne . then end = start ;

FMTNAME= symgetc('fmtname') ;

TYPE= symgetc('fmttype')

LABEL= label;if label= ' ' then label = '!!DEFAULT!!';
```

The only change here has been to use the numeric missing value rather than the character. The formulas are stored in the FSVIEWN catalog.

Finally, the FSVIEWI catalog is used for storing the formulas associated with numeric informats. These formulas are

```
LABEL= label;if label eq . then label = -999999 ;

START= start; if start eq . and end ne . then start=end ;

END= end;if end eq . and start ne . then end=start ;

FMTNAME= symgetc('fmtname')

TYPE= symgetc('fmttype')

HLO= hlo;if hlo ne ' ' and (start ne . or end ne .) then hlo= ' '
```

Browse Option And Print Option

The browse is accomplished by calling the BRSWFMT method in METHODS.SCL. No password is required. The results of using the FMTLIB option with PROC FORMAT are written out to an external file that is then displayed using PROC FSLIST. As the application was designed under MVS and our users were familiar with the ISPF browse facility, using the very similar FSLIST was judged preferable to using the OUTPUT window. The PREVIEW window could have been used here also.

An example of the output from the option is shown in Figure 10.11. This displays the result of browsing a character informat. The printout is obtained from the FMTLIB option in PROC FORMAT, so is familiar to most of our users.

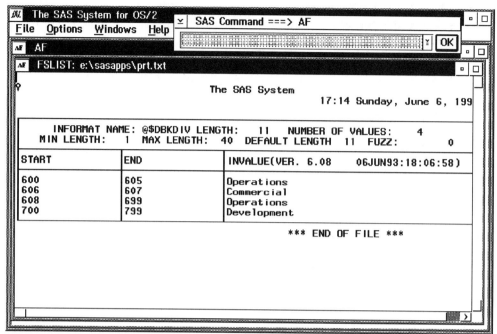

Figure 10.11:   Browsing A Format

The PRINT option is very similar. The difference is that instead of displaying with FSLIST, the output is spooled to a printer. The code in the PRNTFMT method in METHODS.SCL is given from OS/2, but you may replace that with your own code on other systems.

The ADD TEXT Option

The point of this option is to allow users to document what they are doing with the format. Standard use is to specify exactly who is responsible for the format and what jobs use the format.

Figure 10.12 illustrates how the text looks for one of our formats:

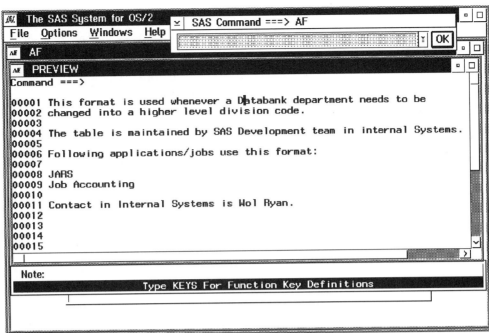

Figure 10.12: Adding Text To A Format

ENTRY: METHODS.SCL Methods For Formats System

This entry defines all the methods in this application that are called by other entries.

***** *SOURCE* *****

```
    makefmt:
    method fsaname $ 8 ;

    /* this method is passed the name of a SAS data set in DD RATESF,
        and creates a (in)format from that data set. No validity checking
        is done here, it is expected that the data set is a valid CNTLIN
        data set with START/END/LABEL/HLO/TYPE/FMTNAME all defined. The
        caller should verify existence of the data set before calling
        this method

        the method explicitly removes any observations with the default
        label value '!!DEFAULT!!'
    */
```

```
      submit continue ;
        proc format library=library cntlin=ratesf.&fsaname ;
          where label ne '!!DEFAULT!!' ;
          run ;
      endsubmit ;

   endmethod ;
   /*---------------------------------------------------------------*/
   dorept:
   method fmtname $ 8;

   /* this method takes the fmtname (ie a valid SAS format name, with
      the $ and @ prefixes where applicable), and prints the format to
      the current external print file (not to OUTPUT window)

      It is expected that the caller has verified the existence of the
      fmtname before passing it into here

   */
      submit continue ;
        proc printto print = &prtfile new ; run ;
        proc format library=library fmtlib ;
          select &fmtname ;
        run ;
        proc printto print=print ; run ;
      endsubmit ;

   endmethod ;
   /*---------------------------------------------------------------*/
   chkuniq:      /* determine if a certain value exists in a field
                    on a database.  */

   method    dsname  $ 17   /* data set name to search */
             fldname $ 8    /* name of field to check against */
             fldval  $ 25   /* value to search for */
             retcode $ 1    /* return code */ ;

      retcode = '0' ;    /* assume nomatch will be found */

      dsid_00 = open(dsname) ;

      if dsid_00 le 0 then do ;
        retcode = '9' /* bad open, return */ ;
        return ;
      end ;

      if attrn(dsid_00,'ANY') ne 0 then do ;
        rc = where(dsid_00,fldname || ' eq ' || "'" || fldval || "'") ;

        if fetch(dsid_00) ne -1 then retcode = '1' ; /* match found */
      end ;
      call close(dsid_00) ;

   endmethod ;
   /*---------------------------------------------------------------*/
   browse:
    method fmtnme $ 8 fmttype $ 1 messlist 3 nobs 4 ;
```

```
/* ensure there is something to browse */

  if nobs lt 1 then do ;
    %errmess(getnitemc(messlist,'NORECORD') || ' Browse')
    return ;
  end ;

  /* for a character format, put the $ in front of the name */

  if fmttype in ('C','J') then format = '$' || fmtnme ;
  else format = fmtnme;

  /* for an informat, put the implied @ in front of the name */

  if fmttype in ('J','I') then format = '@' || format ;

  call method('catlg.af.methods.scl','dorept',format) ;

  call fslist(symgetc('prtfile')) ;

endmethod ;
/*-------------------------------------------------------------*/
editit:
 method fsaname $ 8 fmttype $ 1 fmtnme $ 8 ;

  /* start by extracting the START/LABEL lengths so we can customize
     the FSVIEW window */
  dsid99 = open('ratesf.' || fsaname) ;
  slength= varlen(dsid99,varnum(dsid99,'start')) ;
  llength= varlen(dsid99,varnum(dsid99,'label')) ;
  call close(dsid99) ;

  /* we use a different FSVIEW formula, as well as passing different
     commands to FSVIEW, depending on whether we are going to edit a
     numeric or character format */
  if fmttype in ('C','J') then do ; /* character */
    formname = 'fsviewc' ;
    view=  'autoadd on;format start "$char' ||
      compress(put(slength,3.)) ||
      '.";format end "$char' || compress(put(slength,3.)) ||
      '.";format label "$char'|| compress(put(llength,3.)) || '.";' ||
      'color id pink;color idname pink' ;
  end ;
  else do ; /* numeric */
    formname = 'fsviewn';
    view=  'autoadd on;format start "10.";format ' ||
      'end "10.";format label "$char' ||
      compress(put(llength,3.)) || '.";' ||
      'color id pink;color idname pink' ;
  end ;

  /* set up fields that FSVIEW expects to find in a formula */
  call symputc('fmtname',fmtnme) ;
  call symputc('fmttype',fmttype) ;

  /* display a keys window for FSVIEW */
  call method('catlg.af.methods.scl','legdkeys') ;
```

```
      /* execute FSVIEW with the appropriate commands passed through */
      call execcmd(view) ;
      call fsview('ratesf.'||fsaname||'(cntllev=member)','EDIT',
              'catlg.fsview.' || formname || '.formula') ;
      call endlegend() ;   /* was set up in method above */

      /* rebuild the format table */

      call wregion(10,10,7,65) ;
      call putlegend(2,center('Updating SAS Format Table .. Please Wait',65))
  ;
      call legend('','','','highlight') ;
      call method('methods.scl','makefmt',fsaname) ;
      call endlegend() ;
  endmethod;
  /*-------------------------------------------------------------*/
  prntfmt:
   method messlist 4 fmtnme $ 8 ;

     if nobs lt 1 then do ;
       %errmess(getnitemc(messlist,'NORECORD') || 'Print')
       return ;
     end ;

     /* for a character format, put the $ in front of the name */

     if fmttype in ('C','J') then format = '$' || fmtnme ;
     else format = fmtnme;

     /* for an informat, put the implied @ in front of the name */

     if fmttype in ('J','I') then format = '@' || format ;

     call method('methods.scl','dorept',format) ;
   endmethod ;
  /*-------------------------------------------------------------*/
  legdkeys :
  method ;
     call wregion(19,1,7,80) ;
     call putlegend(2,
         center( 'PF3 -- End    PF4 -- Top    PF5 -- Delete   PF6 -- Bot',80))
  ;
     call putlegend(3,center('PF7 -- Last   PF8 -- Next',80)) ;
     call putlegend(4,
         center('Scroll Right To Add Other Fields If Necessary',80)) ;
     call legend() ;
     call wregion(2,1,15,80,'') ;
  endmethod ;
  /*-------------------------------------------------------------*/
```

The final method, LEGDKEYS, is used to place a function key definition screen at the end of the FSVIEW window.

This entry contains all the error messages that the system will use. The technique of storing the error messages in a named list is used. In this entry, the messages are initially stored in an array. The list is created, then populated in this entry. The entry is called from the initial screen, FMTMENU.PROGRAM.

***** *SOURCE* *****

```
array messages (*) $ 80
  (
    'CATGONE Error: Diary Catalog Is Missing -- Call Support Team'
    'BADPASS Error: Incorrect Password, Attempt  Of 3'
    "BADNAME Error: FSA Name must be a VALID SAS Data set Name"
    "BADTYPE Error: Format Type must be either N or C"
    "BADFMT1 Error: Format Name must be a VALID Numeric or Char Format Name"
    "BADFLDS Error: You Must Complete All Highlit Fields"
    "BADFMT2 Error: You Cannot Use A Numeric To End A SAS Format Name"
    "FSAEXSTSError: The FSA Already Exists"
    "IOERROR Error: I/O Error On FDA, Call Support Team"
    "FMTEXSTSError: The Format Already Exists"
    "PSSCHECKError: Password Verification Failed - Enter Password Again"
    "PSSAGAINPlease Re-Enter Password To Verify"
    'LOGMESS1Unable To Open FDA In Uniqueness Check - FSANAME'
    'LOGMESS2Unable To Open FDA In Uniqueness Check - FMTNAM'
    'NOTABLESNo Tables Were Found To Select From'
    'BEPONLY Error: Valid Values Are "B","E","P"'
    'NORECORDNote: The Table Has No Records, Cannot '
    'NOFSA   Note: FSA Does Not Exist - '
    'SECVIOL1Note: Security Violation -- No Access Permitted'
    'SECVIOL2Note: Owner Is '
    'PSSABRT1NOTE: Password Check Was Aborted',
    'PSSABRT2NOTE: No Access Granted'
    'MAXERRORError: Maximum Length Is 8 For Numeric Format'
    'MINERRORError: Minimum Length Is 3 For Numeric Format'
    'TYPERRORError: Type Conflicts With Name'
      ) ;

init:
  messlist = makelist(dim(messages),'L') ;

  do i=1 to dim(messages) ;
    messlist = insertc(messlist,substr(messages(i),9),1,
                    substr(messages(i),1,8)) ;
  end ;
  call symputn('messlist',messlist) ;

return ;
```

MACRO: ERRMESS.SAS

*****SOURCE*****

This macro should be placed in your SASAUTOS library. It could be replaced by a method if desired; however, as it stands the macro can accept function calls to GETNITEMC. Using a method would require the caller to place the results of such a function call into a variable, then pass the variable (as you cannot pass a function to a method and have it correctly interpreted). The reason for this is that the parameter pass would be at run time, and the function would have had to be interpreted at compile time.

```
%macro errmess(message1,message2) ;
  %if "&message2 "= " " %then %let message2= ' ' ;
  call wregion(10,7,10,70) ;
  call putlegend(2,center(&message1,70)) ;
  call putlegend(3,center(&message2,70)) ;
  call putlegend(5,center('Press ENTER To Continue',70)) ;
  call legend('Message','','','highlight') ;
  call execcmdi('next message','noexec') ;
  call endlegend() ;
%mend errmess ;
```

The macro can be called in any SCL program and generates in-stream code.

LIST: TYPEVALS.LIST

This list defines the values of the **type** variable that are able to be used in the application. Because the application does not currently support PICTURE formats 'P' is not currently in this list. The items placed in the list are I, C, N, J. Respectively, they mean NUMERIC FORMAT, CHARACTER FORMAT, NUMERIC INFORMAT, CHARACTER INFORMAT. They are the values seen in the **type** variable of an output data set from PROC FORMAT.

How The Formats Are Used

To use the formats, it is necessary only to have the LIBRARY libref allocated to your job or session. Every job and user will have read access to the LIBRARY libref, but only users with a legitimate need to maintain formats have the additional write access.

If the LIBRARY libref has been allocated to you, user-defined formats stored in a catalog in that libref are available for use. No extra loading of formats is needed. Programs that require you to use the formats just name the format and SAS software searches the LIBRARY libref for it.

Accessing The Formats System

The following code is used to start the application under OS/2 with only a single user accessing at a time:

```
libname catlg   'e:\sasapps\marts\formats' ;
libname ratesf  'e:\sasapps\marts\formats' ;
libname library 'e:\sasapps\marts\formats' ;
%let prtfile = 'e:\sasapps\prt.txt' ;
dm 'af c=catlg.af.fmtmenu.program' af ;
```

On other platforms, amend the system-dependent library names as required by the platform standards (this may involve using SAS/SHARE as is done in our site under MVS).

Futures

The application is very much in its infancy, and user feedback indicates several changes are desirable. The following are likely to be implemented at some stage:

- ability to specify a start and end date for the use of an observation in a format data set

- ability to edit a format but to specify a date that an observation is to be used, so the default immediate create is bypassed for some observations

- support all other options of PROC FORMAT, such as noninclusive ranges, FUZZ, UPCASE, and so on

- completely implement the requirement for the application to inform the user when a format creation fails

- allow access back to the FDA entry to alter a password

- redevelop using a FRAME-based development methodology.

Chapter 11: FRAME Technology

Contents

Overview

Up until now, this text has considered windows defined by program entries. A limitation of these windows has been that only text can be defined in them and attributes such as subwindows in a program screen do not exist. In Release 6.08, SAS/AF defines the FRAME entry. With this entry type, the entire screen seen by the user is defined by a collection of logical screens called regions. You can fit many regions onto a physical screen and allow both text and graphics to be on the screen at the same time in different regions. When users see the screen, they only see the text or graphics.

Effectively, FRAME allows a graphical user interface (GUI) to be presented to the user. You may have already seen the term GUI used in other texts and magazines. In the FRAME context, the GUI is another way of interfacing an application with its users, using graphics as the primary presentation tool.

Intuitively a GUI is often an easy way for users to view the application they are using. The GUI removes the constraints of having just text on screen and permits the screen designer to set up icons and other graphical entities on screen.

Each region defined in a FRAME entry has a class associated with it. SAS/AF delivers a number of classes and you can add your own, although you are restricted to basing your own on the SAS/AF classes. Classes are provided to allow regions to be treated as text, graphics, icons, push buttons, extended tables, selection lists, and many more.

Since the GUI approach is new in SAS software, there are some questions to consider. Before you decide to use FRAME in an application, ask yourself whether FRAME entries are really necessary.

In a SAS/EIS application, FRAME is essential because it provides an immediate picture to users rather than verbose explanatory text. FRAME entries carry more overhead in setting up and maintaining as they require each and every region to be defined and given the appropriate class. Because the definition is graphical in nature, FRAME entries may be slow to develop on some hardware. For some screens, (for example, a screen requiring just one field entry), FRAME may be 'overkill'.

Each region in a FRAME entry may have some SCL code associated with it, but frequently you can bypass any coding overhead at all as FRAME regions also permit a command to be executed when the region is selected. SCL functions are provided to allow regions to communicate, allowing a user, for instance, to click on an item in a region and cause another region to display information based in the item that was clicked on.

FRAME entries may reduce coding considerably. You can code a region once, define it as a new class, then reuse that class in other applications. No further coding is necessary to reuse the class.

This chapter experiments with an extended table FRAME entry and shows how to develop your own reusable objects. To do FRAME justice requires far more than a single chapter. FRAME is exciting in that it implements features never before available in SAS software, and the intention here is merely to whet the appetite.

You should read the first 3 chapters of *SAS/AF Software: FRAME Entry Usage and Reference, Version 6, First Edition* for an overview of FRAME and the terminology it uses. No attempt is made to reproduce that information in this text.

FRAME Entries -- An Example

This section is intended to get you familiar with the concept of FRAME. In my experience, an SCL feature used in many applications is the extended table. Here I discuss extended tables created using FRAME entries. The principles shown here are applicable to other region types (in fact some other region types are discussed here as well as extended tables).

In a program screen, an extended table fills the entire scrollable area of the entry. The only control you have is to determine where the nonscrollable area finishes and the scrollable area starts. In addition to that, you could also control the window dimensions to make the extended table look like a window over a larger screen. However, you are restricted to operating in that extended table window -- to communicate with any other screen, the table has to finish or branch to another entry.

In FRAME entries, you have control over how much of a screen an extended table uses and what else is on the screen communicating with the extended table.

Let's experiment. Enter the BUILD command in the usual manner (namely, whichever manner you prefer -- there are several. If you don't know any, type BUILD SASUSER.FRAMEEX on the program editor command line) to work on a catalog called SASUSER.FRAMEEX.

Edit an entry called EXTEND.FRAME. You will see a blank screen with a border around the outside. The border is the edge of the master region. The master region defines the borders within which other regions must reside (there is much more to the master region than this -- read the FRAME manual).

Creating A Region In A FRAME Entry

Having typed EDIT EXTEND.FRAME, you will now create a region. There are two ways to accomplish this: click and drag or use the pop-up menu. If you haven't used these before, use click and drag for region creation followed by the pop-up menu to define the region's attributes.

To click and drag, press the left mouse button and drag the mouse to form a rectangle on the screen. Release the button when you have formed the desired rectangle.

One of my 'rules' of using FRAME is to have a good idea before you start of what you want the final screen to look like.

Click somewhere near the top of the master region and drag the mouse to the right and downwards. Notice the rectangular region being created. Until you release the mouse button, that region can be sized as you desire -- after that you need to activate or click and drag as described above.

Make the rectangle about 75% of the master region depth and about 50% of the width. You should have something resembling Figure 11.1.

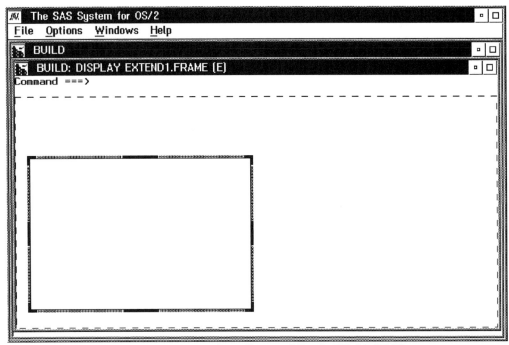

Figure 11.1:   A Region Created In A FRAME Entry

Selecting Region Attributes And Type

Now you need to tell FRAME about this region. Click the right mouse button to obtain a pop-up menu and select REGION ATTRIBUTES. This selection allows you to alter the look and feel of the region. Select the SET OUTLINE option first to change the region border and its border color and title. Use the example in Figure 11.2 to set your outline.

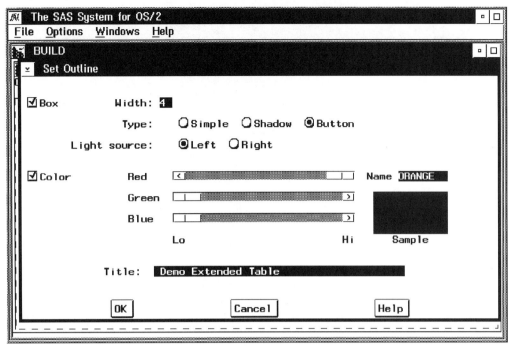

Figure 11.2:   Defining Region Attributes

When you click on OK to go back to the screen, the color is orange, the border has changed, and the region has a heading. Now define the region as an extended table. Pop up the menu again, select FILL, and from the resulting list of available classes select EXTENDED TABLE.

Now comes the fun part of FRAME. Remember in an SCL extended table you had to use SETROW and define various attributes in the GATTR window. The FRAME extended table class does all that here. Click on DYNAMIC EXTENDED TABLE -- you just defined a dynamic table with the size to be defined at run time. Look under PUTROW options -- you have control over just how GETROW will reprocess the table. Change the table name from OBJ1 to EXTEND, and for now leave all other options as they are and press OK to return to the FRAME screen.

The table has changed somewhat. In Figure 11.3, note that a scroll bar now sits on the right of the region. Click on that with the mouse and drag the scroll button. You are emulating exactly what your users will be able to do in the application to scroll through the table.

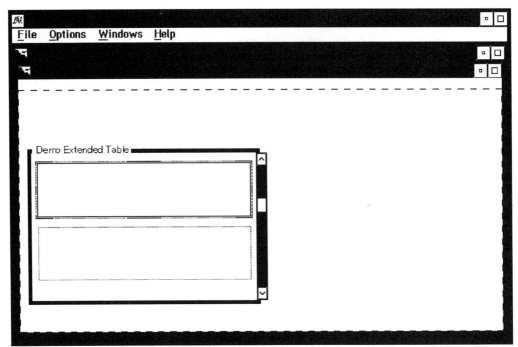
Figure 11.3:   Default Extended Table Layout

The other change is that two boxes have appeared in the middle of the region. The top box is known as the mask row. It will be used to define the attributes of the other boxes in this region. The second box you see is actually the first row of the extended table. At this stage, you have told FRAME that the region is an extended table, but you haven't told FRAME what the extended table will contain. That will be done using the MASK ROW.

Click inside the mask row to activate it. Then resize the region by moving it upwards (click on the bottom handle and slide the mouse upwards) so that it is a single line in height. When you release the mouse button, your screen should show the table with several more lines available, as in Figure 11.4.

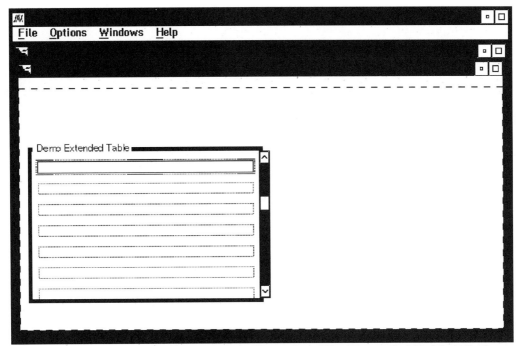

Figure 11.4:   Changing The Extended Table Mask

Click with the right mouse button on the mask row to pop up the menu. Select FILL. You are about to tell FRAME exactly what will be in the extended table. Notice that all the classes are available. In FRAME, an extended table can have graphics, push buttons, icons, and anything else you like from the available classes as extended table entries. For now though, select TEXT ENTRY.

Change the name to TABLEROW and remove the CAPS and AUTOSKIP options. Set the PROTECTION to YES and click on OK to return to the FRAME entry.

At this stage, you may have noticed a certain similarity between what you are setting up here and the actual definition screens that FRAME entries use to define attributes. Those screens are themselves FRAME entries.

Putting SCL Behind FRAME Regions

You are now ready to write some SCL. Type SOURCE on the FRAME entry command line, which allows you to edit an entry called EXTEND.SCL.

By default, when you enter SOURCE on a command line, you will edit an SCL entry with the same name as the FRAME entry. You do not require an SCL entry per region in a FRAME entry, as the single SCL program can communicate between regions.

Enter the following program:

```
init:
  dsid = open('usage.usage') ;
return ;

get1:
  if fetchobs(dsid,_currow_) eq -1 then
    call notify('EXTEND','_ENDTABLE_') ;
  else
    tablerow = getvarc(dsid,varnum(dsid,'keys')) ;
*   call notify('extend','_GET_TOPROW_',toprow) ;
*   call notify('topline','_SET_TEXT_',
                'Top Row Is Record ' || put(toprow,5.)) ;
return ;

term:
  call close(dsid) ;
return ;
```

Note that you could edit any file here; to use the above you need the USAGE libref defined to point to a SAS Notes library. The commented-out lines in the above code will be used shortly.

Let's examine the SCL in detail. There is a new routine that is used only in SCL written in a FRAME entry, CALL NOTIFY. That routine exists to pass messages (values) between regions and to examine attributes of regions. CALL NOTIFY follows a convention where the first parameter is always the region name, and following parameters are dependent on the class of the region. The second parameter always specifies what to do. It is called a method in FRAME terminology, while successive parameters are method dependent.

GET1 is the section of interest. Note how GET1 corresponds with the GETROW section name you used earlier to define the attributes for the extended table. That implies that you can have more than one GETROW section in a program, each corresponding to a particular region. Or to put it another way, you have the potential situation of having multiple extended tables on one screen, each being a single region. Starting to make the program entry look a little dated?

GET1 calls a single method, the ENDTABLE method. It corresponds to the CALL ENDTABLE routine in program entries. In general, use CALL NOTIFY in FRAME, as the SCL equivalents cannot always be used and can cause confusion. For instance, you can't use an SCL equivalent of a method when trying to communicate across regions.

The assignment of a value to TABLEROW fills the extended table with values. After compiling the FRAME entry, use TESTAF to reveal a screen like that in Figure 11.5.

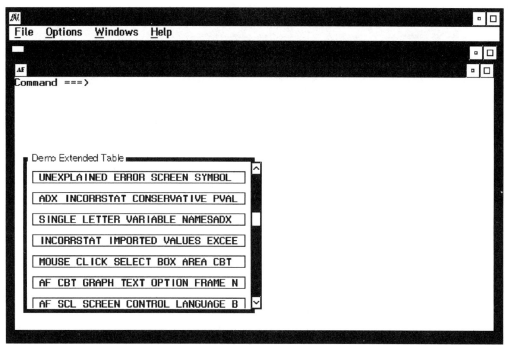

Figure 11.5:   Populated Extended Table Region

Check out the scroll bars. SAS software has provided you with a means of scrolling through a table that looks like the usual operating system means (on graphics-oriented platforms).

Let's remove the extra line between each row. Exit TESTAF and activate the extended table (not the mask row -- that is not the extended table). Pop up the menu and select OBJECT ATTRIBUTES (this option is available in a region after you have used FILL). Change the ROW SPACING option to zero and exit. You will see immediately that the spacing has changed; run TESTAF to verify that.

Adding Multiple Regions To A FRAME Entry

You can add another region. This will be a simple text entry region to tell the user which row is currently at the top. Add a new region above the extended table. Call the region TOPLINE and make it a text entry. It should be protected and have CAPS removed. You need to use the INITIAL VALUES attribute to assign an initial value of 'Top Line Is Record 1'. The screen should look like the screen in Figure 11.6.

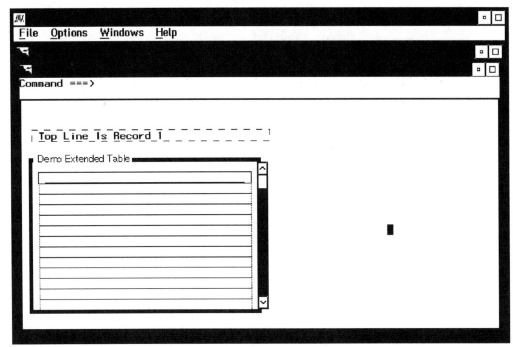

Figure 11.6: Add Another Region

Now uncomment the two commented-out lines of SCL in the earlier program. You are about to embark on some region-to-region communication. The additional code is

```
call notify('extend','_GET_TOPROW_',toprow) ;
call notify('topline','_SET_TEXT_',
            'Top Row Is Record ' || put(toprow,5.)) ;
```

The first line uses the _GET_TOPROW_ method available with extended tables to obtain the number of the top row. In the example, this is analogous to the observation number from USAGE.USAGE.

Now you use CALL NOTIFY to tell the Top Line region what value it should now be displaying. The _SET_TEXT_ method takes the value of the variable TOPROW and uses it to build up the Top Line region's value. Compile the program and rerun it. As you scroll the table, you should see the message in Top Line change to reflect the current top row, which is equivalent to _CURROW_ in an SCL extended table.

You've just been shown a simple way to create a usable extended table and an additional text entry. But a problem arises. Try to scroll to the bottom of the table and you will find you cannot. The scroll bar moves back up when you release it, and you have to keep holding the scroll arrow. So let's do some more experimenting with other region types to get around this problem.

Your objectives are to

- scroll directly to the end of the table
- scroll directly to the top of the table
- scroll directly to any table row specified by the user
- maintain the current scroll bars

Effectively, to scroll to the end of the table you need to issue a BOTTOM command, and issue a TOP command to get to the top.

Adding CHECK BOX Regions

Create a small new region at the right of the table. Fill it as a CHECK BOX. When the CHECK BOX attributes are up, change the name to TOP and give it a label of 'Scroll To Top'. Figure 11.7 shows the CHECK BOX:

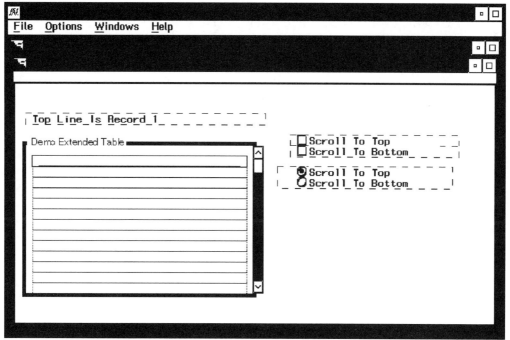

Figure 11.7:   FRAME Entry With CHECK BOX And RADIO BOX Regions

The CHECK BOX (and most other classes) allows you to specify a SAS command to be executed when the region is selected (clicked on). Logically, it would be expected that the command TOP could be executed here to scroll the table back to the top. That is not the case.

An executed SAS command in a FRAME entry is executed as if it comes from the FRAME command line. The word TOP has no meaning to FRAME, only to one of the regions that is contained in the FRAME. Hence you will need a little coding to accomplish the objective of getting to the top of the table.

You need to add a section to the SCL. It will be called TOP and will be executed whenever Scroll To Top is selected. The entry will communicate with the Extend region to tell it to scroll the table to the top. Edit the SCL again by typing SOURCE on the command line.

Add the following SCL, which will execute whenever the Scroll To Top CHECK BOX is clicked on:

```
top:
    call notify('extend','_VSCROLL_','MAX',-1) ;
return ;
```

It selects the _VSCROLL_ method that belongs to the extended table class, and it scrolls the table the maximum distance upwards. Note how the code appears in the top section; an inter-region communication occurs here using NOTIFY as the communication media.

The BOTTOM command is practically identical. Define a CHECK BOX region called Bottom and give it a Scroll To Bottom label. Replicate the code for Scroll To Top, but change the label to Bottom and the -1 becomes 1. Clicking on that CHECK BOX will scroll the table to the bottom (dependent on data set size, this could be quite slow).

When you use TESTAF or execute the FRAME entry and select TOP or BOTTOM you will notice that the CHECK BOX leaves a tick in the box by default. This can be removed by inserting the following code in the labeled sections for TOP and BOTTOM, after the call to the _VSCROLL_ method:

```
call notify('top','_ACTIVATE_',0) ;
```

or

```
call notify('bottom','_ACTIVATE_',0) ;
```

This code deactivates the CHECK BOX immediately after you finish with it.

Using RADIO BOX Regions

The CHECK BOX wasn't the only mechanism you could have used for accomplishing the TOP/BOTTOM code. An alternative would be a RADIO BOX. Let's add that to the screen to compare the two classes. Create a new region under the CHECK BOXES and fill it as a RADIO BOX. Call the region UPDOWN and set the number of items (in the first attribute screen that gets displayed) to 2.

Select the ENTER VALUES text in the box next to the FILL TYPE attribute. This brings up a box containing two button entries that will become the RADIO BOXES. Double click on BUTTON1. Change the item to Scroll To Top and the returned value to TOP. Then double click on BUTTON2; change the item to Scroll To Bottom and the returned value to BOT. Add the following to the SCL:

```
updown:
  if updown eq 'TOP' then
    call notify('extend','_VSCROLL_','MAX',-1) ;
  else
    call notify('extend','_VSCROLL_','MAX',1) ;
return ;
```

So what is the difference between the CHECK BOX and the RADIO BOX in this situation? The RADIO BOX is just one region, while the CHECK BOX requires a series of small regions. Otherwise, they are functionally equivalent in this situation. The RADIO BOX is easier to handle. For instance, if you want to move the RADIO BOX you move just one region, while you have to move multiple regions and maintain multiple SCL labels for the CHECK BOX approach. This comparison illustrates that in FRAME there may be multiple ways to accomplish a task. Other ways you could have accomplished the UPDOWN region include defining an extended table with a top and bottom row or creating a selection list. Experience with FRAME will indicate what's best in a given situation.

At this stage, your screen should resemble Figure 11.7.

Entering Text Into A Region

There is just one further requirement; have the user select an observation number and jump to that observation in the table (in other words, make that observation the top row of the table). Both CHECK BOX and RADIO BOX are not candidates for this task, as they don't allow entry of text. You need a combination of TEXT ENTRY and TEXT LABEL.

Create a region and define it as a text label. Call the region JUMPMESS, change the label to 'Record To Jump To:', and set the justification to LEFT. Exit back to the FRAME entry and create a second region immediately to the right of the first to get a screen like Figure 11.8.

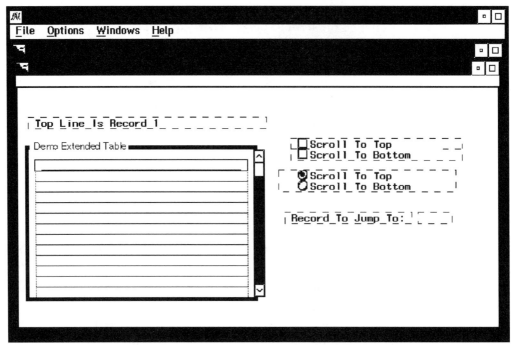

Figure 11.8: Adding TEXT ENTRY And TEXT LABEL Regions

Fill the new region as a TEXT ENTRY with a name of RECNUM, and change the default CHAR attribute to NUM. Use TESTAF to ensure that the field allows data to be entered into it and that the data are numeric only. If you get a message that 'ENTRY DOES NOT HAVE A PROGRAM', exit and compile your FRAME entry.

Return to your SCL program and add the following labeled section:

```
recnum:
  call notify('extend','_SET_TOPROW_',recnum) ;
return ;
```

Notice that the method executes within the section that the user has modified (that is, RECNUM). Thus you do not need to use NOTIFY to extract the value entered in that region. You place the value entered straight into the _SET_TOPROW_ method of EXTEND. Note that this is now a cross-region communication, so you must use NOTIFY to cause the EXTEND region to make the change.

At this stage, you can remove the extraneous CHECK BOXES that were set up as an example earlier. Activate each CHECK BOX and use the pop-up menu to remove each one. Delete the associated SCL.

Adding Columns To The Extended Table

Now let's add some more to the table. You now want to place columns in the table. This corresponds to the standard program entry extended table where columns in the table are defined as variables on the data set.

The columns will be the values of the field SYSTEM in the usage notes database and the field MODULEN. Click on the mask row and drag it to be about 2 lines deep. Now create two new regions inside the mask row to look like Figure 11.9.

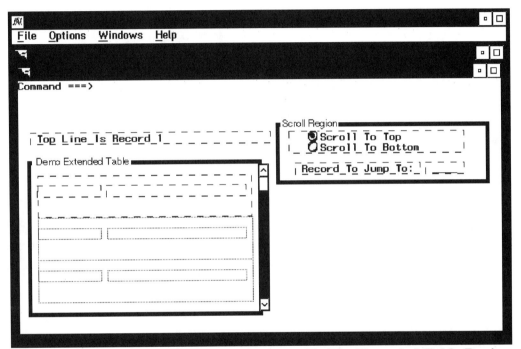

Figure 11.9:   Adding Columns To The Extended Table Region

Make each of these a TEXT LABEL and assign a justification of LEFT and no initial label. Name the regions SYSTEM and MODULEN.

Alter the SCL to add a CALL SET(dsid) in the INIT section immediately after the OPEN. Compile and run the FRAME entry. Notice that the effect of CALL SET, namely to link data set and window variables, occurs in FRAME as it did in PROGRAM entries.

You may now notice that the columns appear to have partial lines around them like those in Figure 11.10. This is due to your having earlier set the BOX attribute in the mask row. Notice that you haven't actually done anything with the mask row other than to place two regions inside it. Click on the mask row, and select REGION ATTRIBUTES. Click on BOX to remove the box. Rerunning now should give you the extended table without any lines.

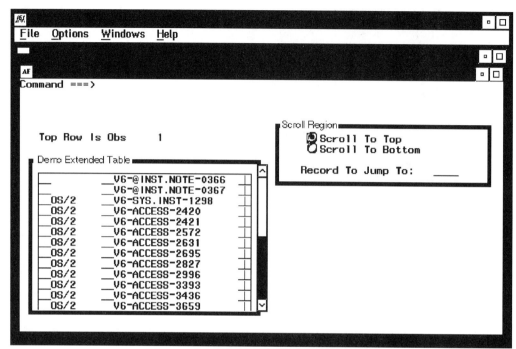

Figure 11.10:   Effect Of Mask Row BOX Attribute

Using A LISTBOX Region

Let's do just more thing to the table. You want to display a list of available products in the usage notes database, as defined by the unique values of the field PROD. The intention is to pop up the list, then allow the user to click on a product and restrict the main extended table in EXTEND to just those observations that have the selected PROD value.

First, go to the program editor and run the following program:

```
proc sort data=usage.usage out=work.prods(keep=prod) nodupkey;
by prod;
run;
```

This creates a small data set containing a list of unique products. That data set will form the input for the region that you are about to create,

Return to the FRAME entry and create another region. In the REGION ATTRIBUTES, make it a box of width 4 with a button border and assign a title of Select A Product. Your screen should look similar to Figure 11.11.

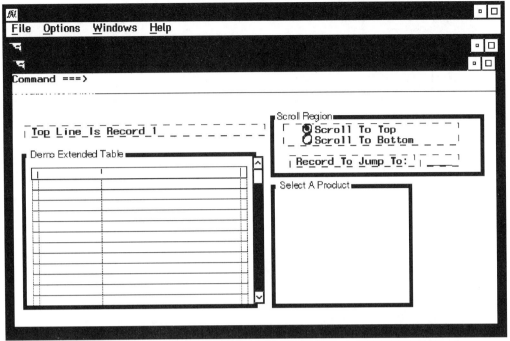

Figure 11.11:   Defining A LISTBOX Region

Fill this region as a list box and name it LISTBOX. Remove the title and click on the downwards arrow in the ENTER VALUES field. This action will pop up a window in which you can enter the characteristics of the list box. Double click on SAS data set, and in the following window enter WORK.PRODS as the SAS data set and PROD as the field name.

Exit back to the FRAME screen where you will notice that the new LISTBOX region has already been populated by the data set values. You need to add a section to the SCL to accommodate a selection from the LISTBOX region. Modify your SCL program so it now looks like this:

```
length text $ 20 ;

init:
  dsid = open('usage.usage') ;
  call set(dsid) ;
  dsid02 = open('work.prods') ;
  call set(dsid02) ;
  call notify('listbox','_ADD_','REMOVE WHERE',1) ;
return ;
```

```
get1:
  if fetchobs(dsid,_currow_) eq -1 then
    call notify('EXTEND','_ENDTABLE_') ;
  else tablerow = getvarc(dsid,varnum(dsid,'keys')) ;
  call notify('extend','_GET_TOPROW_',toprow) ;
  call notify('topline','_SET_TEXT_',
              'Top Row Is Obs ' || put(toprow,5.)) ;
return ;

term:
  call close(dsid) ;
  call close(dsid02) ;
return ;

updown:
  if updown eq 'TOP' then
    call notify('extend','_VSCROLL_','MAX',-1) ;
  else
    call notify('extend','_VSCROLL_','MAX',1) ;
return ;

recnum:
  call notify('extend','_SET_TOPROW_',recnum) ;
return ;

listbox:
  call notify('listbox','_GET_LAST_SEL_',row,issel,text) ;
  if text eq: 'REMOVE' then rc = where(dsid) ;
  else rc = where(dsid,'prod eq "' || text || '"') ;
  call notify('extend','_NEED_REFRESH_') ;
return ;
```

You have made room in the INIT section for a list entry in LISTBOX, which will allow you to remove the WHERE clause. In the LISTBOX section, retrieve the selected text, and then issue a WHERE clause. You tell FRAME that the EXTEND region needs to be rescrolled by executing the _NEED_REFRESH_ method. Run the entry and experiment with the interregion communication.

You now have the basic knowledge of how to maneuver around FRAME entries. The above discussion did no more than look at the tip of the FRAME iceberg -- using FRAME is limited essentially only by your own imagination. When you combine SAS/GRAPH software with FRAME, the results can be both stunning and useful.

Creating Your Own Reusable Objects

In the above example, a RADIOBOX was created that allowed a quick and easy means of jumping directly to the top or bottom of an extended table. This RADIOBOX will be taken a step further in this section -- it will be set up as a reusable object that can be used in your own FRAME entries with minimal programming effort.

It would be useful to read Chapter 7 of *SAS/AF Software: FRAME Entry Usage and Reference* before starting on this section.

At this stage, it is also worth pointing out that in order to work comfortably with customized objects in FRAME, you need a good working knowledge of lists.

Recall you had a RADIO BOX in the earlier example that allowed access to the top or bottom of an extended table at the click of a mouse button.

Effectively, that is all the RADIO BOX allowed. But remember that to accomplish this, a section had to be coded in the FRAME SCL to actually carry out the jump. FRAME and object-oriented programming (the two are NOT one and the same -- FRAME is just one means of using OOP in SAS software) allow us to reuse objects and store the SCL code along with the object so that another programmer can later simply define the object and call a method in that object.

You are going to accomplish the following tasks:

- provide a generic object that can be used in any extended table FRAME application to allow jumping to the top or bottom row of an extended table.

- imbed all code associated with the object within the object, so future users of the object only need to call a method in the object to trigger the processing.

- customize the window normally seen when a region is filled as a RADIO BOX so that users do not need to alter the attributes of the RADIO BOX. You will require only that users enter the region name of the extended table that the RADIO BOX will apply to.

Start by creating a catalog entry to store the new object and its attributes in. This section will store the new object in SASUSER, but in general you most likely want to have a more generic system catalog available. The subject is approached here in a numbered tutorial manner. So just follow the steps, and at the end you should have a working object in addition to those supplied by SAS Institute.

1. ***Create a catalog entry to store the new object in.*** From the program editor or log command line, type

    Build SASUSER.JUMP

2. *Edit an entry called JUMP.CLASS.* This will bring up the CLASS EDITOR. You need to

- change the description to 'Jump TOP/BOTTOM'

- change the parent class to 'SASHELP.FSP.RADIOBOX'

3. *Click on the EDIT ATTRIBUTES option.* This will give you access to the usual RADIO BOX attributes screen. You need to

- change the name to 'JUMP'

- change the NUMBER OF ITEMS to 2

- change the label length to 20

- change the color if you wish

4. *Click on the arrow in the ENTER ARROWS region.* This leads to the usual box containing options for defining your RADIO BOX labels. Click on Enter Values.

5. *Double click on the default Button 1 text.* This pops up a window for you to define your own text. Enter 'Jump To TOP' as the label, and enter 'TOP' as the return value. Then double click on Button 2, enter 'Jump To BOTTOM' as the label, and enter 'BOT' as the return value. Double click on OK to return to the RADIO BOX attributes screen.

6. *Click on INSTANCE VARIABLES in the ADDITIONAL ATTRIBUTES box.* This pops up the existing instance variables. Click on ACTIONS and then click on ADD MODE On.

7. *In the NAME region, type 'TABLE_NAME'.* In the AUTOMATIC RADIO BOX, click on YES. Click on OK to exit back to the RADIO BOX attributes screen. Click on OK again to return to the class definition screen.

   TABLE_NAME will be used to store the name of the extended table that the new RADIO BOX will control TOP/BOTTOM access on. It will be set up so that when developers select the new JUMP object in a FRAME application, they will be prompted for the tablename (it will soon become apparent how).

8. *Click on SET CUSTOM ATTRIBUTES.* Change the CUSTOM ATTRIBUTES to SASUSER.JUMP.CONTROL.FRAME. Change the 'Invoking Custom Attributes Window' to 'REPLACE SUPPLIED ATTRIBUTE WINDOW'. Click on OK to return to the class definition screen.

You have just defined a screen that will replace the usual RADIO BOX screen whenever a developer decides to use the new object. The actual physical screen associated with that new screen will be developed shortly.

9. ***Click on METHODS.*** You are about to define the methods that will be executed by the new object when it gets selected. Note you are not yet coding the method, just defining it.

    Only one method will be used here. The method is used by the programmer to trigger the processing when a user selects the new object.

    Click on ACTIONS and then ADD MODE ON. Enter a method name of 'M_JUMP' and give it a label of 'M_JUMP'. Click on OK to exit back to the class definition screen.

10. ***You have now completed the creation of the new class.*** You now need to build the custom attribute screen and the method for the new object.

    Click on OK to exit the class definition and return to the BUILD list. Type

    ```
    edit m_jump.scl
    ```

    You are about to build the method that will be executed when the new object is selected. Enter the following code:

    ```
    length table_name $ 8 ;

    m_jump:

      method jump $ 3 ;
        call send(_FRAME_,'_GET_WIDGET_',table_name,tableid) ;
        if jump eq 'TOP' then
          call send(tableid,'_VSCROLL_','MAX',-1) ;
        else
          call send(tableid,'_VSCROLL_','MAX',1) ;
      endmethod ;
    ```

The LENGTH statement is necessary. It enables the instance variable defined earlier in the class to automatically pass its value at run time to the method.

You will notice that the method just coded is a normal SCL method. The CALL SEND(_FRAME_ ...) is required to determine the object-id of the extended table that the new object will interact with. You cannot use CALL NOTIFY here, as that function only works from FRAME entries and this is an SCL entry that is not running under FRAME control.

Note how you use the value returned from the new object (TOP/BOT) to determine which method to pass to the extended table.

Compile the SCL and exit back to BUILD.

11. *Now you will build the customized attribute screen.* This will allow the new object to define the extended table with which it will interact. Type

```
edit control.FRAME
```

12. *Set up the customized regions.* You require 4 regions. Set up a FRAME screen and define the regions as follows to look like Figure 11.12.

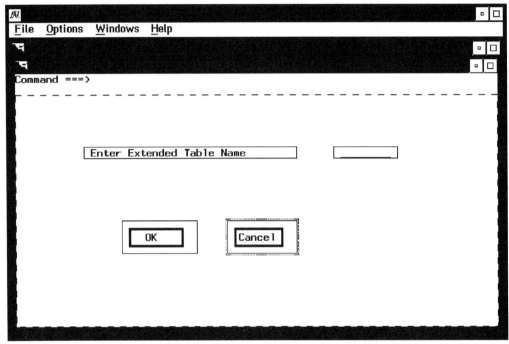

Figure 11.12:   Customized Attribute Screen

Text Label:
Name = LABEL
Text = Enter Extended Table Name
Just = Left

Text Entry:
Name = ENTRY
Type = DSNAME
Selection = ENTER/Single mouse click

Push Button:
Name = OK
Label= OK
Under COMMAND PROCESSING enter a command of END

Push Button:
Name = Cancel
Label= Cancel
Under COMMAND PROCESSING enter a command of CANCEL

13. *SAVE the entry by typing SAVE on the command line and then enter the source window by typing SOURCE.* Enter the following program

```
entry optional= _widget_ 8 _uattr_ $ _class_ 8 ;

entry:

 if entry = _blank_  or error(entry) then return ;

 _widget_ = setnitemc(_widget_,entry,'table_name') ;
return ;
```

You must have the entry statement exactly as defined above because SCL expects it in that manner when you execute the customized window.

Essentially what happens here is that the developer enters text into the ENTRY region. When the above SCL executes, it checks that the text is a valid SASNAME and returns to the user if not. Otherwise, it places the table name into the _widget_ list from where it is associated with the instance variable when the application is run.

Return to the FRAME screen and compile your program. Exit back to BUILD.

14. *Define the new object to the class list that is seen when you use FILL on a region.* Type

```
copy sashelp.fsp.build.resource
```

to copy the default resource library into the current catalog (you won't generally do this; you would usually select a catalog for your custom resource library, copy from SASHELP once, and then always edit that resource file when you added new objects. This process is for illustrative purposes.). Now type

```
edit build.resource
```

15. *Click on ACTIONS and then on ADD.* From the resulting LIBRARY list double click on SASUSER. That will list all the catalogs in SASUSER in the list box on the right. Scroll to the JUMP catalog and double click on it. A list of all classes in JUMP will appear in the bottom listbox. Double click on JUMP.CLASS.

16. You are now back in the resource list box. Scroll to the bottom. You should see the entry Jump TOP/BOTTOM at the bottom of the list, with the word DISPLAY next to it. Single click on the new entry, click on ACTIONS, and then click on MOVE AFTER. Now scroll the listbox to the EXTENDED TABLE entry and click on it. This moves the new entry so it will appear after the extended table entry. Click on OK to return to BUILD.

You've finished! A jump object now exists that can be used in your applications. So let's use it in a FRAME entry. Follow these numbered steps in order:

1. **Tell SAS that you want to use your custom resource list.** Type

    ```
    resource sasuser.jump.build.resource
    ```

2. **Create a small data set for illustrative purposes.** Go to the program editor and run the following program to create a data set to use in the extended table.

    ```
    data work.testjump ;
       do i=1 to 1000 ; output ; end ;
    run ;
    ```

3. **Return to BUILD and edit a new entry called TESTJUMP.FRAME.** Create two regions, and populate them as follows:

    A. ```
       Extended Table
       Name = Example
       Max Rows = 1000
       Row Spacing = 0
       ```

       (Did you notice when you used FILL that the new object is on the fill list?)

    B. Use the new Jump TOP/BOTTOM class, and enter a table name of 'EXAMPLE' in the customized attribute screen. When you return from the FILL, your customized object will appear in the region.

4. **Fill the extended table logical row as follows:**

    ```
    Text label
    Name = tab_row
    no label
    ```

5. **Open the source window and enter the following program:**

    ```
    init:
      dsid = open('work.testjump') ;
    return ;

    get1:
     rc = fetchobs(dsid,_currow_) ;
     tab_row = getvarn(dsid,varnum(dsid,'i')) ;
    ```
    ```

```
      return ;

   term:
      call close(dsid) ;
   return ;

   jump:
      call notify('jump','m_jump',jump) ;
   return ;
```

Note the JUMP section. The label corresponds to the name of the new object. The method that is called is the M_JUMP method that you entered earlier. That method had one parameter, the value returned by the radiobox when the user clicked a button.

Try it out. Compile the FRAME entry and use TESTAF. Scroll the extended table down a few rows. Now click on Scroll To Top and the table goes back to row 1. Click on Scroll To Bottom and the table goes to the end. Magic!

What you have just done is to add new functionality to the base set of objects that SAS Institute supplies with FRAME. This is the crux of OOP, being able to define and reuse objects with minimal coding. Note that you really got by with NO coding in the example above, although a section like JUMP is mandatory for all objects because you still have to call the method. The control over when, but not how the method is called rests with you as the developer.

So you now have a new object to use in your applications. Essentially, the definition of any new object follows the above guidelines, although some are more difficult than others. Sometimes you won't want to customize the attribute window; other times the customization will be vastly more complex than the above.

A Few FRAME Tips

Even though I have only explored the basics of FRAME, there are a few rules that already stand out. These include the following:

- Use the RM DESCRIBE ON command liberally. It is easy to get lost in regions when your screen gets filled with different regions, especially when they are close together.

- You may find that creating all your regions and then filling each one is easier than creating and filling as you go. Creating all the regions allows you to see the 'big picture' before you start filling.

- There may be many ways of accomplishing some tasks using FRAME. Experience will show which works best, so at the start of your exploration of FRAME don't get held up by such questions. You will find that you both need to and want to experiment with FRAME entries, and you will develop a means of seeing what is easiest in different situations.

- When you create SCL with a FRAME entry, it is easiest to compile from the FRAME rather than from the SCL. This ensures you don't overlook compiling. (If you compile from the SCL you may not be compiling the FRAME itself -- sometimes it appears that although the SCL is compiled, the FRAME doesn't do as expected, until a recompile of the FRAME entry occurs.)

- Remember that when a value has to be passed between regions, you MUST use CALL NOTIFY or CALL SEND.

- Don't clutter your display. The cardinal rule of any display window is to keep it readable. FRAME invites cluttering ... it's the 'I can fit another itty bitty region over here' syndrome!

- FRAME makes extensive use of in-memory lists. Essentially, for each region on your screen, at least one list is defined. The length of the list depends on the object class.

  SAS Institute recommends a minimum of 12 megabytes of memory for FRAME. The example work in this text was done on an 8 megabyte 486 running under Version 2.1 of OS/2. Frames were very slow to display, and swapper use was very high. On a number of occasions, SAS software completely abended while I was using FRAME.

  I have also made an attempt to use FRAME in a 4-megabyte Windows 3.1 environment. This is very inappropriate, with FRAME entries taking 1.5–2 minutes to display. The memory resources that SAS Institute indicates are necessary should not be ignored.

  I have noted FRAME applications running and being developed under UNIX in 16 megabytes of memory running very fast with little overhead. The lesson is clear -- FRAME will be expensive on system resources, and this should be kept in mind when deciding whether to use FRAME.

- Above all else, remember that FRAME is just a tool for use in your applications. There is no reason why you shouldn't mix FRAME and PROGRAM/MENU entries. There is also no reason to use FRAME if its use is not warranted. Having said that, FRAME is fun and easy to get carried away with!

Chapter 12: Questions And Answers

Q *I coded an extended table that does as I require except that when the user selects the last record on the screen, the table moves up one line after processing the selection. How do I avoid this?*

A Use the SETCR function. SCL extended tables always move the cursor to the next row by default. If that row is the last row on the current screen, then the screen moves up one row, causing the behavior noted above.

The SETCR function has an option STAY. Using the following command (in INIT, it only need be called once) causes the desired behavior:

```
call setcr('stay','return') ;
```

Q *Why do extended tables sometimes insist on beeping when they write to the screen? Not all my tables do this; they look identical in the way the code is structured, yet one table insists on beeping wherever the screen appears.*

A Usually this happens when a command line is not being used. When a field is in error at the time the screen is displayed, a beep occurs and a message is displayed in the SAS message area. If the command line is switched off, no message area is available so the message does not display (and it is not in the log or message window either). But the beep that accompanies a screen error still occurs. The most usual situation is that a field is not long enough to accept the value being placed into it. Check to be sure that none of the formatted fields have formats wider than the field. SCL does not check the attributes for this sort of error at compile time.

Q *Help! I display an extended table, where the table rows represent observations in a data set. The application users can type over some of the fields, and I use the UPDATE function in PUTROW to save the value they entered over the existing observation. The in-place UPDATE function seems to do anything but update inplace .. my data set still contains the old observation and also contains the modified observation a few observations further on, but has another observation missing. What is going on?*

A In PUTROW, you cannot assume that the row being processed contains the last observation read from the data set. The UPDATE function operates on the last observation read, and PUTROW does not automatically reread the file to position the data set I/O pointer to the observation currently referenced by PUTROW. Indeed PUTROW knows nothing of the source of the rows it is processing; that is responsibility of GETROW.

So the answer is simple. Since **_currow_**maps data set observations onto extended table entries, reread the data set in PUTROW before doing any processing, as follows:

```
rc = fetchobs(dsid,_currow_,'noset') ;
```

The NOSET option is used, as without it all the changes your user just made will be removed by the SET routine (assuming it is in force).

Q *How can I cause a command to be executed on the pressing of a PUSHBTNC field?*

A You need to use EXECCMD. For example, suppose you have a PUSHBTNC in a choice group named SLECTION that is intended to cause an extended table to scroll forward. Assign the button an initial value of FORWARD, protect the button, and in SCL code the following in MAIN:

```
if  slection eq 'FORWARD' then call execcmd('forward') ;
```

You need to be aware of the impact on extended table processing when doing this. The initial selection of the button causes the button field to be treated as modified. Since the key that was pressed to trigger the SCL was an ENTER (clicking on a button is equivalent to modifying a field and pressing ENTER), MAIN will execute followed by GETROW. (See Table 1 in Chapter 5, 'Extended Tables.') However, the command pushed by EXECCMD is executed when the screen is redisplayed, and that is when GETROW has finished. Now the SCL is executed again, this time with a scrolling command (FORWARD) but without a row selected and without any field being modified. This causes GETROW to be executed again. The fact that a push-button field is considered modified when clicked is important because it causes MAIN to execute. This feature can be very useful, but in some circumstances it can be a nuisance, so be wary.

Q *On an extended table, how can I display the total number of rows that will be displayed on the table, as well as the position of the top row currently displayed?*

A The question as put here relates to the screen in Figure 12.1 seen from the programmer's viewpoint.

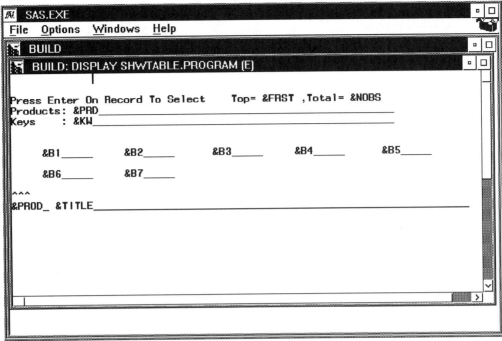

Figure 12.1:   Displaying Total Rows On An Extended Table

You must fill out the two fields in the top right hand corner, **frst** and **nobs**.

Finding **nobs** is quite trivial, assuming the data come from a SAS data set and the table is nondynamic. Either use the NOBS function, or use one of the methods described later in this section for finding the number of observations in the presence of a WHERE clause.

If the data come from a list, **nobs** is the number of elements in the list. Using an external file as the extended table data source means the data has to be read in somewhere (it's easiest to use a LIST) so that a count can be maintained. At any rate, **nobs** is quite trivial for a nondynamic table.

When the screen is first displayed, it is required to display the value 1 for **frst**. Thereafter, the value displayed depends on what action the user takes. However, it will always be the value of **_currow_** for the row currently displayed at the top of the screen.

Finding **_currow_** for that row is not trivial. First, the calculation must be done in MAIN. It cannot be done in GETROW because there is no way of knowing when you are setting up the first row and hence storing the value of **_currow_**.

The solution is to use the CURTOP() function in MAIN. This seems contradictory at first, since the documented order of operation always sees GETROW being executed as the final operation before handing control back to the user. How then can MAIN know what GETROW will set up as the next CURTOP value?

The only way to change **frst** is by scrolling the screen or entering a DOWN or UP command. Refer to the Table 1 in Chapter 5 to see the order of processing in an extended table.

On the face of things, it is only possible to achieve the aim in a dynamic selection table because they process in the order GETROW/MAIN/GETROW and the first GETROW has found the new row that will display at the table top. However, in a nondynamic table, CURTOP() actually returns the value of the row that will be top *after* the next GETROW execution is complete. It isn't actually necessary to call GETROW before MAIN in a nondynamic table. Thus, calling the CURTOP() function produces the correct value for **frst**.

Because the MAIN section will not be executed upon entry to the screen, it is necessary to set **frst** to 1 in INIT. The following is the code required to set up the above screen:

```
init:
  control always ;
  frst = 1 ;
  ...
return ;


main:
  ...
  frst = curtop() ;
return ;


getrow:
  ...
return ;


putrow:
  ...
return ;
```

➡ *You must have CONTROL ALWAYS on; otherwise the MAIN section may not be executed and frst may be incorrect.*

➡ *If you need to do any processing in MAIN that involves the row of the table that was at the top when the user pressed the scroll key, do it before calling CURTOP().*

Q *When tasks can be accomplished in SCL or using submitted SAS code, how do I decide which method to use?*

A In general, SCL code is more efficient than SAS code due to SUBMIT's requirement to load additional SAS modules, and it is thus preferable. This may come down to a decision of whether the code runs quicker one way or the other or whether the programming effort is much less one way than the other.

I do not regard my advice to use SCL code rather than SAS code as an absolute rule. One objective of systems development is to provide quick, functional, bug-free software; if this can be accomplished using SAS code as a tool in the SCL programmer's arsenal, then sobeit.

Q *How can I find out how many observations satisfy a WHERE clause?*

A There are two questions to answer here. First, did any observations satisfy the clause? That can be easily determined by using FETCH and checking for immediate end of file.

While that is the obvious method, this question is a good example of how the obvious may be misleading. In the situation where no observations satisfy the WHERE, the FETCH function will try to read every observation on the database looking for a successful match with the WHERE clause. It should be apparent that as the database size increases, this will become a very expensive means of finding out if any observations satisfied a WHERE.

An alternative method is to be aware that documentation of the ATTRN function in *SAS Screen Control Language: Reference, Version 6, First Edition* is not correct. When a WHERE clause is in effect, ATTRN with the ANY option is affected by the WHERE clause, despite the documentation's stating otherwise. Using the ATTRN function in this case returns a 1 if the WHERE clause returns observations and a zero if the WHERE clause does not return observations. The documentation implies that the WHERE clause does not have an impact on the ATTRN function's outcome, that it should always return a 1 if observations exist in the data set, irrespective of the presence of a WHERE clause.

This is clearly shown in the following example using the SAS Notes database:

```
init:
  dsid00=open('usage.usage') ;
  /* following WHERE has no matches */
  rc = where(dsid00,'modulen contains "987654321"') ;
  rc = attrn(dsid00,'any') ;
  put 'NOGOOD WHERE ' rc= ;
  rc = where(dsid00) ;
  /* following WHERE has one match */
  rc = where(dsid00,'modulen contains "5015"') ;
  rc = attrn(dsid00,'any') ;
  put 'GOOD WHERE ' rc= ;
  call close(dsid00) ;
return;
```

However, from an efficiency viewpoint, if no observations satisfy the WHERE, both methods (FETCH and ATTRN) will perform more slowly as data set sizes increase. Again, be clear that this is a function of the WHERE, which needs to read each observation to ascertain whether any one satisfies the condition. You can minimize the wait time here by using an index on the variable used in the WHERE.

The second question is: Which observations do satisfy the WHERE clause? In SCL, there are 3 simple ways to get this information:

- Submit a short program to SQL or SAS and count the observations, returning the count in a macro variable. For instance, the following will accomplish the task:

```
wherecl = 'wedate between "01sep92"d and "01oct92"d';
submit continue sql;
 reset noprint ;
  select count(*) into :nobs from global.activity
    where &wherecl ;
endsubmit ;
```

Note the immediate disadvantage here, namely the need to ensure that it is possible to reissue the WHERE clause in the submitted code. This will often mean that an extra field needs to be carried in the SCL program to store the WHERE clause.

A further problem exists here in that the SQL will be a second process opening the data set if the SCL already opened it. This is only a problem in general if the SCL opened the data set with member level locking, as the SQL will not be able to open the data set again. Also, if the SCL has fetched an observation and UNLOCK has not been used, the SCL will hold an observation lock and the submitted SQL will fail.

- Alternatively, use FETCH to read observations until an end of file condition becomes true, maintaining a counter to keep track of how many observations exist. This is done as follows:

```
nobs=0 ;
do while(fetch(dsid) ne -1) ;
 nobs=nobs+1;
end ;
```

- A third alternative involves using the LVARLEVEL function to load a list with the values of a variable from the database. This function has a parameter at position 3 that is filled with the number of items in the list. That will correspond to the number of observations loaded from the database.

```
listid = makelist() ;
nobs=0 ;
rc = lvarlevel(dsid,'varname',nobs,listid);
rc = dellist(listid) ;
```

In some situations, use of LVARLEVEL seems very quick. In others, there is no noticeable difference between the 3 methods. Some situations, on the other hand, showed LVARLEVEL to be very slow, which intuition suggests it would be.

I recommend that you develop a site macro or method to accomplish this task, code the technique that you feel most comfortable with, and use that rather than chopping and changing methods. All 3 methods are often similar in terms of efficiency, but the LIST method will require much more memory.

 As an example, you could retain the following method in a site catalog available to all SCL coders:

```
countwhr:
method dsid 3 nobs 8 ;
  nobs=0 ;
  noteid = note(dsid) ;
  do while(fetch(dsid) ne -1) ;
     nobs=nobs+1;
  end ;
  rc = point(dsid,noteid) ;
endmethod ;
```

Essentially, all that is done here is to allow the counting technique to be parameter driven. The calling program needs to open the file, define a numeric field to hold the count, and call the method, passing the data set identifier through and having the count returned.

In the method above, the NOTE and POINT functions are used to ensure that the calling program will have the data set positioned at the same place after the method is executed as before. This is important if the calling program has already started to use the file, as the program may continue to carry out operations assuming that the same observation will be accessed. It should be clear that because the method has to read every observation, when the method is finished the file pointer is set at end of file, so the caller would not be in the same position as before the call.

As an example, issue the following in the calling program:

```
length numobs 8 ;
init:
  dsid00 = open('usage.usage') ;
return ;
```

```
main:
  rc = where(dsid00,'modulen contains "' || scrvar || '"');
  call method(<method location>,<method name>,dsid00,numobs);
  if numobs eq 0 then ... < coding for no obs >
  ...
return ;
```

If using LVARLEVEL, ensure that the variable read into the list has no duplicate values -- that function only loads unique values of a variable and could potentially return an incorrect number otherwise. If using LVARLEVEL in this context, you have to be careful that the variable obeys this rule.

The major disadvantage with LVARLEVEL is that the list may require a lot of memory. Although the list is discarded immediately upon producing the desired information, large numbers of observations satisfying the WHERE will cause problems here. It may seem overkill to load a list with all observations satisfying the WHERE, but in practice it may sometimes be quicker than other methods. If the list itself is also required in the application, this technique kills two birds with one stone.

As the number of observations in a database (physical, not the logical database that satisfies the WHERE clause) increases, all methods will appear to give slower response time to a terminal user. This is because all observations will be read; the impact of the WHERE is only to not permit some observations through for future processing. This is unavoidable because the WHERE clause is only a filter; the exact number of observations satisfying the WHERE is never known until they are counted.

The above caution also applies to the first situation described earlier, where no observations satisfy the clause. In order to know that no observations satisfy the WHERE clause, SAS software must still read all observations (unless an index is present). The WHERE simply permits none through for future processing. The term 'immediate end of file' is rather misleading in that case because the physical end of file only occurs when all observations have been read. The end of file seen by the FETCHOBS is a logical end of file.

 I have to validate a number of fields against a format table. On the first FSEDIT observation to be validated, the validation is very slow, yet it is fast on others. Why?

 This is often due to the overhead of loading a large format table to search against. This has always happened with SAS software, but it only shows up clearly in an online situation because a user has to wait for the SCL to complete.

There is no simple answer to how to get around this problem being caused by large tables. A design consideration may be to take a critical look at tables; for instance, the bottleneck was removed in one JARS FSEDIT screen by carrying two tables, one for all projects in the JARS project register, the other for all OPEN (currently being worked on) projects. The latter was used in the FSEDIT checks and reduced the wait time for the first check considerably because only about 20% of projects on the project register are open at any given time.

SAS software now allows long labels in formats. It may be worthwhile avoiding these on large tables because they will generate more I/O and probably cause even longer load times.

It may be appropriate to remove large formats and replace them with LISTS that seem to be quicker loading and are then maintained in memory. Trade this approach off against the amount of memory that your list will use, but be aware that both the list and the format are kept in memory and the format will often be larger due to its need to carry a label as well as each value.

The list approach is potentially much faster loading because it can be saved as a special catalog entry devoted to list structures.

Question carefully whether you need to use either formats or lists. I have found that WHERE clauses on a lookup data set often provide faster searching. You may need to experiment to find the best solution for your particular situation.

Q *I have an application in which I wish to use push-button menus. Having set my screen up and successfully compiled, I now find TESTAF does not function. What is happening?*

A There are a number of possible solutions here:

● Although it appears undocumented, push buttons have a restriction on their screen positioning. You must leave a minimum of 3 characters to the left of the leftmost push button. For the other buttons, at least 5 blanks must be left after the preceding button. Furthermore, at least 1 blank line must be left between push buttons that are on multiple lines.

This space restriction allows room for operating system-dependent graphic features such as shadowing. Under MVS, it appears as though only 1 character is used, but 3 must be left.

If this restriction is not obeyed, an error message is displayed when the ATTR screen is exited. That message is in the MSG or LOG window. The message is

```
WARNING: 1 error(s) detected in attribute screen. See MSG or LOG window.
```

The program screen will still compile; however, if the button position is not corrected, TESTAF will not work. In Release 6.07 and 6.08, the only message issued is

```
ERROR: Cannot open ddname.catlg.XTESTAFX.PROGRAM
```

● Searching usage notes for errors on TESTAF indicates that if TESTAF is being attempted while the program entry is open for browse, then the above error message is issued. So if push buttons do not appear to be causing your problem, ensure that the program is being tested in edit, not browse mode.

Q *From within an SCL program, I want to know whether a certain catalog contains any entries. If I don't do this, my call to the CATALOG function may cause the user to see a window with no entries to select from.*

A

This is easiest accomplished using the SQL dictionary feature and submitting code. Suppose you wish to know whether the catalog SASUSER.QUERIES contains any entries of type SOURCE. Issue the following SQL submit from within your SCL program:

```
submit continue sql ;
  create table temp as
     select * from dictionary.catalogs
     where libname eq 'SASUSER' and
           memname eq 'QUERIES' and
           objtype eq 'SOURCE';
endsubmit ;
```

You can now use the macro variable **&sqlobs** to see how many observations SQL wrote to TEMP. Thus, in your SCL, use

```
if symgetn('sqlobs') eq 0 then do ;
  .... handling for no catalog entries ....
end ;
else do ;
  .... handling for some entries ....
end ;
```

Note that the SQL dictionary feature in effect gives you a very powerful masking feature over files allocated in your SAS session.

Q *In my application, I want to allow users to access the CATALOG entries for a certain libref. I can accomplish all I want with the CATALOG function, but I want to switch off the command line. I do that using the WREGION function, but now I can't work out how to assign an END key in the CATALOG window.*

A Part of the beauty of SAS software is that window functions are independent of the SAS product. You can use (usually) any window command in any SAS window. The KEYDEF window command exists to overwrite a key value for a specific window.

Using KEYDEF in SCL requires it be called via the EXECCMD function. Use the following code immediately prior to your CATALOG function call:

```
call execcmd("keydef f3 'end'") ;
```

And for an added bonus, when the user sees the CATALOG window, SAS software will have placed the following message on the screen so that the user knows just how to end the window:

```
NOTE: PF3 set to END
```

Note that the effect of the KEYDEF is not limited to the intended window. You have to switch the key back to its setting in the calling window or it remains set in all subsequent windows.

Q *I have to display a window that is defined by SAS software, namely the CATALOG window. But it does not give me the ability to display some text of my own choice to prompt users. How can I display my own text?*

A SAS has given SCL applications access to a number of windows that are actually part of the SAS software shell, rather than being intended purely for applications. It is correct that SAS maintains total control over these windows, and thus it is not possible to place your own application messages in them as you can with SCL function windows like DATALISTx. However, a legend can be displayed at the base of the window. Consider the following example:

```
call wregion(20,10,4,60,' ') ;
call putlegend(2,'Use B To Browse') ;
call legend() ;

call wregion(1,10,4,60,' ') ;
call catalog(..... );

call endlegend() ;
```

This code displays a legend with a prompt for the user, and immediately above the legend it displays the window that the user requires. Note that to make the legend look as much as possible like an extension of the called window, the WREGION dimensions are identical with the exception of the start line.

Q *A user enters a list of values that are checked against a master list. Any entered values not on the master list should cause the user to be prompted to correct the list. How can I show the user exactly which part of the list is incorrect?*

A The FLDCOLOR function will do this. This function can highlight a portion of a text field. Thus, a user can enter a string of data (for example, a list of projects on a project register) separated by spaces, the SCL can compare each one with a master list, and if any are invalid it displays a list showing all projects, but with the selected ones highlighted or in a different color. Figure 12.2 illustrates data entry before validation.

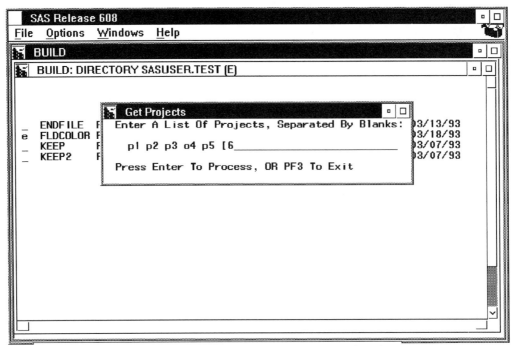

Figure 12.2:   User Data Before Validation

An alternative method is to have a second field on the screen that the SCL program will move any invalid entries into. This is not discussed further; it is simple and works well but has the added overhead of an extra field.

A complete program to use FLDCOLOR in the above context follows. The user can enter up to 10 projects, and each is compared with a master list. If any are invalid, the whole list is redisplayed with just the incorrect portions highlighted. This screen is shown in Figure 12.3.

In the example program, checking for validity of the project number is done using a master list stored in an array. That can be changed to set up any check source.

```
array valprj (20) $ 8 _temporary_ (
  'P1' 'P2' 'P3' 'P4' 'P5' 'P6' 'P7' 'P8' 'P9' 'P10'
  'P11' 'P12' 'P13' 'P14' 'P15' 'P16' 'P17' 'P18' 'P19' 'P20') ;

init:
  control always ;
  rc = field('color yellow alloff','prjlist') ;
return ;

main:
  if _status_ eq 'E' then return ;
```

```
/* switch off any highlighting that may have been put on */

rc = field('color yellow alloff','prjlist') ;

if prjlist eq _blank_ then return ;

/* loop through each entered field, check it against the valid
   entry list, highlight all invalid fields, return to user at
   end of check */

project = prjlist ;
i = 0 ;
do until (project eq _blank_) ;
  i = i + 1 ;
  project = scan(prjlist,i) ;
  if project not in valprj then do ;
    start = indexw(prjlist,project) ;
    rc=fldcolor('prjlist','blue','reverse',start,length(project));
  end ;
end ;

return ;
```

In the above, notice how the FIELD function is used. It is used initially to make the input field a different color from the rest of the screen. Then in the MAIN section, it is used to remove any highlighting that currently exists (for parts of the input field in error). If this is not done, then when the user corrects an invalid part of the string, the highlighting will remain even though the field is now correct.

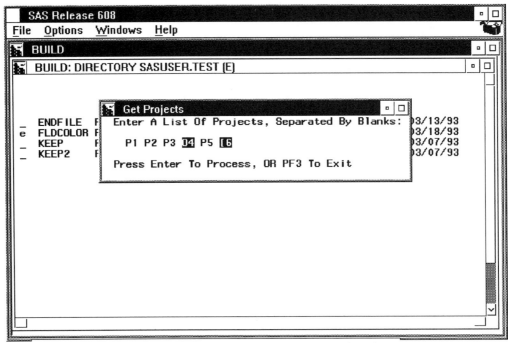

Figure 12.3: User Data After Validation

The code that does the bulk of the work is just a loop that works through the string one word at a time, checking validity and switching on the error flag if the string is invalid.

Note the use of the INDEXW function. This exists in Release 6.07. It returns the position in the first string where the second string is found, but only if the whole second string is surrounded by blanks.

Q *I want to allow the users of my SAS/AF window to enter a question mark which, when I check for it in my SCL, will prompt me to pop up an assisted entry window. However, I always get the SAS window telling me what data type is allowed in the field. Why?*

A SAS/AF has a default prompt character of '?'. If this is not changed, SAS sees the prompt and acts on it, removing the '?' before the SCL sees it. The default action when a '?' is present is as described in the question. It is simple to override; just enter the GENERAL ATTRIBUTES (GATTR) window and change the prompt character to some other character. Changing to blank removes any attempt by SAS to pop up explanatory windows.

Alternatively in SAS/AF, set the NOPROMPT attribute in the ATTR window for the field.

Q *How can I allow multiple developers to access and update SAS/AF and SAS/FSP SCL programs in the same catalog when using SAS/SHARE and still maintain code integrity?*

A You cannot accomplish the entire requirement. FSEDIT is specifically designed NOT to allow a user to edit and save an SCL program created through MODIFY when running under SAS/SHARE.

However, you can have multiple developers working on the same SAS/AF catalog and maintain integrity. This is done by allocating the catalog under a SAS/SHARE server and ensuring that whenever a developer enters a screen, the LOCK command is used to deny other users access to that screen.

The LOCK syntax is LOCK <4-level catalog name> <CLEAR>. When first accessing the SAS/AF catalog member, issue the LOCK command entering the full 4-character catalog name, but without the CLEAR operand. No other developer will be able to access that member, so you maintain code integrity.

When you finish with the member, exit in the normal manner and then re-enter the LOCK command with the CLEAR operand so that other developers can access the member.

Ensure that when a member is accessed, the developer accessing the member enters the LOCK command. If this is omitted, and a subsequent developer enters and locks the member, integrity problems can occur. The following sequence of events can occur:

1. user X enters the member and does not lock.
2. subsequently user Y enters the member and locks the member. At this stage, user X cannot save the member but can make changes to the image copy that has been loaded.
3. user Y changes the member, exits saving the changes, and clears the lock.
4. user X exits the member, saving the changes.

Unfortunately, all the work done by user Y was in vain. When exiting and saving, user X knew nothing of the fact that user Y changed the member because BUILD loads a member into memory and does not subsequently need to refer back to the member on disk. The image that member X is working on knows nothing of the existence of user Y, and consequently it destroys the work done by user Y.

In the above circumstance, the fault clearly lies with user X. Had user X immediately locked the member, user Y would not have been able to access the member until user X had finished. In that case, both users would have successfully edited and saved.

 My application generates an extended table from which users select a row for further processing. The table is based on a data set that is updated by users. That data set is getting very large, and my users are getting frustrated at the amount of time it takes to scroll to the item they want to select. How can I avoid this problem?

 There are two possibilities here. The first involves no coding and is thus attractive from a developer's viewpoint. That is to show the user how to use the display manager KEYFIELD and FIND commands. Together, those commands will search the extended table, making the top row the first one that satisfies the user's search.

Alternatively, you can cut down on the amount of data shown and thus the processing overhead by issuing a WHERE clause before reading the database. To do this, you must prompt the user for some key that will be used in the WHERE clause.

An example is a project register that has a keyfield **sponsor**, defining the customer sponsoring (that is, paying for) work done on projects. At some stage the user may want to pop up a list sorted by sponsor. To go directly to projects for sponsor '450', for example, the user enters the following sequence of commands on the extended table command line:

```
keyfield sponsor
f '450'
```

Of course, **sponsor** must be a field on the extended table. Be aware that the search will succeed on the first occurrence of 450, even if that occurs as a substring of a larger string. Thus a sponsor of 6450 would be considered a successful match.

The alternative would be to have the user enter the sponsor value into a field in the nonscrollable area, then on pressing ENTER issue a WHERE command for GETROW to operate on.

The screen in Figure 12.4 is seen from the user's viewpoint at a terminal. In this example, it is possible to start with a table of the entire data set, subset using WHERE or use KEYFIELD/FIND, go back to the full data set, and even issue and use KEYFIELD/FIND while a WHERE is active.

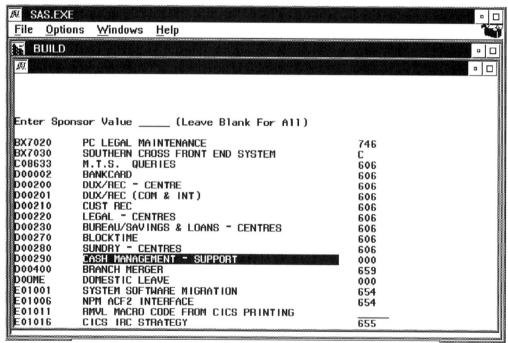

Figure 12.4:   Table Without Subsetting

The screen in Figure 12.4 is at the start of the application. No WHERE has been issued, and the user sees all observations. If the user now enters 450 in the **sp** field, the on-screen list is restricted to just projects sponsored by department 450, shown in Figure 12.5.

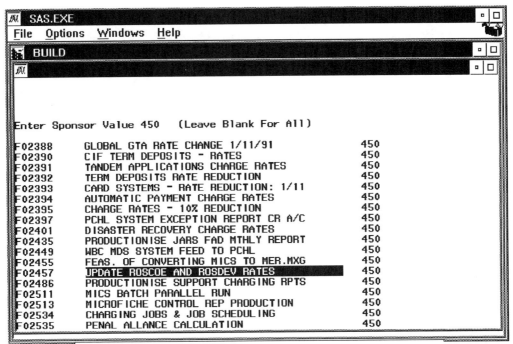

Figure 12.5: Table Subset To One Sponsor

Suppose the user now wants only projects beginning M0. The user can enter the following on the command line:

```
keyfield project
f 'M0'
```

Here is the code to accomplish the selection activities just described:

```
init:
  control always ;
  dsid00 = open('library.projlist') ;
  call set(dsid00) ;
  call setrow(0,1,'N','Y') ;
return ;


main:
  if modified(sp) and sp ne _blank_ then
    rc = where(dsid00,'user eq "' || sp || '"') ;
  else if modified(sp) and sp eq _blank_ then
    rc = where(dsid00) ;
return ;
```

```
term:
  call close(dsid00) ;
return ;


getrow:
  if fetchobs(dsid00,_currow_) eq -1 then call endtable() ;
return ;



putrow:


<<< your PUTROW code >>>


return ;
```

Q *On screen I intend to have a list of up to 7 variables, and my users can enter a number beside up to 3 of these. The number indicates an ordering for future processing; in other words, they may number a variable from 0 to 3, where 0 implies no further processing of that variable. The non-zero numbers will define a sort order of variables for a report. How can I code this?*

A This task is tailor-made for array processing. Suppose the variables are called **var1** to **var7**. The user will see the screen in Figure 12.6 and is required to enter a number between 0 and 3 beside each variable.

First, note that there are several separate tasks to accomplish here:

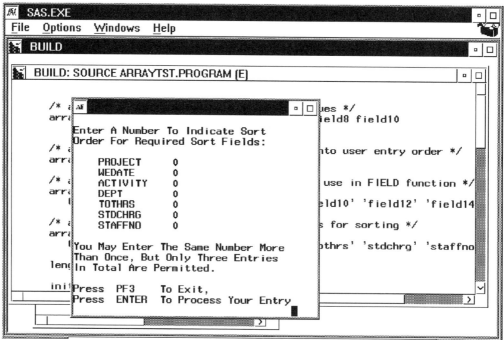

Figure 12.6:   Allowing Users To Order Variables

- check to be sure the number entered is valid, that is between 0 and 3.

- verify no more than 3 fields are given a number.

- be sure at least 1 field is given a number.

- create a variable to hold the list of field names arranged in sort order.

In this example, assume that the user can enter a number more than once, in other words, that some variables are in the sort list, but relative position does not matter. Thus a user may assign 2 fields to number 1, meaning that it is of no concern which order they appear in, as long as they are at the start of the sort list.

The following program accomplishes all tasks:

```
/* array to hold entered sort indicator values */
array sortnums {*} $ field2 field4 field6 field8 field10
                  field12 field14;

/* array to hold SORTED fieldnames sorted into user entry order */
array sfield {7} $ ;

/* array to hold names of screen fields for use in FIELD function */
array scrnvars{7} $
   ('field2' 'field4' 'field6' 'field8' 'field10' 'field12' 'field14');

/* array to hold names of possible variables for sorting */
array fieldn {7} $
   ('project' 'wedate' 'activity' 'dept' 'tothrs' 'stdchrg' 'staffno');

length sortlist $ 7 sortby $ 30 ;

init:
  control always ;
return ;

main:
  if _status_ eq 'E' then return ;

/* initialize, cleanup up old messages */
  sortby = _blank_ ;
  call wname(' ') ;
  sortlist = _blank_ ;
  if err then rc = field('color cyan alloff',scrnvars(err)) ;

/* change any blanked out entries back to zero */
  do i=1 to dim(sortnums) ;
```

```
    if sortnums(i) in (' ' '') then sortnums(i) = '0';
    sortlist = sortlist || sortnums(i) ;
  end ;


/* error if no entries selected for sort at all */
  if sortlist eq '0000000' then do ;
    call wname('ERROR: Select At Least One Field') ;
    return ;
  end ;


/* error if any entry outside range 0-3 */
  err = verify(sortlist,'0123') ;
  if err then do ;
    call wname('ERROR: Enter 0,1,2,3 Only') ;
    rc = field('color yellow highlight',scrnvars(err)) ;
    return ;
  end ;


/* error if more than 3 sort fields selected */
  if length(compress(sortlist,'0')) gt 3 then do;
    call wname('ERROR: Maximum 3 Fields Allowed');
    return ;
  end;


/* all ok, attach sort indicator to field name and sort */
  do i=1 to dim(sortnums) ;
    sfield(i) = sortnums(i) || fieldn(i) ;
  end ;

  rc = asort(sfield) ;


/* extract 2nd bytes onward of sorted entry to get the sort list */
  do i=1 to dim(sfield) ;
    if sfield(i) ne: '0' then sortby = sortby || ' ' ||
       substr(sfield(i),2);
  end ;


/* hereon will use the sort list in its intended manner */
  put sortby=;


return ;


term:
return ;
```

Q *In my application, I intend to allow the ability to drop fields off a SAS data set, in other words, I want to emulate the SAS DROP or KEEP statements. I tried the following program, but it didn't work. Can I accomplish this task using SCL, or do I need to use a submitted DATA step?*

```
init:
  control always ;
return ;

main:
  dsid = open('work.activity(keep=project dept activity tothrs
    stdchrg cntllev=member)','U') ;
  do i=1 to nobs(dsid) ;
    rc = fetchobs(dsid,i,'abs') ;
    rc = update(dsid) ;
  end ;
  call close(dsid) ;
return ;
```

A The reason that the above did not work is that the KEEP on the SCL open command is for read purposes only. When the UPDATE occurs, it is done in place, and the original fields not in the KEEP are unchanged. The KEEP only stops the fields from being loaded into the SCL data vector.

The task is actually very simple, but you have to remember the rules that SAS software places on operations that manipulate data (as opposed to the header area) of SAS data sets. These rules include that fields cannot be dropped or kept by in-place operations, only by a complete rewrite of the file.

Operations that will do a complete rewrite include COPY and SORT. SORT is not considered here, as it will generally require much more work to copy and sort a file than to carry out a COPY. The code that will accomplish the copy task is

```
init:
  control always ;
return ;

main:
  rc = copy('work.activity(keep=project activity tothrs
                          stdchrg )',
          'work.activity') ;
return ;
```

I am here taking advantage of a nondocumented feature of COPY, namely that a COPY can be to the same data set as is being copied.

This procedure was also done with SORT to compare the resource usage. Under OS/2 running Release 6.08, a 19,587-observation data set used 14 seconds elapsed time to accomplish the KEEP using SORT and 4 seconds to accomplish with COPY. Note that SORT also has extra overheads of SCL OPEN and CLOSE and may require the FORCE parameter if the data set is already sorted.

Both methods may require that you obtain an exclusive lock on the file being modified if it is possible for other users to be using it.

Q *How can I hide a push button in a program entry and under program control reveal the button when a certain condition occurs?*

A This seemed such a simple thing to *want* to do. After a few hours of experimenting, I discovered that it was not simple. The simple answer appears to be that you can't. FRAME entries will allow this, but program entries appear to be unable to cope with this.

Q *My application requires a unique identification number on each observation in a data set. At present my users manually enter that number in FSEDIT, but frequently they make mistakes. They should be entering the next number in sequence, but the database now has many gaps. How can I automate this procedure?*

A The first solution presented is simple. Assume that your identification variable is called **idvar**. It must be numeric. In your FSEDIT SCL, detect a new observation using the OBSINFO function. In SCL, reopen (in input mode) the file being edited. Use the VARSTAT function to obtain the maximum number using the MAX statistic. Increment by 1 and place this in your **idvar** field, which should be protected.

The code to implement this solution follows. Note that the code is in INIT. This means that on accessing a new observation, this user will see the id number immediately. The **idvar** field should be protected.

```
fseinit:
  dsid = open(<dataset being edited by FSEDIT>) ;
return ;

init:
  control always ;
  if obsinfo('new') then do ;
    rc = varstat(dsid,'idvar','max','bigidvar') ;
    idvar = bigidvar + 1 ;
  end ;
  ... rest of init ....
return ;
```

```
   ...
   fseterm:
     call close(dsid) ;
   return ;
```

This program has two drawbacks. The first is that the id variable must be numeric, which is frequently not acceptable. The second is that the time required to obtain the value of MAX may be excessive.

➡ *The note about excessive time is an important design consideration. Frequently code is developed and tested on test data sets that are necessarily quite small. Algorithms that work well in testing on small data sets may perform poorly in production. That poor performance may NOT be immediate. In the above example, coding the VARSTAT would see it generate early idvar values rapidly. But as more observations are entered on the database, performance will be degraded to an unacceptable level. This is a design consideration.*

There are better ways to achieve the aim. It is difficult to code a generic means of doing this, but one of the following should be adaptable in any system.

You need a secondary data set, <LIBREF>.COUNTER. This will hereafter be referred to as COUNTER.

COUNTER will have either 1 or 2 fields, depending on whether you have a numeric **idvar** or a character **idvar**. The fields are as follows:

When IDVAR is NUMERIC. . .

the single field, called **counter**, is itself numeric. It will always contain the last **idvar** value on the data set that you are generating values for.

When IDVAR is CHARACTER. . .

there are two fields. One is called **counter** and is itself numeric. The other is called **prefix** (although you may use it as a suffix) and is character. The length of that variable and its values are application specific.

Fetching IDVAR When IDVAR Is Numeric

You require the following code in INIT:

```
   fseinit:
     dsid = open(<DDNAME>.counter) ;
   return ;
```

```
init:
  control always ;
  if obsinfo('new') then do ;
    rc = fetch(dsid) ;
    idvar = getvarn(dsid,varnum(dsid,'counter')) + 1 ;
    call putvarn(dsid,varnum(dsid,'counter'),idvar) ;
    rc = update(dsid) ;
  end ;
  ... rest of init ....
return ;

...
fseterm:
  call close(dsid) ;
return ;
```

This code just identifies the most recent value of **counter**, increments it into **idvar**, then places the new value back into **counter**. It is very simple, very effective, and always very fast as only one observation is ever on the **counter** data set.

Fetching IDVAR When IDVAR Is Character

Now consider the situation where **idvar** is character. This is more complex, as there are a number of ways that **idvar** could be structured. For example, **idvar** could be character values followed by the numeric counter, or the numeric counter followed by character values, or both a character prefix and suffix. You also store **counter** as numeric, but convert it to character to create **idvar**.

Assume a prefix is present for the counter. The situation will be as follows. The user will not get an **idvar** value displayed on entry because the prefix will be unknown at that time. Instead, the user must enter the prefix, and then the MAIN section will obtain the rest of the number.

This is the situation in Databank's JARS system. Each project falls into one of the following categories: Maintenance, Internal project, External customer project. Hence there are 3 prefixes, M, I, E, and each is always followed by a 5-digit code.

The COUNTER data set will have 3 observations. Each will have a different value for **counter**, and the **prefix** field will have the value I, E, M. At a given point in time, COUNTER may look like this:

PREFIX	COUNTER
M	2136
I	6234
E	1976

Here, as before, **counter** is the last number that has been assigned to an **idvar** value.

The user will enter a 1-character prefix (actually even more characters can be entered, but the code will substring off just the first); then the COUNTER data set provides the next number. The code follows:

```
fseinit:
  dsid = open('<libref>.counter','u') ;
return ;

init:
  control always ;
  ... rest of init .... 
return ;

main:

  if obsinfo('new') then do ;

    if substr(idvar,1) not in ('M','I','E') then do ;
      .... issue error message .....
      return ;
    end ;

    rc = where(dsid,'prefix eq "' || substr(idvar,1) || '"') ;

    rc = fetch(dsid) ;
    counter = getvarn(dsid,varnum(dsid,'counter'))+1 ;
    idvar = substr(idvar,1) || put(counter,z5.) ;
    call putvarn(dsid,varnum(dsid,'counter'),counter) ;
    rc = update(dsid) ;
  end ;
return ;
...
fseterm:
  call close(dsid) ;
return ;
```

This isn't that much different from the **idvar** being numeric case. Because there are more observations in the COUNTER data set, a WHERE is used to return the observation for the entered **idvar** prefix. The other main difference is that **idvar** is prefixed with the user's entry, and the PUT function used to create the numeric part of **idvar**. Note the Z5. format, which ensures that the returned id has leading zeros.

 Q *I used the CENTER function to place legend text. I expected this would center the text in the legend window, but I get a blank window instead. Why ? The code I used was*

```
call putlegend(2,center('processing, Please Wait')) ;
```

A The CENTER function has two arguments, the first being the text and the optional second being the length of the output field. If you let the length default when used as an argument in a PUTLEGEND (or other usage that results in the output's not being written to a variable), the CENTER function is not placing its output to a field with a known length and sets the length of the output field to zero.

To get your text centered then, use the width of the legend as the second argument to the CENTER function.

Q *Is there any way to prevent users from leaving a screen? Users have no need to open other windows from the screens in my application, but they frequently enter commands that could jeopardize my database's integrity, for instance the DIR command.*

A Provided that NO other screen (including HELP) should be accessible in the application, use the SAS/AF attribute NO EXIT found on the general attributes screen. This attribute prevents the user from issuing any command that would result in the opening of a window. You can still use CALL DISPLAY to open other windows under application control.

When you use NO EXIT, some of the changes that occur in AF behavior include the following:

- HELP opens a window, so it is no longer available.
- When a command that would open a window is issued, SAS/AF takes control before the SCL is executed.
- Commands that would open a window are discarded, and MAIN will not execute unless a field is altered.
- Setting NO EXIT removes the ability to submit code for immediate processing. The code is stacked up and submitted at the end of the entry.

To provide HELP screens with NO EXIT, you need to use CALL DISPLAY. Since you cannot issue the HELP command (including from function keys or PMENUS), you will need to assign another command, HELPX, to a key. With CONTROL ENTER switched on, you can search for that command and call the appropriate display window.

When you use NO EXIT, don't forget its impact. I spent a whole afternoon trying to track down why my HELP screens and KEYS screens would not work, only to find I had forgotten that NO EXIT was switched on!

As an aside here, a related issue has been that users often accidentally trigger GROW/SHRINK mode and get confused about what is happening. Again, a SAS/AF attribute, DIALOG, can be used. This effectively switches off GROW/SHRINK mode.

Q *I tried to issue an EXECCMD function with a color argument to change the background color of a DATALISTC window in a program entry. The code I used follows:*

```
init:
  dsid = open('work.test') ;
  call execcmd('color background green') ;
```

```
     varname = datalistc(dsid,'test','Pick One','N',1) ;
     rc = close(dsid) ;
   return ;
```

The color did not change in the DATALISTC window but did in the underlying program entry window. Why did EXECCMD not get carried out on the next opened window, the DATALISTC?

This is a good example of how the obvious is not necessarily what occurs. According to all written descriptions about EXECCMD, the above code should work. However, there is a difficulty here with timing. The next window opened is actually the program entry window, and this is what gets its background changed.

It is interesting to note that the SCL debugger causes things to be a little different here. When you use the debugger on the above code, the DATALISTC window does change its color!

Please explain when I should use CALL EXECCMD('end'), as supposed to _STATUS_='H' to force an end to an SCL program.

EXECCMD arguments do not execute until the window is redisplayed, and EXECCMD will cause more processing, as the SCL MAIN section will be run again. Setting _STATUS_ to 'H' and immediately issuing a RETURN is much more efficient because the program halts immediately.

When you issue an EXECCMD('end') from the INIT section, the display screen still displays and then immediately disappears. Using _STATUS_ does not display the screen, so the process looks cleaner from the user's viewpoint.

Issuing EXECCMD('end') in MAIN re-executes MAIN, which could stack up another END (if the EXECCMD gets executed again) if you are not careful. This means that as well as the current program entry ending as you intended, the calling entry may also end. There may be situations where that is desirable.

My preference is always to use the _STATUS_ variable.

When you use _STATUS_ = 'H', the TERM section is not invoked automatically. If you carry out processing such as closing files in TERM, you will need to force that section to be executed. An example that will not work properly is the following:

```
init:
  dsid = open('work.test','i') ;
  if getvarc(dsid,varnum(dsid,'check')) eq 'N' then _status_ = 'H' ;
  call set(dsid) ;
return ;

term:
 call close(dsid) ;
return ;
```

To successfully close the file, use this code instead:

```
init:
  dsid = open('work.test','i') ;
  if getvarc(dsid,varnum(dsid,'check')) eq 'N' then do ;
    link term ;
    _status_ = 'H' ;
    return ;
  end ;
  call set(dsid) ;
return ;

term:
  call close(dsid) ;
return ;
```

Chapter 13: A Potpourri Of Hints And Notes

- SCL lists exist in Release 6.07 and later releases of SAS software.

- To read a catalog entry in a data set, under MVS you can use

```
filename incatlog 'pgm=sasreadc' pgmread='<catalog name>';
```

followed by a DATA step referencing INCATLOG as the fileref in an INFILE statement. This allows INPUT statements in the DATA step to read lines from the catalog SOURCE entry. Thus you can use methods in this book to save text in a SOURCE entry and use standard DATA steps to report from that text.

Alternatively and under other platforms, copy source entries to the preview buffer using CALL PREVIEW('COPY' ...), then use CALL PREVIEW('FILE'...) to save a catalog entry to an external file from where it can be easily read by a DATA step. Don't forget to issue a CALL PREVIEW('CLEAR').

- If data sets appear not to be closed at the end of an FSEDIT entry when the close is in TERM, try using CONTROL TERM in the INIT section to force TERM to be executed.

- Certain internal tables in SCL have a size limit of 32K, so if you get errors indicating 'DATA SET SIZE EXCEEDED' you have reached this limit and need to consider another means of accomplishing your task. You may need to break large PROGRAM, SCL, or FRAME entries into smaller programs.

- Comments are not included in compiled code, so they have no impact on system memory at run time. There is no need to feel constrained when using comments.

- Using the RESIDENT option on an entry's general attribute screen in SAS/AF can significantly increase memory usage and use of virtual memory -- be wary in systems with constrained memory.

- If you use the SCL debugger, recompile all programs before production with the DEBUG OFF option; otherwise it is possible that the user could see debugger screens in the application, and that extra unnecessary code would be generated.

- You do not *need* a PUTROW section in an extended table; it is only necessary if you wish to carry out some processing on selected rows. A GETROW section, or its equivalent in FRAME entries, is always necessary.

- If your users are running an application and you change an entry in that application, then any user who has not yet accessed that entry during a session will see the new entry, not the entry that existed at the beginning of the session.

- If you attempt to edit a program entry and place a lock on the entry using LOCK <four level name>, any application that attempts to use that entry will receive a program halt. It is preferable to have a separate development and production version of your application, with migrating from development to production being done when no one is using the production version.

- Using CALL DISPLAY or REFRESH in an SCL program will cause procedure-specific entries on the command line to be cleared before SCL sees the command line contents.

- In Release 6.08, SUBMIT blocks in an FSEDIT program will be executed at the point that they occur in the program source stream; prior to that, code in SUBMIT blocks is not executed until the FSETERM section.

- Executing the WHERE function does not bring the first record found into memory. It only defines a filter, and FETCH or FETCHOBS is still necessary to actually get the first record.

- Still confused about the order in which events occur in SCL, especially with extended tables? Use the SCL debugger. It shows (by default) each statement being executed and is an excellent way to verify your program flow. In particular, you can see the order in which the various sections get executed with extended tables.

- The AFA (or AFAPPLICATION) command is an excellent way to have users start an AF program from a function key. This is very useful when you have a window not controlled by SCL (for example, the PREVIEW window) and you want users to start an SCL process from that window.

- If you define a LIST entry, and your SCL has a program field that uses that list (if, in other words, the list is defined using =LISTNAME in the LIST attribute), SAS will always carry out any prompting on that field before it executes SCL. Thus, if an application permits an EXIT using PF3, and the user has entered a prompt character into a field with a selection list defined, the list is popped up even when the user has requested an exit. The exit from the program screen is carried out only after the list is exited. This situation is annoying, but avoidable when you use SCL code to call the list instead of using the list attribute (which means a lot more coding).

- To write text into a legend window with the text centered, use the SCL CENTER function. For example, if your legend window is 50 characters wide, you can use PUTLEGEND in the following manner:

```
call putlegend(<line number>, center('Press PF3 To Exit',50))
```

The second argument is the length that the first argument will be centered in.

- It is often desirable to have a field on screen with a meaningful name but to have less characters available for input than there are characters in the field name. By default, the length of the field name plus any underscores will be used for data entry. By using the meaningful field name as an alias and making the screen name a less meaningful name of the required length, you can accomplish the two aims of having a meaningful name in your code but less characters available for the user to enter data into.

- When using LOCATEC/N, always check the return code to ensure that a record was found. If you don't, and you attempt to read data immediately using, for example, GETVARx, the program will *halt* if LOCATEc failed. LOCATEx only loads a record when a match has been found, so don't assume a match without checking the return code.

- Non-window variable names are not restricted to 8 characters in length and can use underscores in the variable name.

- Although the EXECCMDI routine permits a number of commands to be stacked with semicolons between them, the results may not be what was intended. In this situation, the first command is executed, and then the SCL following the EXECCMDI continues. Further commands are only executed when the entry window is redisplayed. You are better off issuing multiple EXECCMDI calls, as these will be processed as expected.

- When you are using the debugger, you may get unexpected results from EXECCMD. The debugger does not process commands issued by EXECCMD or EXECCMDI, as the debugger flushes the command stack when it takes control.

- When you are using FSEDIT, the FSEINIT and FSETERM sections do not process SCL functions that are window related because no window is yet present. Move such commands (the CURSOR command, for example) to INIT or TERM.

- Since SUBMIT IMMEDIATE returns immediately to the application window, it is pointless to use this with CONTROL LABEL, as it will cause any following labeled sections to be ignored.

- You can cause extended tables to leave space between the table rows by using the TSP option on the ^^^ line. By using ^^^ TSP=2, you will cause two blank lines to be inserted between each row of the table.

- When you start an application with a PROC DISPLAY, you need to be aware of the impact on submitted SQL code. Submitted code is stacked, and it executes only when the application finishes. The reason for this is that SAS software cannot start a DATA or PROC step while one is already running. This means that SAS-to-SCL communication is impossible with code that uses SUBMIT CONTINUE when the application is started with PROC DISPLAY.

- You may find that using lists to store parameter values makes your application code more flexible. Lists enable a value to be retrieved in any entry, with it only being stored once.

- Do not use FRAME entries with less than 12 Mg memory available and plenty of disk space. FRAME will run on a 386 PC, but a 486 is recommended.

 Additional sources on the topics discussed in this book include the following:

- *SAS/AF Software: FRAME Entry Usage and Reference, Version 6, First Edition*

- *SAS/AF Software: Usage and Reference, Version 6, First Edition*

- *SAS/FSP Software: Usage and Reference, Version 6, First Edition*

- *SAS Procedures Guide, Version 6, Third Edition*

- *SAS Screen Control Language: Reference, Version 6, First Edition*

- *SAS Screen Control Language: Usage, Version 6, First Edition*

- *SAS Technical Report P-195, Transporting SAS Files between Host Systems*

- *SAS Technical Report P-199, Using SAS Screen Control Language in Release 6.06*

- *SAS Technical Report P-216, SAS/AF Software, SAS/FSP Software, and SAS Screen Control Language: Changes and Enhancements, Release 6.07*

- *SAS Technical Report P-242, SAS Software: Changes and Enhancements, Release 6.08*

- *Observations: The Technical Journal for SAS Software Users*

- *Proceedings of the Annual SAS User's Group International Conference*, 1991 to present

Index